Unsinkable

ALSO BY DEBBIE REYNOLDS

Debbie: My Life

Unsinkable

a memoir

Debbie Reynolds
and Dorian Hannaway

HARPER LUXE

An Imprint of HarperCollinsPublishers

FIRST HARPERLUXE EDITION

HarperLuxe™ is a trademark of HarperCollins Publishers

Library of Congress Cataloging-in-Publication Data is available upon request.

ISBN: 978-0-06-222301-2

13 14 ID/RRD 10 9 8 7 6 5 4 3 2 1

For my children,
Carrie and Todd

Contents

Foreword by Carrie Fisher   xi

Preface   xv

Part I

1. Third Time Is a Charm, or Three Strikes, You're *Out?*   3
2. Debbie Does Virginia   15
3. Postcards from My Daughter   25
4. Move Over, Hiltons—Reynolds Is in the Hotel Business!   31
5. The Star Theater   43
6. Fear and Loathing in Las Vegas   57
7. A New Day   65
8. Happy New Year?   69
9. Raid on Roanoke   77

10. Under the Elephant's Tail 85
11. Mother Plays *Mother* 108
12. Looking for Mr. Wrong 118
13. Divorce American Style 126
14. Hail Mary Deal 127
15. Black Wednesday 133
16. Bottoming Out in Beverly Hills 138
17. On the Road Again 146
18. Family and Faith 156
19. *These Old Broads* 167
20. I'm Princess Leia's Mother 186
21. Hollywood & Highland 198
22. September 10, 2001 203
23. Museum, Interrupted 211
24. On to Pigeon Forge 215
25. Another Day in Court 222
26. June 18, 2011 234

Part II

Debbie Does Eighty 253
Miss Burbank 1948 262
MGM: "More Stars Than There Are
    in Heaven" 276

Acknowledgments 407
The Films of Debbie Reynolds 411

Foreword
by Carrie Fisher

My mother has an amazing memory. She doesn't seem to remember things utterly and all at once. Her recollections can come gradually, or they've been known to come to her intermittently, even late at night and suddenly—maybe on a plane, when entering an elevator, deciding not to exercise, not to go to bed yet, to spend time reading, watching TV, or returning calls, while eating or alone.

The bottom line is that she's never quite gotten to that bottom line. In the end, the end gets farther and farther away. Just when you think you've heard her last word on a subject—a vivid and vast assortment of reflections—you find that you've been happily swept up into another anecdote long forgotten, hoisting memory's anchor, embarking on a new long-forgotten cruise, sailing storied seas on the S.S. *Other Hand.* Or she's embroiled in some new epic misadventure—one of her kids abruptly gets married, the other chats gaily about her electroshock therapy, a fan catches fire. I mean, what the hell! She lives two lives—one of them public, the other private. Some she lives concurrently, others one at a time, in or out of order. Always, she is who she is: a good person, a kind person—which would be a fine thing if these were qualities that are consistently rewarded. But as most of us know, they are not. Which is one of the things very vividly demonstrated in this book.

My mother has lived a long and at times unendurably eventful life. Yet she keeps living it, keeps enduring, applying makeup, trying not to remember how unreal it all seems at times, writing checks, sleeping late, voting Republican *and* Democratic, answering the "who the hell could *that* be" phone. Did she really make all those movies, marry those morons, sing those songs, dance those dance steps, pretend to know all those people she didn't know from Adam, Eve, or Uncle Wally from Tucson? Singing for more than a few suppers, skipping breakfast, even lunching with ladies who had, at some point, been men?

This isn't a tell-all—what book is? This book is what all memoirs are—a tell-some. It's not the telling that counts, though, as much as who's doing the telling and from what point they are telling it. Well, as you know, my mother is doing the telling here and telling her story from a point in her life where she can see farther and better than ever before.

I'll stop here so you can go and enjoy reading her story as much as I enjoyed reading it and contributing my colorful and, at times, annoying part of it. After all, I'm her daughter and her neighbor, and I have custody of her granddaughter.

So hoist this introductory anchor and cruise down memory lane with Debbie, a journey flooded with extraordinary anecdotes from an extraordinary woman. I oughta know.

Preface

In 1988 I wrote an autobiography entitled *Debbie: My Life.* At the time I had recently married my third husband. My life was chaotic, but I was very happy. I called my new husband "brave, loyal, and loving." How wrong I was!

When I read the optimistic ending of my last memoir now, I can't believe how naive I was when I wrote it. In *Unsinkable,* I look back at the many years since then and, in the second part of the book, share my memories of a film career that took me from the Miss Burbank contest of 1948 to the work I did in 2012. I was a simple kid who was thrown into the wonderful world of show business. I've loved every moment.

These are my recollections. If you remember things differently, send me your version—but only if it's funnier.

Thanks for sharing this journey with me. To paraphrase Bette Davis: Fasten your seatbelts. I've had a bumpy ride.

Part I

Chapter 1

Third Time Is a Charm, or Three Strikes, You're *Out*?

I t was going to be a perfect day.

In May 1984, I got married for the third time. Like my first two husbands, Richard asked me to marry him soon after we met. I held back.

When I was a young contract player at MGM, I met a handsome man who was the biggest recording star of the 1950s, Eddie Fisher. He was a success in records and also in the new medium of television with his program *Coke Time with Eddie Fisher.* When we got married, the press called us "America's Sweethearts." Eddie was my first love—and my first divorce. Eddie's best friend, movie producer Mike Todd, spent a lot of time with us while we were dating. Mike fell in love with Elizabeth Taylor. Eddie and I stood up for Mike and Elizabeth when they were married. When Mike was killed in a horrible plane crash, I took care of their children while Eddie comforted Elizabeth. Then Eddie left our two small children and me for Elizabeth. (You knew you'd be hearing about them in this story, didn't you? The scandal made headlines around the world. People still talk about it to this day.)

My second husband was a very wealthy businessman, Harry Karl. His family owned a chain of shoe stores worth many millions of dollars. Harry was older than me, but he courted me until I said yes to his proposal. He gave my children and me stability and a family life that lasted for many years. I let him take care of all our business while I took care of our home and his wardrobe. The trouble with Harry was that he loved gambling more than he loved me and our family. He squandered all of his money and then went through everything I had earned. When I found out—thirteen years into our marriage—everything fell apart.

When Richard proposed to me, it had been twenty-six years since Eddie Fisher left me for Elizabeth Taylor, in 1958. That seemed like a lifetime ago. The nightmare of my second marriage had ended ten years before, and after being a rich man's trophy wife I'd vowed never to marry again. I'd worked to pay off millions of dollars of Harry's gambling debts, and I'd rebuilt my life. At fifty-two, I didn't want to spend the rest of it alone, afraid of loving again. I'd known Richard less than a year, but marrying him felt right. We seemed to be kindred spirits. I was comfortable with him. We talked for hours and hours, yet it seemed like minutes. I was happy to be in love again.

So a few months after Richard proposed, I decided to take a chance and marry him.

That being said, I was glad when Ruta Lee gave me a copy of her prenuptial agreement, to protect myself just in case. I've known Ruta since my early days at MGM. She'd played one of the seven brides for seven brothers in the musical of the same name. Leave it to my famous bride girlfriend to have a prenup handy, but then, we do live in Hollywood. After all I'd been through, Ruta thought it would be wise for me to ensure that I wouldn't get hurt again. Richard read it for a few hours, then signed it, to prove that he loved me for myself, not for my money.

I was booked to perform on a cruise leaving from Miami for a week that May, so we decided to get married in Florida and spend our honeymoon at sea. This arrangement was good for me because I thrive on working. It was good for Richard because he enjoyed watching me work. I planned a small wedding, with only my closest friends and family. My mother, Maxene, and my brother, Bill, along with my son, Todd, my daughter,

Carrie, and a few friends, were flying in. Several days before the wedding, Richard and I checked into a large suite at the Ambassador Hotel. My good friends Nancy and Joe Kanter agreed to let us have the ceremony at their beautiful bay-front home on a nearby secluded Miami street. Nancy and I made all the arrangements quickly and quietly, without informing the press.

The day before the wedding, Carrie's plane arrived from London, but she wasn't on it. Carrie called to say she wasn't able to come. This was a difficult time for her. She and Paul Simon were ending their marriage of a few months after being together for many years. She'd recently had a tubular pregnancy, had lost the baby, and had been very ill following the surgery. On top of that, she was devastated that I was marrying again. Carrie didn't know Richard, and she still felt damaged by my second marriage to Harry Karl. I was disappointed by this news but also worried. At the time Carrie was living at the edge but hadn't yet begun to send any postcards.

The next day everyone bustled around getting ready for the ceremony. My mother wore a dusty pink chiffon dress. She was very excited for me. Ret Turner of Bob Mackie's design house created a sea foam green chiffon dress with sheer sleeves and crystal and pearl beading around the scoop neckline and cuffs for me.

My friend and hairstylist, Kelly Muldoon, was with me for my show and to be my matron of honor. She fastened some white blooms in the back of my hair at the hotel, and we went over to Nancy and Joe's.

Daddy was eighty-one and too frail to travel, so Todd gave me away. In Daddy's absence, my son had "the talk" with my groom. Even though Todd was only twenty-six, he warned Richard that if he did anything to harm me, Richard would have to answer to him. Richard laughed nervously.

Before I knew it, it was time for the ceremony. In the early evening, Todd walked me down the stairs at Nancy and Joe's home, my arm linked through his as we made our way to the living room and out onto the terrace overlooking the bay where everyone had gathered. My bridal bouquet was a mix of white lilies and lilies of the valley. Delicate as they were, my hand shook a little as I held them, from nervousness. I kept thinking, I know I can do this. He loves me. Let life in. I reminded myself to breathe.

As the sun was setting in the cloudless sky, casting a glow over the proceedings, I brought the ring to Richard's finger and promised to love him till death do us part. For some reason, I couldn't get the ring on. I bent down and began to twist it onto his finger. Was this an omen? Finally I twisted that sucker on. Everyone clapped and cheered. Then we all went into the house to toast the new Mr. and Mrs. Hamlett.

The flowers and our wedding cake were beautifully arranged on a round table in the dining room. Three tiers of white cake sparkled as we cut it. Richard pushed a big slice in my mouth, and some of the icing landed on the exposed area just below my neck. Richard happily licked it off and we laughed. I smiled for the camera as pictures were taken, the actress in me putting on a good show, but I was thinking about Carrie, consumed with concern for my daughter's well-being. I asked Todd to get her on the phone in London. Todd joked with his sister before passing the phone to me.

"Hi, dear. It's your mother. Debbie," I said. I chatted for a moment about everything that was happening, told her I was sorry she was missing it.

Carrie explained that she had come down with a bad cold that had gotten worse from traveling by plane.

"Feel better, dear," I told her. "Here's your new stepfather."

Richard talked to Carrie for a few minutes and handed the phone back to me.

"Bye-bye, dear, I love you. Wish you were here," I said cheerfully and hung up.

But Carrie's voice had frightened me. Her words were slurred, and by the end of the conversation she wasn't speaking at all. I suspected that taking pills had been more satisfying for her than boarding a plane to Miami.

Worried, I looked at Todd, who instinctively knew what to do. He said he would go to London and get Carrie and bring her home. Something told me he wouldn't arrive there in time.

I asked him to call Carrie back.

The phone rang and rang and rang. I panicked. I knew she was in her hotel room, and I was certain she had accidentally overdosed on her prescription medications. I called the hotel's concierge.

"Hello, this is Debbie Reynolds. My daughter, Carrie Fisher, is staying at your hotel. I've been calling and calling, but she doesn't seem to be answering."

I begged him to go to Carrie's room to make sure she was all right.

"I'm sorry, Miss Reynolds," he interrupted, "but we have no way of knowing that you are who you say you are."

He continued talking but I didn't hear him. Did he really think I was some crazy fan pretending to be Carrie's mother?

It was close to one in the morning in London, and somehow I had to save my daughter. Who did I know there who could help? Frantic, I asked the concierge,

"Would you go to Carrie's room if Ava Gardner came to the hotel and went with you?" In the moment of silence it took him to process this and agree, I prayed that my good friend would be true to her reputation, still awake in the wee hours and sipping champagne at home.

Thank goodness she was.

"I'll sure as hell take care of it," Ava said when I explained the situation to her. Ava had handled everyone from Frank Sinatra to bullfighters in Spain. I was confident that one London concierge would be no match for her.

I went back into the dining room, where my wedding reception had been going on without the bride, and pulled my host Nancy aside.

"Carrie may be sick in London," I confided. "I have to get back to the hotel to make sure she's all right."

I smiled and posed for pictures with my new husband and my friends a while longer, not letting on that I was scared to death about Carrie. Then Richard and I prepared to leave.

Somehow the press had found out about the wedding; cars full of reporters and paparazzi packed the driveway and surrounded the house. I just wanted to get back to the Ambassador to make sure Carrie was safe.

With my best man at the wedding—and in my life—
my son, Todd Fisher.

With my *last* husband.

Joe called his friend at the sheriff's station to clear a way for us, then drove the short distance so fast that the car wheels barely touched the pavement. It seemed like we were flying through every back alley, and each minute felt like an eternity.

More press had gathered at the hotel entrance. We escaped the mob and hurried up to our suite, where we spent the rest of the night on the phone with Ava in London.

Ava had rushed to the St. James Hotel the instant after we'd first spoken. When she and the manager opened the door to Carrie's room, they found my daughter asleep on the floor, face down, all of her clothes still on, including her shoes. The television was playing and all the windows were open, chilling the room. Ava called a doctor, who gave Carrie the medical treatment she needed. Carrie had not overdosed, although she had taken many more pills than a person should, maybe because she felt so sick from her cold.

Ava stayed with Carrie until she was sure she was out of danger. In our last phone call, many hours later, I thanked Ava for taking care of Carrie and making sure she was safe. I knew that words could never express how grateful I truly was. I trusted that my dear friend would understand.

Then, resilient as ever, Carrie got ready to fly back to the States. Instead of going to London, Todd went to Los Angeles and met his sister at home. However briefly, for this one instant, everyone was settled. Once I knew Carrie was truly safe, I felt guilty, caught between concern for my daughter's welfare and wanting to devote my time to my new husband, and wondering if our marriage had triggered this episode. I was a wreck.

Richard and I had to leave for the cruise ship later that day. After we settled into our cabin, I collapsed, exhausted and drained, into a deep sleep.

I'm not a morning person. I'm barely an afternoon person. I woke up after my delayed wedding night alone in our cabin. Where was Richard? After a while, I got dressed, put on my makeup, and ventured onto the deck.

There was my new husband seated at a table with three lovely ladies; they were laughing and seemed to be flirting with him. Richard looked tall and handsome and very relaxed. As I approached them, he stood to welcome me with a kiss on the cheek.

"Debbie, these are some friends of mine from Roanoke," he said, introducing them to me. "They're going to Bermuda with us."

"Pleased to meet you," I said. "Isn't this a lovely surprise?"

The sun was shining brightly, but I felt a shiver. Sometimes you don't see the storm clouds as they're forming on the horizon. I didn't know it at the time, but my new husband had all the makings of a champion tennis player—a great racket, fast moves, and a lot of balls.

Chapter 2
Debbie Does Virginia

Time sure flies when you're having fun. The cruise was smooth sailing after those first bumpy days. I never noticed the ladies from Roanoke again. My new husband stayed out in the sun so long, lounging on the deck with his Virginia girlfriends, that he looked like a lobster. I just threw wet towels on him to ease his suffering. I guess I won't go down in history for my nursing skills. And I guess third-degree burns, no matter how painful, don't keep a person from gambling. At checkout time back in Florida, I noticed a very large sum for charges in the ship's casino. I chalked it up to entertainment and his excitement at being a newlywed.

Soon after our arrival back in Los Angeles, my friend Phyllis Berkett gave Richard and me a reception so my friends could meet Husband Number Three.

My Hollywood pals turned out in force to meet the new man in my life—partly out of curiosity, I'm sure, since no one knew him very well, including me. Garry Marshall and his wife, Barbara, were there. Florence Henderson, Pat and Tom Bosley, Patty and Dick Van Patten, and many of my other friends came to wish us well. I wore my most recent wedding dress, which was perfect for a dinner party. Richard looked wonderful in a white jacket, his skin having returned to its normal color. If anything, he was looking a little pale.

All was just lovely for the first half of the party. During dinner, Richard said to me, "I'm not feeling well. I have to lie down." We went into one of the bedrooms. He felt hot to the touch as I supported him to the bed, so I took his temperature. He had a high fever. I called the doctor, who recommended that we go straight to a hospital.

There is a famous hospital south of Los Angeles in La Jolla called Scripps that specializes in diagnostics. I hired a car for the drive, and Richard lay in my arms all the way during the two-hour trip, burning up. He was admitted that night. Back at the party, my friends had had enough drama and left shortly after we did. I can only wonder what they thought was going on in my new marital adventure. This guy didn't look like he was going to make it through round one with me.

Once Richard was settled in at Scripps, the doctors found that he had a hole in his heart that was leaking. He was in critical condition. For the next twenty-four hours, he was medicated through an IV. I slept in an adjoining room and prayed that he would get better. The doctor at Scripps had developed a new treatment for this type of heart disease that kept Richard from needing surgery. I stayed with him day and night for the next few weeks. It was an incredible bonding experience. I was enjoying my new role of loving wife and protector. My husband needed me, which made me feel that we were strengthening our relationship. We were off to a rough start, but it drew us closer.

When Richard was strong enough to travel, we flew to his home city of Roanoke, Virginia, where he was admitted to a hospital. The medication was working, and Richard preferred to finish his treatment near where he did business. I stayed at his house in Roanoke, a huge mansion by any standards. Richard had designed this house himself and built it on an impossible, slanted lot at the top of a hill. It had a large bay window that overlooked the valley below. Sometimes we were above the clouds. Now I knew what a bird feels like, soaring above the earth looking at the view below.

During the day I spent my time with Richard and his family and friends at the hospital. Richard owned a real estate business, and the builders who worked on his projects came by with updates. Every day I would bring him special food, including candy and other sweets, and clean clothes and underwear from home.

I became friends with the many people I'd met in Roanoke before we were married, when Richard had driven me around town, showing me all the places that he owned or wanted to develop. I loved seeing real estate; when I was married to Harry Karl, I used to travel around Hollywood looking at properties. Of course, once I bought places they somehow evaporated when my second husband became their overseer. By all accounts, Richard had done well in Roanoke; at least that was the impression he gave me.

Elizabeth Taylor had relocated from Hollywood to Virginia when she married John Warner. Although she loved John very much, she was miserable living the quiet life in the country while he was in Washington, DC. She was separated from all her gay-boy friends, who weren't interested in hanging around the farm of a Virginia senator. She was lonely without them. I found Roanoke to be a lovely community full of friendly, unassuming people. Richard's mother and sisters were especially kind to me. But it was a huge contrast to the world we inhabited in Hollywood.

Sometime after Richard was released from the hospital, I gave a dinner party in Roanoke for his family, beautifully done up by a local caterer. I laid out the table with my good china and silver that I'd shipped in from the West Coast. "What are all these forks for?" Richard's grandma asked as she sat down. Like Elizabeth, I had to adjust to a life that wasn't as fancy as the one we shared in Beverly Hills. Still, I was determined that if we were going to spend long periods in Virginia, as my new husband wished, we would be the King and Queen of Roanoke, not just part-time citizens of Los Angeles.

As the Queen of Roanoke, my duties included shopping for the house and preparing dinner, a new experience. I'd always had people cook for me. My reward was when my husband came home to share the news of his day, after he was finished reading the newspaper. Although it took me three hours to get a meat loaf prepared, I enjoyed making a meal for Richard and me. I put the salad plates in the refrigerator and set the table with flowers and ivy that I picked from the mountainside. I approached this with the same dedication that I approach any role that I play. After dinner, we would go upstairs and watch TV and make a lot of love—not at the same time usually. Our evenings were lovely, and it was a very happy time.

When my marriage to Harry Karl was unraveling, I'd tried to figure out what I was doing wrong. My first two husbands couldn't have been more different. Eddie was young, brash, and energetic. Harry was older, more romantic, and not athletic at all. You would think that I could have made *one* of them happy in bed. In an effort to avoid a second divorce (before I discovered that the real problem had nothing to do with our sex life), I'd decided to enlist the help of an expert.

Years before, I had made friends with a lovely woman I met at a charity benefit. Cheryl was the mistress of a very wealthy man. I called her and asked for her advice. Cheryl suggested that I consult a friend of hers who was a "professional." Really? I'd never met a pro, although I would find out later that my second husband had a visit from one every day, disguised as a manicurist. Harry's nails weren't the only things getting trimmed professionally.

I went to visit Cheryl's friend, a tall, slender brunette who reminded me of the actress Linda Darnell. Being in the movies, I'd learned over the years how to work with props, but I wasn't ready for the lesson I was about to receive. The lady took out an assortment of playthings that would have filled a floor at Toys R Us. There were big things, little things, balls, gags, handcuffs, scarves. Things that hummed, things that buzzed. I think one of them whistled "Dixie." In vivid detail, she explained exactly how to use each device to satisfy a man. Part of me longed to return to my innocence before I felt I had to go to school to be a good lover. Gone were the days of just hugging and kissing. Now I had to learn this routine, like a dance step combination. Then I pictured myself twirling a baton in high school—figure eights, up, down, into the air, catching behind my back. I could do this.

After my lesson, I threw myself into the practical application of this new knowledge with my second husband. But it was already too late to save our marriage. When the FBI shows up at your house and puts boards across the doors and windows to seize the property, it doesn't really get you in the mood. Besides, Harry may have gotten a frisky Debbie confused with his morning polishers.

Now that I was committed to a new man and beginning a new life, I enthusiastically put what I'd learned to good use, much to Richard's delight. To be or not to be was no longer a question for the happy Mr. Hamlett. Adventurous sex is like having an affair within your marriage. Prior to this, I'd felt that loving someone was enough. I learned that pleasuring a man is all part of being a good hostess.

Once Richard's health was restored, I worried about him more. I was determined to support him in any way

I could. I was more than willing to lend him thousands of dollars for his business. Sometimes after finishing a gig, I would FedEx my entire paycheck to him in time to meet a payment on one of his loans. My lawyers always made sure that they drew up contracts for him to sign outlining the terms of the loans and the collateral on his properties. Richard complained about having to sign notes. He told me that the lawyers were putting too much pressure on him. I chose to ignore what was probably the first of many red flags, telling myself that I was loving my husband while I was ignoring his behavior.

His illness had been a traumatic time for him. He seemed to be the Bionic Man. I probably went along with a lot of things I wouldn't have had I not been worried that the stress of his business would affect his newly discovered heart condition.

The loans I gave him seemed to relieve his stress. Sometime later, we were lying in bed talking while I rubbed the top of his head. He loved when I did this; it relaxed him. He told me that since we'd been married, he had never felt so secure, that since I had taken care of all his debts, he felt free for the first time in his life. I loved him so much at that moment. He made me feel needed and special. It didn't matter that the hundreds of thousands of dollars I had lent him came from my retirement fund. He assured me that the money wasn't getting enough interest there and said that he would invest it for me in some good properties. He was my husband. He loved and needed me and told me he was deeply appreciative of my help. I was happy that I had been able to lend him the money. In addition to a new husband, I had a new business partner. Like Richard, I felt safe.

But I was lonely during the long days when Richard was at work. After two months of being a combination Florence Nightingale and Stepford Wife, I was eager to get back to my career. So I returned to work.

Onstage with my show, doing what I know best.

Chapter 3
Postcards from My Daughter

Although Carrie had missed my wedding to her new stepfather, they became close in the years afterward. One Christmas, Carrie and Todd gave Richard a very expensive briefcase with an engraved plate on it that read WORLD'S GREATEST STEPDAD. Family life was good. We all went on vacations together. I had taken the children to Europe many times when they were young; now I wanted to introduce Richard to the places I loved overseas.

We took a trip on the Orient Express as well as vacations in Rome, Venice, and many other exotic locations. Rene Russo was Todd's girlfriend at the time. She's a lovely girl who just added to our fun on the trip. Todd took home movies of us as we toured everywhere like a normal family. As normal as we could be with three movie stars on board. When we weren't traveling, I split my time between Roanoke and Hollywood.

By the late '80s, everyone was busy. Todd was building a new ranch north of Los Angeles. Carrie was making movies. When she performed in *When Harry Met Sally,* she arranged for Richard to play her father in a cameo role, walking his real-life stepdaughter down the aisle as her fictional father. I guess Eddie Fisher wasn't available.

While they were all occupied, I was on the road in a multicity tour of Meredith Willson's *The Unsinkable Molly Brown,* the musical that was the basis of my movie version. It was 1989, and Richard and I were coproducers. He enjoyed branching out from real estate and gave himself a salary of $20,000 a week. As one of the producers, he felt he deserved it.

As producer, he fired the scenic painters and hired house painters to work on the sets. He cut corners, made mistakes on union contracts, and acted like the amateur he was. Most of the time I was too busy to notice, which was my mistake in hiring him.

The show reunited me with Harve Presnell, my costar in the movie, and touring was exhausting. Performing in all those dance numbers and acting in almost every scene kept me busy. In addition to doing all the live shows, I had to vocalize every day for an hour before I went in to get my hair and makeup done. Harve just cleared his throat, did a few scales, then went onstage and sang. All of that took less than a minute. He had an incredible instrument that didn't require the upkeep my voice did.

The work was extremely hard. Our director, John Bowab, had taken the stage play and reworked it to resemble the film version. He was right that the audience would be expecting to see their favorite numbers from the movie. In spite of the challenges of the long dance numbers and lots of singing, the company got along well together, and that made the hard work and the road fun.

One evening in San Francisco we all went out for drinks after the show. Hours later we returned to the hotel and helped each other into our rooms. Gene Ross, who played my grandpa, had had a few too many, and as he dug into his pants pockets in the hotel hallway his pants dropped. We were all laughing too hard to help the poor guy find his key, which of course was in a trouser pocket that was now around his ankles.

While I was busy on the road, my daughter spent her time launching a new career as a writer. In 1987 Carrie's first book, *Postcards from the Edge,* had been published. "Loosely" based on our relationship, it's a hysterically funny romp about drug addiction and fame—just another day around our house. Bravely, with great intelligence, Carrie went public with her story, and the book was a best seller. Carrie was already a famous movie star and the poster child for outer space hotties (from having played Princess Leia in the *Star Wars* films); *Postcards* made her the poster child for dealing with addiction. As happy as I was about her new writing career, I was even more delighted that she had been through a successful rehab and was living a sober life.

Adding to this success, *Postcards* was optioned, and Carrie wrote the screenplay for the movie. Mike Nichols was the director. Meryl Streep was cast as Carrie's counterpart, Suzanne Vale. I asked Mike if I could read for the role of the eccentric mother.

"You're not right for the part," he told me, turning me down cold.

Excuse me? I'm not right to play myself, a part that I'd been creating—admittedly, unwittingly—for my daughter for decades?

Mike gave the part to my good friend Shirley MacLaine. Ironically, Shirley had also been up for the part of Molly Brown. She played a better hooker than a hillbilly, but she was under contract to Hal Wallis at Fox at the time, and they wouldn't let her make the film. Shirley always claimed I'd stolen the role from her by undercutting her price. When I was married to Harry Karl, people sometimes assumed we were so rich that paying me to work was optional.

I have known Shirley since we were both in our twenties. When I was pregnant with Carrie, Shirley was expecting her daughter Sasha. Still, Shirley asked if she could come to my little house in the San Fernando Valley to "study" me for the role. For two days she trailed after me, scrutinizing my every move. I couldn't turn around without bumping into her. Her research worked: Shirley is wonderful in the completed film.

The movie opened in September 1990. Richard was in Roanoke, so Todd was my date for the premiere. (I love going to premieres where my only job is to be the proud mother, not the anxious actress.) Shirley, Meryl, Carrie, and I smiled for the cameras on the red carpet. I wasn't thrilled to see them show me with no hair near the end of the movie, or putting vodka in my breakfast drink, but that's part of their story in the movie, not mine. There had been a fair amount of improvising during filming, and I was surprised by some of the exaggerations on the screen that weren't in Carrie's book. But I was thrilled that it was a wonderful success for my daughter.

At the party afterward, a woman came over to me, took my hand, and looked sadly into my eyes.

"I'm *so* sorry," she said.

I stole a perplexed glance at Todd, who stood next to me, giggling.

"Don't be sorry, dear," I said. "It's only a movie."

With Shirley MacLaine at the premiere of *Postcards from the Edge. Ron Galella Ltd./Getty Images*

Chapter 4
Move Over, Hiltons—Reynolds Is in the Hotel Business!

On July 17, 1992, Carrie gave birth to a beautiful daughter she named Billie Catherine. I was thrilled to have a grandchild, content in my marriage, and tired of being on the road for forty or more weeks every year. A while back, Richard and I had formed a corporation so that we could look for a venue where I could perform all the time. Three months after Billie was born, Richard heard that the Paddlewheel Hotel in Las Vegas was going up for auction. If we could buy it, not only could I have my own showroom, I could also create a museum in the hotel to house my collection of Hollywood memorabilia. Since the early '70s, I had bought thousands of costumes and props from MGM and Fox Studios and assembled the largest private collection of movie memorabilia in the world. Preserving this had been my passion for years.

It sounded like a really good idea. It would give us security, and I knew that I would do whatever it took to make it happen.

It was a spectacular October day when I went to the Great Western Savings and Loan on Victory Boulevard in Studio City and got a cashier's check for $200,000, the amount I needed to qualify to bid on the Paddlewheel. It was all my savings, but Richard assured me that if we won the hotel, we could get a loan to cover the mortgage. I left the bank practically floating with exhilaration and drove across Victory under a clear blue sky to my dance studio in North Hollywood.

DR Studios has been my second home since I opened it in 1979. When I bought the building, a former post office on Lankershim Boulevard, I wanted to create a rehearsal space where dancers could work and be treated well—with clean showers and bathrooms! From the beginning we've had free parking, a lounge area with fresh coffee, dressing rooms, and six big rehearsal studios with high ceilings and pianos in each room. I'm proud to say that everyone from Bette Midler to Madonna to Usher and Janet Jackson has rehearsed there, and nowadays we offer classes in hip-hop as well as tap. Michael Jackson rehearsed his *Thriller* video there under the direction of our friend Michael Peters, a brilliant choreographer. After doing some business in my office, I skipped down the stairs, got into my car, and drove to the Burbank airport to fly to Vegas to meet Richard, who was waiting for me at the small two-bedroom apartment where I had lived since the 1970s, a condo on the twelfth floor of a beautiful building near the Strip.

We were both buzzed about the auction. An older Las Vegas establishment, the Paddlewheel stood on a six-acre lot, a few blocks midway between the Strip and the Convention Center, and had 196 rooms. My head was spinning from the numbers. If we could buy the hotel for $2 million, it would still take a lot of money to create a showroom and museum in addition to renovating everything else in the place. Richard told me that he could and would handle this. After all, real estate development was his business. And I was his partner.

The hotel was already crowded with other prospective buyers when we arrived. I'd been going to auctions for decades to build my memorabilia collection, and each one had its own personality. The Paddlewheel auction was full of businesspeople. Since it was taking place in Las Vegas, I imagined each of us as taking a gamble.

There were about twenty bidders to start. I raised the paddle in my hand high as the offer went from $1 million to $1.1 million. Suddenly only ten people were bidding.

And then four. When the bidding reached $2 million, it was only me and one other person. The tension made me light-headed. The person bidding against me went to $2.1 million. The auctioneer announced the final bid. I looked to Richard, then raised my hand.

"Two million, two hundred thousand," the auctioneer announced, and paused.

I held my breath.

"Going once. Going twice." Gavel down. "Sold!"

Adrenaline rushed through my veins—or was it fear? Excitement?

All of the above.

There was a moment when I had doubts about taking on this enormous project. With the help of all my savings, Richard and I had bought a hotel in Fabulous Las Vegas. My $200,000 deposit was nonrefundable, and now we needed another $2 million. Richard again assured me that we could get the financing we needed, on my name alone.

After Richard and I won the Paddlewheel, a piece of property next door to the hotel went up for sale. Seated beside me at the auction was Ralph Engelstad, the owner of the Imperial Palace Casino, which was famous for housing his huge automobile collection. He leaned over and asked me if he could borrow my paddle. (He'd come to the auction to see what everything would bring and hadn't planned on bidding, but on impulse he decided to buy the lot.) I was taken aback but gave him my paddle, feeling like a real schnook. Mr. Engelstad won the lot for $800,000—in *my* name. He always thanked me for letting him use my credit line to buy it. Even so, I remained nervous until his secretary hand-delivered his check to me the next day at my new hotel. If he'd changed his mind, I'd have been in real trouble, since my purchase of the hotel had cleaned me out.

Shortly after the auction, Richard and I went back to Roanoke for a visit. Our friend Bootie Bell Chewning picked us up at the airport.

"We bought a hotel! We got it! We got it!" I called out, waving enthusiastically to Bootie as we came down the escalator.

"You'd better cover your ass," Bootie advised me quietly as we hugged.

"Everything's going to be fine," I assured her, wondering why she would say such a strange thing. "Richard and I have it all covered."

Now that we owned the hotel, the real fun began. There were meetings, meetings, and more meetings. Richard was in charge. I was the movie star wife, showing gentlemen into the office. I was never invited to sit in, but I went ahead and let him do that because I felt he knew more about running a hotel business than

I would as an entertainer. We were both so excited. Richard was like a kid in a toy shop because he held all the reins.

One of the first things we did was enter into an agreement with Edward Coleman and Ronald Nitzberg to arrange financing for the hotel and bring their expertise to selling some of the hotel rooms as time-shares for people or companies to use for a designated amount of time each year. Coleman, an attorney, would also serve as general counsel for the hotel. As part of Coleman and Nitzberg's generous compensation, they received salaries, commissions on the time-shares, and stock in the venture, as well as positions on the board of directors. They arranged for a Canadian company to lend us some of the money we needed. The hotel would be renamed the Debbie Reynolds Hotel and Casino.

While Richard tended to the business and financial end of things, I threw myself completely into every detail of the creative planning. My dear friend Jerry Wunderlich (famous Hollywood set designer of films such as *The Exorcist* and *Ordinary People,* my film *The Singing Nun,* and episodes of the TV shows *M*A*S*H, The Twilight Zone,* and *The Man from U.N.C.L.E.*) dropped everything and moved to Las Vegas to help. Billy Morris, another friend from our

MGM days, came along to assist with the design and installation. Our plan was to open the hotel rooms by the following June, in time for the 1993 summer tourist season, and to qualify for a gaming license. Once that was done, we'd add a showroom where I could perform, and then a museum to display my Hollywood memorabilia collection.

We had one overall goal: make it fabulous!

The theme was Hollywood. Since the front of the hotel already included a giant paddlewheel, we transformed it into an enormous movie reel, with a "strip" of "film" that stretched around the facade. Each frame was a huge color image of a different famous star that we bought for a song from Bally's Hotel and Casino. Previously known as the MGM Grand, Bally's was getting rid of the former hall decorations as part of their ongoing renovations. There were so many pictures that I was also able to hang some throughout the hotel.

There was so much work to be done. Every inch of space needed renovating. I wanted the front lobby to be welcoming and elegant. Jerry converted it from a dingy, dark cavern into a beautiful showplace, replacing the old wooden floor with white marble. Warner Brothers gave me huge ottomans that I had reupholstered and positioned under huge crystal chandeliers that had been used in *Gone with the Wind, Marie*

Antoinette, and many other famous MGM movies, all from my collection. My son, Todd, redid all the lighting. My brother, Bill, restored the chandeliers, which sparkled against the newly painted powder-blue ceiling. Jerry used crystal candlesticks as ornaments. He created a huge floral arrangement in a large silver vase that Harry Karl had bought for $8,000 for our house when we were married. Other treasures from my decades of collecting found new lives in my hotel. I moved silent film star Harold Lloyd's Steinway player piano into the lobby to play music all day, with a seated wax figure of Lloyd himself on the bench.

It wasn't all flower arrangements and beautiful music, however. When we took possession of the hotel, the kitchen was flooded with standing water. There were rats and mice in all the pipes, some not such good swimmers. I put on high yellow rubber waders and went in to help clean up the mess. The switch from movie star pitchwoman to kitchen help came more easily than I would have expected.

The entire hotel received a face-lift worthy of Hollywood. Every room had to be refurbished. Steve Wynn had recently bought the Dunes and planned to liquidate its contents and implode the building to make way for the Bellagio. At the end of January 1993, Jerry and I went to the Dunes auction to see what we could find that might be right for our place. We bid for and bought booths for the showroom and chairs, tables, and lamps for our hotel rooms. All the income from my Los Angeles dance studio—every penny I earned—went into overhead, furniture, and fixtures.

Meanwhile, Richard was preoccupied with the retail space. For some reason, he was treating the hotel like a mall. He leased out the restaurant, all the retail space, and even the casino. We hadn't gotten a gaming license yet, so we hired a gaming firm to run the casino. They gave us a tiny percentage, less than 10 percent. All this in addition to leasing out some of the hotel rooms as time-shares. Richard kept me busy greeting all the folks he lined up to invest. I was part of a great dog-and-pony show as he made deals faster than I could count them.

Richard brought in people from Virginia to help with the work. Our neighbor Anne Bell, who had been so kind to me during Richard's hospital stay in Roanoke, came and created murals, cutting life-size figures out of wood and painting portraits of our favorite stars on them. We installed these in the hallways on every floor. Anne is a wonderful artist, and I was proud to have her beautiful work at our hotel.

Many of my friends also pitched in to help. Donald Light, a good friend from New Jersey, came for a visit and never left. He quit his job back east and moved to Vegas to run the hotel gift shop. His mother, Agnes, came along to keep Donald company. She passed the time knitting in the shop while Donald worked. Everyone thought she was my mother. I loved having her there because it gave the hotel the welcoming, homey feeling I ultimately wanted to convey to the guests.

So many people were working for us. The transformation process was exhausting. It was also exciting and a lot of fun.

As expected, there were also problems.

There was confusion about getting a valid license for construction. Richard had a Virginia license, but it was no good in Nevada. When the Las Vegas Building and Safety Department asked Richard to take a test to be certified, he refused. Instead, Todd and his friend Victor Smith got a general contracting license so we could do our own work at the hotel, but Richard insisted on being in charge.

Richard brought in three young men from Roanoke to refinish the doors for the individual rooms. They poured paint stripper down a drain that went through the kitchen out into the street. People in the neighborhood began complaining to the Nevada Division of Environmental Protection, which traced the pollution directly back to us through the sewer lines. This resulted in fines of more than $52,000. We had to use 55-gallon drums to clean up the hazardous waste. I could have bought new doors for every room for that price. Before I could ask Richard to fire the trio, the FBI stopped by and picked them up. Apparently they were wanted for various felonies back in Virginia.

Richard hired someone to paint over the mirrored elevator doors with gold leaf. The painter took a lot of time to complete his painstaking designs. After a few days he was finished. Then Richard hired someone else to come in and paint over the beautiful gold leaf with plain gold paint.

Richard asked the man who did the stucco work on the hotel exterior to renovate the swimming pool. Todd was the first person to swim in it. As his foot hit the bottom, bubbles of gray gunk rose to the surface. Todd reached his hand out to the wall of the pool; it fell apart under his touch. Instead of concrete, the man Richard hired had used stucco to line the pool— another $30,000 literally down the drain. I went over Richard's head and hired Frank Basso, a contractor who had done work for me in Vegas for years, to redo the pool properly. Frank was our favorite concrete guy. He'd already done a lot of good work for us around the hotel.

It was hard for me to keep track of everything. I saw a lot of questionable activity, but Richard got so defensive when anyone challenged his authority or judgment that I thought it best not to upset him by doing so myself. Like all of us, he seemed to be working so hard to get the hotel opened. The fact is, I was still colorblind when it came to red flags.

But my faith in Richard's ability to build our dream hotel was crumbling like the stucco in that pool.

I'm so happy to have this drawing, as I truly loved
my little hotel. The Paddlewheel Hotel became
the Debbie Reynolds Hotel and Casino.

Chapter 5
The Star Theater

You can imagine my relief when the Debbie Reynolds Hotel and Casino finally opened the last weekend in June 1993. Not every room was ready for occupants, but we were in business. We still had to build the showroom, and then we had to think about the museum—one thing at a time.

My friend Rip Taylor, the comedian, was our first tenant. He'd agreed to be my opening act. As soon as we started refurbishing the rooms, we'd broken down the walls between two rooms on the first floor to create a one-bedroom suite for Rip. While we were building the showroom, Rip and I performed in a little lounge on the first floor we named Jazz and Jokes. I would spend my days circulating in the hotel and greeting people, signing autographs, and doing whatever I could

Todd and me at the Star Theater. This is a jewel of a
theater. I loved performing there. Great memories.

to personally encourage business and get the word
out that my hotel was special. In the early evenings,
I'd be onstage in our Jazz and Jokes lounge after Rip.
Sometimes we'd sing a song together after I came on.

Jazz and Jokes featured a wonderful trio of musicians: my pianist, Joey Singer; my drummer, Gerry
Genuario; and Bob Badgley on bass. They played all
the great music from the 1930s to the present. There
was no cover charge; people just paid for their drinks
and had a good time. Word got out that our hotel was

a fun place to visit, and everyone stopped by. Steve Wynn came in one night with Bob Wagner and Stefanie Powers. Norm Crosby would stop by and tell jokes and ad-lib with me. I wasn't taking any salary for performing, but I enjoyed making everyone happy. And it was the only place where I could perform until the showroom was built.

I wanted my son to design the showroom, which would be on the first floor of the hotel and which we decided to call the Star Theater. Todd had toured with me since he was a child, when I did my act around the world. He was an expert at sound and lights. But Richard was reluctant to have anyone else oversee the work, as he had been with the renovations. I didn't think I had to give my husband Todd's credentials, but we agreed to meet and discuss it over dinner at my favorite restaurant, Piero's.

Dinner started off pleasantly enough. We chatted about the hotel as well as the progress that Todd was making on his ranch in California. Todd was willing to stay in Vegas to help build the Star Theater.

"What do you know about building a showroom?" Richard challenged him.

"I've seen the inside of hundreds of places with my mom," Todd answered calmly. "She's played every place from the Palladium in London to big Broadway theaters and little shitholes in Nowhere, USA, and everywhere in between. I've spent years on the road with her. I know where she was happy and where she wasn't. What do you know about sound? Or lights? And what do *you* know about showrooms?"

Richard responded that he planned to buy the sound equipment from the Dunes.

"No way," Todd said. "That stuff is old and worthless. Mom needs a great sound system."

Richard became agitated and started yelling at Todd. Todd hadn't ever worked with Richard, so he was as surprised as I was by Richard's vehemence. Finally, Richard reluctantly conceded that Todd knew more about showrooms than he did.

"But I don't want you in my business," he told Todd, just a bit too loudly.

"Why would I be in your business?" Todd responded. "You're working in the rest of the hotel. I'll just be building the showroom."

Everyone agreed that Todd would stay out of Richard's "business" and build the showroom in a few months, to open the last Saturday in October.

There we were again, taking on big projects with short deadlines.

Todd plunged head-on into construction. He asked me about my favorite places to perform, which were the Desert Inn in Las Vegas and the Crystal Room at Harrah's in Lake Tahoe. Todd measured the showroom at the Desert Inn, then flew to Tahoe to do the same at Harrah's. He was determined to build a "picture frame" for my show. "You're the painting," he said. "I want the frame to be beautiful too." He envisioned a room with five hundred seats, which would resemble the Rat Pack rooms where Todd's father, Eddie Fisher, had sung and where I also enjoyed performing. We had purchased black booths from the Dunes that had to be completely rebuilt with maroon upholstery to fit the Star Theater's decor. Our showroom was bigger than the showroom at the Dunes, and we had to build additional booths from scratch. I like to connect with my audience like Al Jolson did. Todd built ramps and railings around the booths, so I could leave the stage and walk through the theater to talk and joke with the people who came to see me.

Things were moving along at a breakneck pace, and there was more than enough work to keep everybody busy. The hotel was doing well enough for the time being. Rip Taylor and I entertained in Jazz and Jokes, singing and telling jokes for hours every day. It kept the guests happy, and I loved doing it.

Suddenly, Todd began to get calls and visits from folks with the Las Vegas Building and Safety

Department, about noncompliance with codes. He was pulling permits and using professional, licensed contractors, and we couldn't understand why we were being interrupted all the time to answer their questions. Todd dealt with them so often that he became friendly with them.

"Who's Richard Hamlett?" someone from the code office asked Todd one day.

"That's my mom's husband," Todd answered. "Why do you ask?"

"We've been getting complaints about your construction."

Todd wasn't surprised to hear this, because Frank Basso had told him something similar. So much for staying out of each other's business.

Todd settled that with Richard and left me out of it.

But there was something more serious that he couldn't keep from me. One day in the showroom Todd was talking with a young man who worked for Billy Walters, an associate of Richard's. This person was bragging about how the hotel belonged to him and how Debbie would be working for him. Todd called me to ask if the hotel was in my name.

"Of course it is," I said.

Todd told me about these statements. Billy was one of the people who'd lent us money. Every paycheck

I'd earned for personal appearances since we'd bought the hotel had gone into this venture—*plus* as much as I could borrow by taking out mortgages on my dance studio in LA and my other properties, *plus* loans from all my friends. I had sold my jewelry and my artwork and borrowed against my many antiques. My share of the investment was in the millions. Todd said he would go to the title office to find out what was going on. When he came back, he told me that Billy's assistant was listed as the owner of my hotel.

"That's not possible," I said.

"Believe me," Todd replied. "If I'm telling you that it's in this guy's name, it's in this guy's name."

How could this be?

I confronted Richard, who suggested that we go see Billy, acting as if he wasn't quite sure how this had happened.

So Richard and I drove over to Billy's house in Las Vegas. Billy and his wife, a very pretty blonde, welcomed us. After sitting and exchanging a few pleasantries, I said, "Billy, why isn't the hotel in my name?" Billy looked at Richard, who was looking away from all of us. I continued. "I don't understand why on earth that is. You made us a *loan* so we could buy the property, not you. We never agreed to this. I don't understand any of it."

Billy mumbled something that didn't answer the question.

I turned to Richard and asked, "Is this your doing?"

Richard wouldn't make eye contact with me.

"If this doesn't go back in my name immediately, I'm leaving," I threatened. "Today. Right now. Put the deed back into my name—*only* my name."

Richard was quiet on the ride back. Was I supposed to be an employee at my own hotel? I chose to believe that Billy had talked Richard into something. A few days later, Todd called the title office and the property was back in my name.

Everyone turned their attention back to the work at hand. Money was going into the hotel as fast as I could borrow or earn it. Progress on the showroom moved along quickly. It looked like the Star Theater would open on schedule. In the final weeks, Todd had two crews working around the clock to finish in time. I couldn't afford to pay people time and a half, so my production company hired them during the day and if they wanted to work another shift, their second paycheck came from the hotel payroll. The week before opening night, Richard decided that we needed to raise the floor at the bar in the back of the showroom three feet, to be level with the rest of the room. He and Todd got into a fight about it.

"We'll never make the opening if we tear out the back of the showroom to pour concrete for that," Todd told Richard angrily. "What difference does it make if the waitresses have to walk down a few stairs to get to the bar?"

Richard remained adamant, and Todd came to me, warning, "If we rip out the whole back of the showroom, it will take weeks until we can open."

I shut Richard down, which only caused more tension all around. It was getting more difficult for me to ignore the many problems at the hotel that seemed to be Richard's fault.

By this time, I had tapped every friend I had to help with the opening of the hotel. My accountant, David DeSalvo, was working in the showroom. My friend Margie Duncan had flown in from LA and was working alongside us. I wouldn't have been surprised if Spielberg and Lucas were there, doing the windows. I was running the vacuum cleaner in the hallways outside the rooms. Todd was Scotch-taping wires together in the showroom. People were running around getting the lights and sound set for the first show. The new fiber-optic curtain Todd had ordered hadn't arrived.

In the middle of this madness, I was rehearsing a new show for the Star Theater. We couldn't do it at my hotel since the theater was still under construction, so

I rented a suite in a nearby motel where we could work in the afternoons. My drummer Gerry had a rehearsal plank that he used instead of a drum kit. For three weeks, we worked getting ready for opening night. I put off paying the dancers and musicians until we were open, hoping that the showroom would support itself after that.

But on opening night, I didn't have enough money to pay them, and the ads had been placed and the tickets sold.

I called my friend Phyllis McGuire, who lent me $20,000 to get the doors open. One of the popular McGuire Sisters singing trio, Phyllis was always so generous about lending me money when I was in a jam. Opening night arrived, and Todd's crew was still cleaning up the showroom. I spent close to two hours serving champagne to the guests waiting in line for the show and making sure everyone had a good time while Todd and his group worked away inside.

Finally everyone went into my new jewel of a theater. Rip Taylor took the stage and told jokes. But when he came to the end of his act, Todd was still working on the wiring in the sound booth. He waved to Rip, signaling for him to keep going. Rip vamped for almost an hour more and was really stretching by the time Todd secured the last of the wires with Scotch tape.

At last Rip introduced me.

"Debbie will be here in a minute. She's been through a lot. Can you believe that Eddie Fisher left her for Elizabeth Taylor?"

The crowd laughed, as they do whenever Eddie is mentioned near me.

"Screw Eddie Fisher," Rip joked.

"I did—twice," I said from backstage.

The audience laughed loudly.

When I finally walked onstage, I didn't care that there was no curtain for my entrance. It didn't matter that we'd had no time for a sound check. What a relief to be on my own little stage at last.

I looked at everyone, comfy in the recently upholstered maroon seats. The booths in front of the stage were called Kings Row. Then there was a row of tables, and directly behind them was Queens Row, a name I knew would please some of my fans. Richard was seated in Queens Row, right in the center of the showroom.

After my first song, I went downstage to greet the audience.

"Hi, everybody. Welcome to my new theater. Isn't it beautiful?"

Those wonderful people who had waited on line for hours for my opening night cheered loudly.

"Thank you for coming. What a great night. We made it—we made it! We worked so hard to get ready for the show. I haven't had this much stress since Eddie followed Elizabeth down the Nile."

The audience laughed. I continued to talk to them like they were my friends—which is how I think of them—and was pleased at how responsive they were. They really seemed to be enjoying themselves.

Things went fine until about the middle of my act. As I was performing, Richard stood and walked to the back of the showroom, past Todd in the sound booth, and out the door. He was hard to miss: over six feet tall, with all that gray hair, striding up the center aisle in my spotlight.

I was stunned to see him leave, but didn't miss a beat. Continuing my conversation with the audience, I joked, "They say sex is like bridge. If you don't have a good partner, you'd better have a good hand."

I paused.

"And some say sex is like air. It doesn't seem important until you aren't getting any."

As the audience laughed, I thought about a tall, gray-haired man who wouldn't be getting any for a long time. How dare he walk out of my show?

More singing, dancing, and joking around until opening night drew to a close. I thanked my audience again, then waved to Todd in the back of the room and thanked him for all his hard work. I basked in the applause, feeling a sense of accomplishment.

Afterward, we had a party for everyone who'd helped to make the Star Theater happen. The party went on until the early morning light, with no sign of my husband, who'd never returned after walking out of my show. I didn't have time to worry about him. I was so relieved that we had actually managed to open on time, thanks to Todd and all my friends. I'd made it to the end of a very long night in spite of my fatigue and my husband's premature evacuation.

Todd had been in the theater when Frank Basso, our concrete guy, stopped by after the show. He asked Todd if he had seen Richard, and Todd told him about Richard's early departure.

Frank laughed. He already knew what Todd's answer would be.

"Richard bet me ten thousand dollars that you guys wouldn't get the place open in time," he said. "I waited for him in the parking lot tonight. My truck was blocking his car when he came out. I knew he would try to skip out on me. We got into a big fight. I don't think I hurt him too badly. He's not much of a fighter."

This baffled Todd, although it might have explained Richard's desire to pave the showroom at the last minute, as well as all those calls to the building inspectors Todd had heard about.

"Is he all right?" Todd asked Frank.

"He's fine. Ten thousand dollars lighter and pretty pissed off, but he's fine."

Apparently my husband was somewhere in the city of Las Vegas, licking his wounds caused by betting against me. Meanwhile, I was laughing and drinking with my friends.

Chapter 6

Fear and Loathing in Las Vegas

With the Star Theater finally open and the hotel operational, I needed time to catch my breath. Events had been moving so fast in the past year, but mostly things seemed fine—if I didn't look too closely. I had finished my shows for the second night without a hitch.

It was at least two in the morning. A glass of white zinfandel wine in hand, I sat looking through the open French doors that led to the balcony, at the other end of the living room of my Vegas apartment. From my seat at the little round glass dining table, I could see over the small balcony to the glittering lights of the city. I'd always loved this apartment that I'd bought after my divorce from Harry Karl in 1973. It was small and cozy. I poured another glass of wine and thought about the past few days.

Chaos at the showroom finally turned to joy as we managed to open, only a few hours late. Then my husband walked out in the middle of my first show, and I hadn't seen him since. I'd heard rumors that Richard had a mistress at the Stardust Hotel, loud whispers people must have known I'd notice, that he was having an affair with Jane Parker—that she'd come to Vegas from Roanoke with Richard to help him pass his free time while everyone else was working around the clock to finish the showroom in time for opening night. I didn't want to believe it. Why would Richard be cheating, and with her? I'd met her and didn't think much about her. How could he find the time when we were so busy? I guess people can always find time for affairs.

And now my lawyer had sent me a copy of the deed to a Bel Air property I'd bought, on Angelo Drive. Somehow Richard's name had been added to it. It knocked me back to the days during my second divorce when I was totally broke and in debt for millions, faced with complete failure in every aspect of my life. It was the worst loss I'd ever felt, and I never wanted to repeat it. After that experience with Harry Karl, I'd insisted that all new property I bought be registered in my name only. It was true that I'd bought this one because Richard and I were planning to build a new home in Bel Air. But when I saw the deed to the lot in both our names, that old feeling of insecurity washed over me again.

As my mind raced about deeds, dalliances, and debt, I decided to wait up for Richard and confront him, hoping that he would show up. The more time that passed, the more anxious I grew. I sipped more wine, to soothe my nerves.

It was almost four in the morning; if he didn't get home soon, I'd pass out at the table.

Finally I heard someone at the front door. I sat quietly as Richard closed the door behind him and latched the security chain. I was dreading the coming confrontation. But I wanted to know where he'd been, and why his name had been added to the deed.

Richard's appearance made things easier for me. He looked and smelled like sex, his gray hair tousled just enough to make me think he'd recently tumbled out of bed. He smiled when he saw me, that charming smile I used to love. Now it made me angry. I was sure he was hiding something.

"What are you doing up so late, darlin'?" he asked innocently.

"Waiting for you to come home," I said. "Where have you been for the past day and a half?"

Richard glanced at the empty wine bottle.

"I was working."

"At a brothel? You smell like sperm. I hope it's yours."

Richard looked at me wearily and said, "You've been drinking."

"You bet I have." I held up the deed to the Angelo Drive lot. "Why is your name on this? You do not own this property."

"It's *our* property," Richard said, his blue eyes filled with anger.

I glared at him as he sat down across from me at the table.

"No, it's not *ours*. I paid for it. It's *my* lot. You need to sign *this*."

I pushed my lawyer's paper across the table at him.

Richard reached for my hand. "Why don't we go out on the balcony and talk?" he said.

"I'm not going anywhere with you. This conversation is over."

"We can talk about this outside," Richard insisted and tried again to get me to cross the few steps to the open French doors. My hands gripped the table edge in defiance.

The setting was perfect: my handsome husband and I sitting at a lovely glass table that had once been in a movie, while outside the night was turning to that beautiful hue just before dawn. I could feel my marriage hanging in the balance.

"Let's get all this out in the open," I said. "Who have you been seeing? Do you really have a mistress? If you can have a mistress, I should be able to keep the lot that I paid for. I think you can sign it back to me; I think I deserve that. You walked out of my show on opening night. You've done a lot of bad things at the hotel. You presented yourself to me one way and now you're somebody else. So sign this paper and get out."

"Come outside and let's talk," Richard repeated, his skin flushed with rage.

"No! Sign this paper. I want my property back."

Richard stood and stormed up and down the small living room. My head was spinning from anger, disappointment, and a bottle of wine. Finally he came back to the table and said, "All right. I'll sign it. Come outside and let's be friends."

"Sign it," I said, "and then we'll be friends."

Richard scribbled his name hastily across the deed papers, then took my hand to lead me to the balcony. The look in his eyes scared me. Why did he seem so intent on getting me out on the balcony, which is only about three feet wide—not enough room to have a friendly conversation? Was he thinking about my million-dollar life insurance policy with him as a beneficiary? I could practically see the dollar signs floating above his head, like he was some corny cartoon monster.

At that moment, through the haze of my cheap wine, I was sure he was going to toss me off the balcony. One shove and all his troubles would be over. I pictured myself plummeting twelve stories to the pavement.

"I have to go to the bathroom," I said, pulling away from him. "You go out on the balcony and I'll meet you in a few minutes."

I ran to my bedroom and looked for a place to hide. I didn't know if I could find one, but I wasn't going anywhere near Richard or the balcony.

I opened my closet and quietly closed the door behind me, then shimmied up a pole to the top shelf, where I kept my big luggage and quilted bags, and slid behind the bags, arranging them in front of me so I was completely hidden. After all the work I'd been doing the past few months, I was down to ninety-five pounds, tiny enough to fit behind the duffels and the variety of big satchels. All I could do now was pray.

I shook with fear as silence enveloped the apartment. Time passed. I held my breath as I heard Richard walk through the apartment, slamming doors and calling my name. I really did have to pee; I wished I'd taken a minute to go to the bathroom. But I felt that saving my life was more important.

No sound for another hour or so. The wine had long since worn off. How could I have been so stupid?

How could this be happening to me again? My mind raced through the events of the evening. Richard didn't deny having a mistress, and he was certainly angry. I imagined him telling everyone, "Poor Debbie. She had so much stress from the opening of the hotel. She was drinking heavily. She must have fallen off the balcony. I wish I could have saved her." The stress and the drinking were true. People would believe it was an accident—just a sad case of another drunken ex-movie star. What a great story for the tabloids. I bet I would have been on magazine covers at the supermarkets for weeks! I could almost see the show Richard would put on afterward: the grief-stricken widower busily revealing all the debts I'd accrued at the hotel, sighing through tears, "It must have been too much for the old girl." It would have been a perfect crime.

Finally I heard the front door close. As quietly as possible, I climbed off the top shelf, lowered myself to the closet floor, and curled up there for another twenty minutes, staying very still. God, I had to pee. Hoping desperately that Richard was really gone, I crept down the hall to the front door. The security chain was hanging loose, a sign that he had left and I was alone in the apartment. I said a silent prayer, blessing my daddy who had put that security lock on the condo door soon after I moved in. I slipped the chain back in place and bolted the door, sure now that it was true that Richard had a girlfriend down the block at the Stardust Hotel.

After finally using the bathroom, I called security and instructed the office to remove my husband's name from the parking garage and building pass lists and never to let Mr. Hamlett back into the building.

Chapter 7
A New Day

I 'd told Richard to leave and locked him out of my apartment, and now it was time to lock him out of my life. My third marriage was over.

Eddie Fisher had left me for Elizabeth Taylor, humiliating me in front of the world. But the most hurtful thing that Eddie did was ignoring our children. He wasn't mean or vicious to us, just absent. My second divorce was different. Although Harry Karl wiped us out financially, he was simply an unfortunate man oblivious to the fact that he was harming the children and me. The third time I'd married the devil.

Why didn't I see this coming? Especially after all the times that I'd saved Richard's ass by lending him money. My eyes were wide open when I'd taken him on as a project, even though when I married him I didn't know that he needed propping up. I did what I thought I had to do in order to be a good wife. Thank God my lawyers always drew up notes for him to sign and I could recover the money somehow when we sorted all this out. I felt the failure everywhere I looked. And this time I'd feared for my life as well as the security of my family.

I knew I'd have to meet with Richard to figure out the next step. We owned the hotel together. We'd cosigned loans. That would take time to unravel. I'd been so busy raising money to finish the hotel that I hadn't paid attention to all the details Richard was handling. I did what I do best—I entertained our guests every day, in the lobby, in the showroom, or in the Jazz and Jokes lounge. I did what I always do—work. Telling jokes and putting on a show through every heartbreak. And then I work some more.

Richard had left my apartment two nights before. I hadn't heard a word from him since. I called Jane Parker's room at the Stardust to leave a message for my husband, and he called me back. What a surprise. We agreed to meet at the coffee shop in my hotel. I wanted it to be in a public place.

As we sat at a small table in the coffee shop patio just outside the lobby, in full view, this big man suddenly looked very small to me. He stared at me, those blue eyes as cold as ice. Time stood still. Finally I said, "What do you want to do? Do you want a divorce?"

"I'm in it for the money," he replied. "I'm not leaving. You'll never get rid of me."

I let the words sink in. As many times as I've been betrayed, I never get used to the feeling.

"I want you out," I told him calmly.

"You can't get rid of me," he said. "I control everything. It's all in my name. You're just a figurehead. You're nothing. And I don't love you."

That's obvious, I thought. But I said, "I'm not asking you that. I know you don't love me—you're keeping a mistress right up the street. You had the nerve to bring her here from Virginia. We're done."

"She's not my mistress," he corrected me smugly. "She's the woman I love." Contempt was all over his face.

"I hope you're very happy, and I hope I never have to see you again the rest of my life," I said.

Richard smirked. "I'm going to get the money first," he said. "I'm going to get all the money."

"I hope you won't," I said, praying to God, please don't let this happen to me. "I'm going to fight you as hard as I can."

"You can't," Richard assured me with a smile. "That son of yours isn't clever enough to beat me."

He sounded like he had it all sewn up.

"Thanks for coming by," I said.

Richard stood up, took my hand, and kissed it, then turned and walked away. I sat and watched as he passed the poles in the patio that Todd's wife had painted and strolled past the swimming pool that had collapsed, out into the sunny Nevada day, leaving with his pockets full.

Although I never wanted to see him again, I knew it couldn't be avoided—we'd see each other in court, if no place else.

I'd been in this movie before.

Chapter 8

Happy New Year?

There's an old saying: be careful what you wish for. My wish for a hotel where I could work and put down roots had come true in 1992, and I had welcomed 1993 with such optimism, certain that my dream of stability had finally become reality. Instead, it had cost me my marriage, and once again I was facing the unknown. In November, I arranged for Richard to be paid $270,000 as a buyout of his interest in the hotel, which he was thrilled to take as he ran back to Virginia. In December, the $2 million loan we'd taken out to finance the hotel came due. Todd and I were looking for new money people to pay off the old money people.

They also say that with a new year comes a fresh start, and this was my first New Year's Eve in the Star

Theater. Rip Taylor was great as he laughed and joked 1993 away. I put on my game face and did my show. When it was over, we moved the party to Jazz and Jokes to ring in 1994. My trio played. Old friends joined us, and we sang until 5:00 A.M. Everyone had a great time. I had too much fun to think about resolutions. I rolled into bed around 7:00 A.M. I had a matinee that afternoon and needed sleep.

It was also my first New Year's Eve in ten years without Richard. One of the best things about being married is that you always have a date for New Year's Eve. Despite everything Richard had done to me, when I finally came down from all the parties, I began to miss the rat. Part of me had hoped to hear from Richard during the holidays. When I didn't, I realized there truly was no chance of saving our marriage. So much had happened, but the romantic in me still wanted to believe that somewhere in that black heart of his, Richard had loved me.

Dream on, Tammy.

I wasn't the only one feeling Richard's absence. When Richard's cronies heard that he was back in Roanoke, I guess they got nervous. Suddenly there were people coming out from under every rock in the Nevada desert claiming to have some kind of ownership in the hotel or a note from Richard that was due. I wondered how much money Richard had raised using my name, even before we bought the hotel.

In January 1994, someone sued me for breach of what he claimed was his brokerage agreement, saying that he had brought in all the time-share players and now he wanted a cut. I won the suit, but it took time, money, and energy to fight it.

In March, hoping to stem the tide of lawsuits as well as foreclosure, we merged with a privately owned Colorado corporation called Maxim Properties, which put up cash to help bail us out of the original loan.

The managers were fighting over just about everything, all trying to fill the void left by Richard's departure. As chairman of the board, I was the referee. It was hard to concentrate on the business at hand, and even harder keeping peace while the vultures circled overhead. Instead of fighting with one another, we should have been thinking of ways to make the hotel profitable. It seemed like there was a new battle daily. It could be anything: the investors, the shareholders, or a belligerent bartender. It was hard for me to balance it all. Every day consisted of endless meetings followed by shows at night. I just wanted to perform and get on with my life. How had Richard found the time to lead *two lives?*

The answer to that question apparently was even more interesting than I could have guessed.

One day some gentlemen who worked for Caesars Palace arrived in my Star Theater dressing room and asked if I knew where my husband was. I could honestly answer that I had no idea—it had been weeks since we'd last spoken to each other.

"Mr. Hamlett has some debts at Caesars that need to be settled," they informed me.

I was astounded that, in addition to cheating on me with his mistress, Richard had found time to gamble. The Nevada desert is full of the bones of folks who skipped out on their casino debts, and I could tell that these guys meant business.

Out of annoyance, I suggested that they might find him with his "lady friend" at the Stardust. Part of me wished that they *would* find Richard and "handle" him. I assumed that he must still be in Roanoke, but I wasn't about to share that with these hoodlums. As angry as I was at Richard, I didn't really want to see him get killed. But I wouldn't have minded seeing him run for his life. Another part of me suspected that no one would ever find a trace of Richard Hamlett if he didn't want them to.

My better self prevailed. I replied emphatically, "You won't be getting any payment from me on Mr. Hamlett's debts."

The guys from Caesars said their good-byes and stalked out.

Everyone in Vegas knew about the troubles I'd had with Harry Karl. Soon they would know I had stepped in it again with my third husband. I was grateful to be left out of this particular mess.

Weeks passed. I knew I would have to get a divorce lawyer and serve Richard with papers. The longer I waited, the more money he would want from me. Daddy had raised me to finish every job, but I needed help to finish this one. Even though I was afraid of Richard, even though I knew there was no hope and every day brought a new problem, some part of me still loved him. I knew that explaining my situation would be really difficult.

Finally, after making and breaking several appointments with a legal firm, I showed up and faced the music.

And then, of course, Richard called me. He wanted to know what was going on. He told me that he wasn't really happy without me. Hearing his voice again brought up all the emotions I'd been feeling, all the hurt and shame—and a lingering sliver of affection for him even though I believed he must be lying.

I got off the phone as soon as I could and turned it over to my new attorney to handle.

Now that we both had lawyers, I had a sinking feeling that Richard was juggling our assets so I would come out short in the divorce, even though I hadn't filed yet. In spite of everything that had happened, Richard was still claiming ownership of the hotel. I warned my lawyers and accountants that Richard was up to no good. I was sure that he was spending all his time getting ready for court. Meanwhile, I was drowning in problems at the hotel, trying to unravel all the awful business deals he'd arranged.

In early April, he called and asked me to sign over a property that he'd had me purchase as an investment right after we were married, an office building/shopping mall center in the Peters Creek area of Roanoke. Richard had managed the property for us.

"Why would I do that?" I asked him.

"Because I hold the note on it. You have to sign it over to me or I'll be forced to foreclose on it."

God, how I hated him when I heard that.

"How do you hold the note?" I asked evenly, glad that he couldn't see me gritting my teeth. "I paid off that property years ago."

"There are expenses and taxes due. I don't want to foreclose on you, but I may have to. Just sign the paperwork over to me and I'll take care of everything."

I just bet you will, I thought.

"I need a little time," I said. "Let me get back to you."

Richard agreed, explaining that he was going to a San Diego clinic for prostate surgery.

My lawyer advised me to hold off on signing anything Richard gave me. I kept flashing back to my other divorces. I, the Girl Scout who did not believe in divorce, was now headed for my third.

A few weeks later, Richard called again, threatening to foreclose on me if I didn't sign the Peters Creek papers. He said he was still in the clinic but was going to Virginia soon to handle the foreclosure. His phone calls were coming every week now. By the middle of May, I knew I had to do something to find out his intentions. We owned so many properties together.

By the end of the month, the phone wires were burning up all over Roanoke. I got a call that Richard had bought a new Lincoln for himself and a new Jaguar for Jane. Did I know that he'd charged drinks at the Elephant Walk in Roanoke using a credit card with my name on it? Richard's family told me that he and his girlfriend were leaving on May 24 for a two-week vacation in Europe, and one Roanoke friend added that their plans included traveling on the Orient Express. How ironic. Richard would be showing Jane the places that I had shown him only a few years before with my family. He'd been calling to tell me about his prostate surgery while he was actually taking off for Europe.

But I had no time to ponder the irony in my life. I wanted to know where Richard was getting the money to do all this.

My lawyers found out that the Peters Creek property was indeed in Richard's name. Time was slipping by, and I had to find out exactly where matters stood. I needed proof of all the dirty tricks Richard had played while we were married.

I had a matinee on Sunday. I decided that after I'd done my show, I would take matters into my own hands.

Chapter 9
Raid on Roanoke

When the going got tough, the tough got going . . . to Virginia. I sent out a call to action and rented a small plane to fly to Roanoke. My friend Margie Duncan flew to Vegas from Los Angeles to join me. Her son, Mark Rich, was already working at the hotel. Todd and his friend Fred Pierson filled out the passenger list. We were on a mission to get what was rightfully mine out of Roanoke. It was Sunday, May 29. We left right after my performance. We could be back in Vegas in two days, in time for my next show.

Supposedly I owned a dozen properties in and around Roanoke. Richard acquired them, my attorney carefully wrote loan papers and promissory notes securing the sales, and I paid for everything. But I was convinced that Richard had been juggling the real estate. I feared that there would be no way to prove my ownership without his records of the transactions. Richard's bookkeeper was prepared to let me copy whatever I needed from his office.

Margie, Todd, Mark, Fred, and I sat crowded on the plane with computers, portable copy machines, and reams of paper balanced on our laps. Somewhere in the Midwest the pilot had to stop to refuel; I couldn't afford a plane big enough to make the cross-country trip in one jump. I don't think any of us got any rest, crammed in as we were.

Our plane landed at 2:00 A.M. Eastern time. Bootie Bell met us at the airport and drove us to a little hotel in Roanoke, where we managed to get a few hours of rest before friends picked us up and drove us to the house I'd shared with my husband. I hadn't been there since we separated. As we pulled up the driveway, I knew that my key wouldn't work anymore.

Todd tried the front door lock—no luck. He surveyed the house for an open window or door that might have been left ajar. Some of our neighbors waved to me as they were leaving for work, saying, "Nice to see you, Debbie."

"Nice to see you too," I replied, waving back and smiling. "I'm here to surprise Richard for our anniversary."

That sounded good. Wave and smile.

Margie's son, Mark, was terrified that we would be arrested and thrown into a Virginia jail. Todd and I had no concern about that. I was still legally married to Richard, and I had paid for this house three times over. I should be able to visit it, with or without a key.

Todd finally dislodged a window in the back by taking it off its track. He climbed in, opened the front door, and let us all into the house.

"Hi, darling, I'm home. Surprise! Happy anniversary," I called out as I crossed the threshold. It seemed like an eternity since I'd been happy there. As I looked around the living room, I saw my good china in crates, and large gondolas full of the costumes from the *Molly Brown* tour. Everyone went to a corner of the house to start gathering information that could help in my divorce settlement.

I took the bedroom. When I went into my closet, I discovered another woman's clothes. My things were scattered all over the floor—scarves, makeup pencils, eyelashes, and wigs, lying there in a mess. All my rollers and cosmetics had been taken out of the bathroom and tossed on the pile. If they bothered Richard's girlfriend so much, why didn't she just throw them away? Did they think I was coming back for them? Maybe it felt good just to fling them around and close the door. You can have Richard, I thought. Just leave my eyelashes alone.

But there was no time to worry about that now. I had work to do.

In the desk in our bedroom, I found notes from his lady friend that Richard had saved, with intimate details of their sex life together. They made me blush. She wrote with such passion—about how wonderful he was, how romantic.

I was glad she'd found it worth writing home about. The screwing I'd got as Richard's wife wasn't worth the screwing I was getting now.

We decided to rent a truck to ship my things back to Las Vegas. Todd asked Mark if he would drive, and Mark agreed on the spot. He didn't mind making the trip alone. We boxed up everything of mine that we could find—files, costumes, and china. The boys got the truck and loaded it all in. No more fancy dinner parties with my good china for Richard's granny.

As we were leaving the house, I decided to write Richard a note:

DEAR RICHARD,

I flew in to surprise you for our anniversary. I was worried about your health since you told me about your impending operation. Obviously you are feeling better since you took a trip to Europe.

So my trip should not have been in vain, I have
saved you the trouble of shipping me my Molly
Brown costumes and my good china.

DEBBIE

I left the note in the middle of the living room floor.
Once we finished at the house, Bootie drove us to
Richard's office, where the bookkeeper arranged to let
us in to copy the files that Richard kept at work that
covered my involvement in the business. These files
were not the same as the files we'd found at the house.
Todd went to work copying them, as well as the hard
drive from the computer. My business partner husband
had been less than honest in informing me of his deals.
It seemed my properties were no longer in my name or
Richard's. He'd been backdating the deeds while transferring the real estate to his girlfriend, Jane Parker.
Some of them were even in their relatives' names. I
fantasized what it would be like to unravel all this and
leave Richard with nothing—which is more than he'd
had when he married me.

While we were at the office, Richard's property manager came in and saw what we were doing. Although he
was loyal to Richard, when I told him I was there to
surprise my husband for our anniversary, he didn't say
another word. I think he knew that same husband and

his girlfriend were off on a European holiday. I doubt that he knew it was probably paid for with my money.

Our next stop was the county treasurer's office. In Richard's files we had found copies of paperwork from a lawsuit brought by Richard's first wife, who was suing Richard's girlfriend, Jane Parker, over her loss of the Peters Creek property—the same property Richard was now threatening me with foreclosure about. The papers were dated 1992, and actually named Jane as Richard's "paramour." They said Richard had put the property in Jane's name, then in his brother's name. How could she lose the property when I'd bought it in 1984? If this sounds confusing, it was. It took a long time to figure it out. Apparently this game of "deed roulette" was a favorite of Richard's. What was clear was that this didn't look good for my claim to ownership.

I wanted copies of all the deeds, to help my lawyers unravel exactly what Richard had done. The treasurer showed me notices to Richard from the county, for overdue taxes in the amount of $31,183.10. I'd always given him money to pay the taxes, just like everything else. I shouldn't have been surprised that he apparently kept it and left the property with a lien. Maybe it was a mixture of shock and fatigue or a sense of doom about this upcoming court case, but I found myself getting emotional about Richard's treachery. I couldn't make myself believe that someone who'd said he loved me, who'd married me and put on quite a show for the first few years of our life together, could completely betray me. How long had this been going on? Why didn't I run and hide when he told me we couldn't just be lovers because he wasn't "that kind of guy"? Was he really that patient and calculating as he systematically emptied my pension account to invest in his own companies and numerous other properties, all the while acting the part of a loving husband? It baffled me.

It wasn't just the girlfriend, although through the Roanoke grapevine I'd heard about more than one lady who was involved with Richard. Whether it was a toothless waitress from the waffle house or his lady Jane, Richard was never without female companionship of some kind. Hell, my first husband left me for Elizabeth Taylor. At least that made sense.

Thinking back to our long late-night phone conversations, I wondered if any of these women lay patiently beside Richard while he chattered away with me. Sometimes we stayed on the phone for hours, just shooting the breeze and—I thought—enjoying each other's company while we were apart. How rude of Richard to make his girlfriends wait through those long chats with his wife. Where were his manners?

Once we were all packed up, we headed for the airport. As we said our good-byes and thanked Bootie and other friends, I wondered when I would see them again. In court? Would they come to Vegas to visit? I was so grateful that they had helped me expose Richard's antics so I could hope to recover from all this.

No one slept on the return flight to Vegas. We had more room because Mark was driving back everything we could load onto the rental truck. After we landed, I headed for the hotel to get ready for my evening performances. My show always goes on. Thank God for my audiences. At least I have always been able to count on them.

Chapter 10
Under the Elephant's Tail

Richard never called me after my raid on Roanoke. Not a word about my note or retrieving my belongings. I never got back the things I couldn't take with me (including a chandelier I really loved that was in another house), even though I sent Richard everything he'd left behind in Las Vegas and at our house in LA. The trip had been rough on me. My head was swimming with all the Roanoke information. In spite of his health concerns and fabulous European vacations, Richard had been very busy, thank you. The files and paperwork from his Virginia offices would keep my legal team working for quite some time. And when I was back in Las Vegas, I knew I had to confront the failure of my third marriage.

A few days after we returned, I had a spell of global amnesia similar to one I'd had over a decade before, in

March 1983, when I was performing on Broadway in *Woman of the Year*. It happened during my Saturday matinee. Five minutes before the end of the first act, I blacked out. I kept performing, but for those few minutes I had no idea what I was saying or singing. And then I collapsed onstage. When the curtain came down, paramedics rushed me from the Palace Theatre to Roosevelt Hospital, where the doctors told me I'd experienced a rare form of amnesia, which might have been caused by exhaustion or stress. I'd replaced Raquel Welch, had to learn the entire show in only a few weeks, and had been performing eight times a week, so it made sense that I was exhausted. The doctor said it was unlikely to happen again.

Yet here I was, years later, alone in my apartment, unable to remember anything. I knew where I was, but I didn't know what to do. I could speak, but I made no sense. The disorientation lasted only a few minutes, but I felt weak for a few hours. It scared me that all this pressure was affecting my health. I didn't do my show for the next few days while I rested, took Valium and aspirin, and prayed that I would heal.

Hoping that I could relax and maybe even have some fun, my high school friend Paula Kent Meehan invited me on a cruise to the Mediterranean. My friends Margie Duncan and Jerry Wunderlich met us in Nice, in the south of France, and from there we sailed to Saint-Tropez and other wonderful port cities. Paula's other guests included the president of L'Oréal and a Saudi prince. Everyone pampered me and was thrilled I was aboard. It was a wonderful break from all the stress I'd been going through.

When I got back to Las Vegas, I had dinner with my piano player, Joey Singer. At the end of the meal, the waiter returned my credit card. It was maxed out. Joey kindly paid the check.

That was what my life had come to: cruising with royalty one day and dead broke the next. There was no money anywhere, and I couldn't work any harder.

It appeared that Richard had been transferring the properties we owned into his brother's and girlfriend's names and backdating the deeds so they wouldn't be included in his holdings when it came to determining our divorce settlement. He'd supposedly done the same thing to his first wife. I felt that he must have had an accomplice at the registrar's office in Roanoke. Deeds don't backdate themselves.

The details of Richard's deceits were too much for me. Feeling threatened at every turn, I stopped sleeping. I worried about my health. And all of those hotel investors! I was lost in the midst of animals running madly around me and grabbing any funds they could get their hands on. My rage was so deep, even as my heart was filled with hopelessness. I told myself I should be in LA, helping Carrie with my granddaughter, Billie. I felt I was an absolute failure to my children. I had made every possible wrong decision, and I was in deep, almost unbearable pain.

The legal team advised me that it would take months to prepare the divorce filings. It was so complicated and distressing. This is going to kill me, I thought. But I had to keep going. I couldn't leave this mess for my family. I told myself I could start over once I got rid of Richard and his dirty tricks.

In late September 1994, I served Richard with divorce papers. It didn't take long for him to contact me. He called, acting nice, asking about the status of things. Whose name was the hotel in? Where was all the stock? It took a lot of effort for me to keep my distance and not fall for his lying charm again. I focused on staying calm while he gave me the third degree.

And then it was time to turn my attention back to the hotel business. We tapped every resource we could think of to keep afloat. I asked all my friends for help. More loans. More contracts. Everyone received stock in exchange for their investments. Todd suggested that we put on a fashion show of items from my collection, to announce that the hotel was going public and pre-sell stock to credited investors. No one had seen the amazing costumes and Hollywood memorabilia I'd been collecting for decades.

We put on quite a presentation. The fashion show took place on the first floor of the hotel, right outside the entrance to the Star Theater. Models dressed in the costumes I had collected strolled by the folks who might determine the fate of the museum construction. Marilyn Monroe's subway dress from *The Seven Year Itch* came to life again as a young model twirled the skirt in the show.

I took back the management of the hotel's restaurant. The kitchen was a nightmare, but we managed to hire a chef and several ex-convicts as cooks and kitchen workers. Todd installed hidden surveillance cameras to make sure that we weren't robbed. The tapes showed our ex-cons working while our security guards hauled big boxes of steaks out to their cars. Everyone was stealing from me except the men who'd been in prison, who appreciated the second chance offered by a job at the hotel.

I worked through the rest of 1994 holding my breath, hoping that the next year would bring some resolution to all these problems. But 1995 turned out to be what I now call the Year Under the Elephant's Tail.

There was a bright spot: Todd was creating my long-hoped-for museum in the hotel, and in February, Bennett Management & Development, a Syracuse, New York, firm that had been in business since 1980, gave us a two-year loan for $525,000 to use in the construction of the museum and for general corporate purposes. Kennedy Capital Management in St. Louis lent us the remaining $400,000 we needed to finish everything.

Aside from the museum, I felt like I was stranded under the wrong end of the elephant without my raincoat and umbrella from *Singin' in the Rain,* flooded under a cascade of lawsuits and a shit storm of epic problems from every direction. With Richard finally out of the picture, Todd and I did everything we could to clear the foxes out of the henhouse.

We hired the vice president of administration for Sahara Resorts to be the president of our hotel, and Joe Kowal to help drum up interest in the hotel's stock. A former professional hockey player, Kowal had been involved in the successful public launch of the Los Angeles Koo Koo Roo chicken restaurants.

Desperate for money to pay off the existing mortgage and keep the doors open, in March we sought advice from Bennett Management. They said they would help us with another loan, but only if Todd became the hotel's CEO.

Todd and I looked at each other in disbelief. As much as I trust my son, it never occurred to me to put him in that position. He was much better at technical things that required his designing skills.

When we returned to Vegas, I suggested to Todd that we get another opinion. Todd agreed.

Steve Wynn is one of the best hotel operators in the world. He had played a key role in the 1990s resurgence and expansion of the Las Vegas Strip by successfully refurbishing existing resorts and building new hotels such as the Golden Nugget, the Mirage, Treasure Island, the Bellagio, the Wynn, and the Encore—all Vegas institutions now. In addition to knowing the business, Steve's a terrific man. I wrote him a note, asking if he would meet with Todd and me, and reminding him that once at a party when we were talking about my hotel, he'd offered, "If you ever need any help, just call me." Boy, did I need him now.

Ever gracious, Steve agreed to see us.

Todd and I were escorted into Steve's office on the top floor of the Mirage. I began by explaining that we needed help getting a loan to keep my hotel open. We also needed help to get a gaming license. I explained the trouble with the hotel management. Then I asked Steve to recommend a new CEO. As I told my story of crazy deals at the hotel, I became increasingly emotional, until I couldn't keep my composure another minute and began to cry.

"There's no place for that in business, Debbie," he said gently. Reaching for the phone on his desk, he pointed at Todd.

"How old are you?" he asked.

"Thirty-four," Todd answered.

Steve turned to me and said, "He should take over. You need to throw all these people out. Get rid of all these players."

There it was again.

Todd and I looked at each other, taking a moment to let the idea sink in.

"I don't have any experience running a hotel," Todd told Steve.

"So what?" Steve responded. "You're old enough. And you won't rob your mother like you say everybody else has."

He pushed a button on the telephone on his desk. When his assistant answered, Steve told her to get the head of the gaming commission, Chairman Bible (isn't that a fun name for a gaming mogul?), on the line, and they discussed helping me obtain a license for the hotel.

When you apply for a gaming license in Nevada, not only must everyone in the company be above reproach, you also have to have enough capital to pay for the license. As I recall, the minimum license fee was around $2 million at that time. I had banks that would lend me money for the hotel if we had a gaming license, but I had no money for the license. It was a classic catch-22. I borrowed money on my house in North Hollywood, and more money from my dance studio. But we had never been granted a license, even though Richard, Todd, and I had flown to Carson City, Nevada, in 1993 to meet with the gaming board at least three times. It may have been because of Richard's history in Virginia that he had kept secret from me. He'd had felony charges brought against him where he pleaded guilty although the charges were eventually dropped. He explained them away, blaming someone else for giving him a bad deal. I didn't read the Roanoke newspapers, so I didn't know about his troubles there.

It was very frustrating, because I knew that other places got their gaming licenses easily. And I'm not just talking about casinos. I'd drive down the street and see a sign that said SUPER SHOOKIE or PUSSY'S PARLOR or some other little joint had just opened a new gaming room. I'd run in and ask, "How'd you get your license?" "We just applied for it," they'd say. "Oh? Was it expensive?" "Yes." But they got it.

Even with Steve Wynn talking to Chairman Bible on our behalf, our situation didn't change.

Todd and I decided to take everyone's advice and make Todd the CEO, and Bennett lent us another $340,000 for general corporate purposes, to be paid back, like their first loan, in March 1997.

Meanwhile, Todd was building the new museum in the hotel, working closely with Joe Bianci, a lighting designer with a background in theater who had been my lighting director for many years, and Donald Light, when he wasn't running the gift shop. They slept on cots in rooms on the ground floor of the hotel. It was a dorm of gifted, talented friends. They broke out a seven-thousand-square-foot space that could have been used for a small comedy room, but my designer friend Jerry Wunderlich said we could make it work. And he and Todd and Joe did exactly that.

Before they started, Todd had showed me the plans and explained that the museum would be like a ride at Disneyland. "Just build it," I said.

Their concept was to display the collection within a 125-seat theater. They soldered together the floors and built stages with 35mm screens that revolved like a carousel and showed clips from the scenes with the costumes in them. Todd got the original movies and installed surround sound. I did a green-screen voice-over that introduced the film clips. The lighting was designed around the screens. While a film clip ran, the lights would come up on a costume or prop from that movie. The sets, the costumes, and the mannequins came alive as the film clips ran. When you entered, it was reminiscent of the old Pantages and Egyptian movie palaces in Hollywood. It was just spectacular—a brilliant little gem of a museum. Todd was so proud of it, and I was so proud of him.

It had been a long time coming.

In 1961 a group of people in the motion picture industry began plans to build a museum to honor film history. Legendary silent-film star Mary Pickford (the first actress known as "America's Sweetheart"), director Mervyn LeRoy, producer Sol Lesser, and many others of us in the industry contributed money and support. As with the Motion Picture Home, we all wanted this to happen. The project was to be called the Hollywood Motion Picture and Television Museum.

Mary Pickford and her second husband, Buddy Rogers, were an important part of this venture. Mary was a collector. I remember visiting her and Buddy at Pickfair, their Beverly Hills estate that had been named after Pickford and her first husband, Douglas Fairbanks Sr. Buddy gave me a tour of their barn. It was crammed full of costumes and wonderful mementos from the early days of movies. Unfortunately, the barn wasn't holding up well; I could see daylight coming through loose wallboards.

The plan was for the museum to be built on Highland Boulevard, on the grounds of the Hollywood Bowl. Stars such as Bette Davis and Fred Astaire and director Cecil B. DeMille donated their papers, scrapbooks, and memorabilia. The planning committee decided the site was too small and proposed moving it across the street. Both of these lots were available, and everything was a go for the construction of a $6.5 million museum.

Then there was a problem.

An ex-Marine named Stephen Anthony lived in a rundown shack of a house on the edge of the proposed building site. Using the power of eminent domain, the city condemned Mr. Anthony's property and offered him $11,500 to move. This didn't sit well with Mr. Anthony, who barricaded himself inside his house and shot at anyone who came near it.

The standoff lasted sixty-three days. On the night of the Academy Awards, Mr. Anthony was watching the show in his condemned house with his lawyer. As Sidney Poitier was announced the winner of the Best Actor Award for his brilliant performance in *Lilies of the Field,* two undercover Los Angeles policemen managed to get inside. They jumped Mr. Anthony and put him in handcuffs. The house was already surrounded by dozens of police, who took Mr. Anthony away to jail, where he was held for six months.

This incident divided the Hollywood community. Most of the public believed that Mr. Anthony was a hero who shouldn't have been driven from his home just to build a museum for a bunch of dead movie stars. Many actors agreed. The courts ruled that Mr. Anthony was a squatter, living on a property that had been condemned. Faced with a firestorm of controversy, the city's Board of Supervisors pulled the funding and construction was never begun.

The City of Los Angeles then put all the artifacts that had been donated in the City Jail (talk about irony), where they remained for many years. Conditions at the jail were horrible. The roof leaked, and no care was taken to preserve these valuable items. Let's hope Mr. Anthony received better treatment. Fred Astaire tried to get his tap shoes back. Bette Davis called me from her Connecticut home and insisted, "You must go and get my scrapbooks. I gave them my fucking scrapbooks. Where are they?"

When I went down to the jailhouse, the people in charge wouldn't release Bette's property. I told them that since Bette was alive and cursing, she had a right to have her things back until a museum could be built. The answer was still no.

That was the first unsuccessful attempt to get a Hollywood museum built.

Years passed with no activity. Then, in 1970, I read in the *Hollywood Reporter* that MGM was planning to auction off their land, their wardrobe, their scenery, and all their props. I was still under contract there, so I went to the office of the president, Jim Aubrey, to find out what was going on.

"We're in the real estate business now," he told me.

MGM was selling Lot 2, where *Singin' in the Rain* had been filmed. So many other famous films had been shot there, and now MGM was looking to liquidate their holdings to raise money. The old studio system had indeed come to an end. I couldn't believe what I was hearing.

That was the year I began to collect in earnest.

My idea was to turn Lot 2 into another Disneyland. I remember the day Walt Disney opened his theme park. "I sure hope this works," he told me. "I've put all I own into it." Disney had mortgaged everything, including his home, to fund this park for children and the young at heart. He and I went on the "It's a Small World" ride together, both of us crying because it was so wonderful. There we were, a studio head and twenty-three-year-old Debbie Reynolds, weeping in our boats as we rode through the magical realization of his dreams. I'm glad it was dark in there. Walt Disney certainly had the courage to back his dream, and I hoped to follow his example.

Harry Karl and I went to see his good friend Al Hart, who was then president of Citibank in Beverly Hills. Citibank gave me $5 million to buy Lot 2. But my offer wasn't accepted, and someone else bought the property for the same price. Undaunted, I asked Jim Aubrey if he would sell me some of the costumes and props prior to the auction. He told me to "find a seat and bid like everybody else."

The mood at MGM was horrible in those days. It was incredible to me that the studio was scrapping its history. All the music files were sold to a company that used them for landfill under the new 405 freeway being built. Films from the studio libraries were burned in big metal rubbish barrels. These included scenes that had been cut from great MGM movies. Clothes were tossed into boxes and sold to thrift stores. Costumes that cost $20,000 to construct would be bundled together and the lots sold for $200 to costume houses all over the country, and not only in big cities. It broke my heart that so many of these unique creations would probably become Halloween costumes in a very short time, as no one knew their true value.

I bought everything I could afford. The MGM auction lasted for three weeks. I was there almost every day.

Soundstages full of items were sold. I got a tiny fraction of what was offered. The rest was scattered to the four corners of the world, never to be seen again. Someone in Texas bought the paddlewheel boat used in *Show Boat*. I wonder how they got it home! Another Texan outbid me for the brass bed from *The Unsinkable Molly Brown*. He told me that his wife had a stronger connection to it than I did. I still don't understand that. When my costumes from the movie went up for sale, the audience yelled, "Give them to her." The auctioneer finally conceded and let me have them for a few hundred dollars.

The following year 20th Century Fox did the same thing. Jerry Wunderlich put me in touch with the president of Fox, who allowed me to pick out anything I wanted prior to the public sale. That's when I bought all of Marilyn Monroe's costumes, which became the most famous objects in my collection.

All these things had to be warehoused safely. I met with Irwin Karz, a friend from MGM who owned the Garden Court Apartments on Hollywood Boulevard, near Grauman's Chinese Theatre. Irwin shared my love of Hollywood memorabilia and offered to let me store everything at his building. Anne Baxter, George Peppard, and North American Van Lines helped me move all the furniture, props, costumes, and set pieces I had purchased to Irwin's five-story building. He and I

Moving day for my collection. George Peppard and
Anne Baxter even came down to help us.

hoped to transform some part of it into a permanent
home for the collection.

Unfortunately, the security there wasn't good. Many
of the things I had bought at auction disappeared,
including a lot of the furniture.

When Harry Karl and I divorced, the bank gave me a choice between keeping our house or keeping my collection. Everything was out of the house in four days—including me and the children.

I kept trying to find a location for the museum. I entered into an agreement with the City of Los Angeles to renovate the Pan Pacific Building, a landmark structure in the Fairfax District, in the center of Hollywood near the Farmers Market and CBS Television City. This would have been a perfect location. But the city decided not to go forward with the project. It was a bitter disappointment.

Now finally, all these many years later, I had my museum.

Opening night was set for April 1, 1995, my sixty-third birthday. Things went pretty smoothly in terms of making the deadline. Still, I did not actually see the presentation Todd had prepared until that night.

It was a gala affair. Paula Kent Meehan flew up in her jet, filled with guests for the party. So did Bob Petersen, owner of the Petersen Auto Museum in LA. Roddy McDowall, Esther Williams, Ruta Lee, and so many of my Hollywood friends came to Vegas to wish me a happy birthday and see the new museum. When we sat together in the theater, we all saw the presentation for the first time. It was thrilling as the carousel revolved around us in our seats, with costumes and film clips appearing and then passing out of view. Of course I started crying. Seeing everything so beautifully show-cased made my heart sing. It was a triumph—a wish come true and the perfect birthday gift.

But we were still in the middle of a cyclone of trouble at the hotel. Todd was busy fending off more lawsuits. I had paid cash for all the furniture and fixtures, and now I was getting bills from leasing companies I knew nothing about. Richard had taken out loans on the hotel's physical assets, so that I was now leasing what I had already paid for and, according to these compa-nies, the payments had come due. Richard was gone, and with him all that money. I wondered where it had gone. For more $10,000 bets that he lost?

Just to make things concise, let me give you a run-down of some of the litigation I faced in 1995. In prepar-ing to write this book, I went through forty-five boxes of files and reams of legal documents to piece together this time in my life. I was sued by most of the time-share holders—more than three hundred lawsuits—in addition to employees, vendors, managers, creditors, and (to add insult to injury) lawyers. It would be much too boring, not to mention confusing, to slog through the endless details. Instead, I'll give you, for lack of a better term, the "highlights."

The first two important lawsuits came from two of our original associates.

On April 14, Ed Coleman sued us for breach of contract. He got nothing.

On April 28, Ron Nitzberg sued for breach of contract, claiming we owed him $245,000. We counter-sued him for breach of fiduciary duties and contract. I won that one.

In May, Todd became the CEO of the Debbie Reynolds Hotel and Casino, and we terminated our contract with the Canadian company, which had furnished the services of our original time-share guru. Todd discovered some large cash transfers that had been made from the hotel account to an account in Canada. There were personal charges for a Hawaiian vacation on a company credit card. The guru left but the problems at the top had trickled down. There was one croupier who was giving herself two chips for every single chip she collected in the casino. The employees' dining room was losing $75,000 a month. Todd fired one hundred of the company's three hundred employees. The new president was a very nice man and not corrupt, but Todd cut his salary in half to reduce expenses.

No lawsuits in June—hard to believe. Then in July we were sued twice.

August was the hardest month for me personally. In 1993 one of my best friends had invested in the hotel. When we got into trouble and I couldn't pay him back right away, I offered him stock as collateral. On the advice of his management company, he refused. Instead, he took me to court to recover his investment. It was heartbreaking for me as well as a bad choice on his part. All my other friends took the stock, and I personally paid everyone back as soon as I could. This friend and I finally settled, but we didn't speak for a few years. I was devastated, and so was he. For some reason he believed that I actually had money when he sued me.

In fact, that same month I personally guaranteed a third loan from Bennett Management, for $2,865,000, without knowing how I would repay it. The proceeds were principally used to pay off existing debt, including the $525,000 they'd lent us in February and the $340,000 from May, and for general corporate purposes. The new loan was due August 1999. (As it turned out, Bennett was running a Ponzi scheme. In 2000 they were prosecuted and convicted, so we never had to pay them back.)

September brought us a suit from YESCO, the company that put up all the signs outside the hotel. One of their employees told Todd that YESCO had written a check to Richard as part of the deal. Why on earth would they pay Richard for something he hired them to do? It became a big legal mess, with me in the middle. Todd had to beg YESCO to leave the signs up while we straightened everything out. I wrote them a check for the $75,000 they said they had given Richard, and we worked out the rest. Then YESCO got in line with everyone else as we moved forward. Their suit for more than $700,000 was finally settled.

In addition to all that, we had to deal with our own inexperience. In December we issued options for 750,000 shares of stock to a man named Peter Bistrian and an associate, unaware that Bistrian was a convicted felon who'd served time for bank fraud. He and his associate never paid for the shares, and the following April Bistrian was in prison again, after pleading guilty to selling phony shares of another casino company in 1993. "He had a pretty good reputation," Todd says, but he wishes we'd done more checking.

As Todd told the Las Vegas Sun in April 1998, the principal blunder was probably the choice to focus on time-share units rather than gaming, because people go to Vegas to gamble. Everything else is incidental. But we'd never been able to get our own license.

Looking back, I believe I was acting with my heart instead of my brain during the time when all this was happening. I believed that if I fought hard and kept working, eventually the hotel would be a success and everyone would benefit. I never imagined that the hotel could fail.

Dreams are funny when you're chasing them. My dream of a loving husband and a stable life with a permanent place to work had eluded me again.

The museum at my Las Vegas hotel for my collection—
a dream come true.

Chapter 11
Mother Plays *Mother*

Nineteen ninety-five continued to be the year under the elephant's tail. There was no avoiding the ongoing deluge of problems—the hotel troubles, the divorce battles. Through it all, I kept working as best I could. When I hit the stage each night, I could forget my difficulties for a few hours while I entertained my audience.

Sometime in the fall Carrie called to tell me that her friend Albert Brooks was casting a new movie, to be entitled *Mother*.

"You're perfect for it, Mama," Carrie encouraged. "Albert said he'd meet you."

I understood Carrie's reasoning. For as long as I can remember, all the young people around me have called me Mother. The chorus kids in *Irene*, the actors in my movies—all have connected to my motherly side. This makes me very proud, as I believe it's one of my best qualities.

"I don't know your friend, dear," I admitted. "I've been so busy, I haven't kept up."

Carrie went on to tell me more about Albert, emphasizing that he was brilliant and how right I was for the part. I vaguely remembered meeting Albert at some point with Carrie, but she has so many talented friends, he was only a name now. It was difficult for me to think about doing a movie at that time; when I wasn't performing nightly at the hotel, I was giving concerts in other cities.

Carrie sent me a copy of the script to read. Several days later she called to find out if I'd looked at it. When I told her the script was still downstairs at the reception desk, she strongly urged me to read it.

Finally, the next day, I retrieved the script. It was about a neurotic science-fiction writer who moves back in with his mom to solve his personal problems after two failed marriages. I was a bit troubled by how different the character of the mother was from me, but I knew I could study the part and play her well. Albert's script was so good that I agreed with Carrie that I should read for him.

It had been a long time since I auditioned for a part. The studio system had kept me working without screen tests or auditions once I proved myself. I'd read for some sitcom in the 1980s, for a group of twenty-somethings who asked what acting experience I had, which didn't exactly endear them to me. If the casting landscape hadn't changed since then, I wasn't optimistic about my prospects with Albert.

I was the only person there to meet him when I arrived at his office at Paramount. I read two scenes, and he told me I had the part.

"You can't just say that," I protested. "Who's the director?"

"I am."

"Well then, who's your boss?"

"Me again, and I'm telling you the part is yours."

I couldn't believe what I was hearing. One of Carrie's friends was telling me I had the lead in the movie without consulting anyone else. Could he *do* that?

"I can read another scene," I offered. I was prepared to read several. "How about the one in the restaurant?"

He said that wouldn't be necessary.

Much later Albert told me that my behavior during that meeting assured him he'd made the right choice: I was already bossing him around.

I returned to Las Vegas with mixed emotions. Who would take over for me at the hotel while I was on location? I hadn't had a lead movie role in years. There was so much at stake; I wasn't sure that I could handle it. I thanked God that Lillian Burns Sidney, my coach from MGM, was available to work with me.

Todd arranged to book a revue into the Star Theater while I was away doing *Mother*. Production was set to begin at the end of the year. Until then, I continued to work every job in sight to save the hotel from bankruptcy.

On days off from my showroom I would work one-nighters elsewhere to make money for the hotel. One Saturday in November I was onstage performing in Riverside, California, doing a show for a group of doctors, when suddenly I felt horrible pain in my stomach. I hadn't experienced anything like it since I gave birth to Todd, who'd weighed over nine pounds. Somehow I got through the show and had my picture taken afterward with many of the doctors there. Even though I was in a room full of physicians, I would never presume to ask them for medical advice. I decided to wait until I got home, hoping that some rest would make me feel better. It was a two-hour drive from Riverside to my house in North Hollywood. I slept in the back of the limo all the way.

The pain woke me up at nine the next morning. I called my doctor, who was also sick and couldn't come over. I decided to check into the emergency room. Annie Russell, a friend and fellow actor from the *Molly Brown* road company who'd flown in from her home in New York to help with my lines for *Mother,* went with me to St. Joseph's Hospital in Burbank. Sick as I was, I insisted on doing the driving.

The next thing I recall is looking up and seeing a curly hairpiece that was tilted to one side of a head. The curls seemed to be moving of their own accord. I was obviously delirious. I closed my eyes and groaned, thankful that I hadn't passed out at the wheel.

"What kind of drugs do you do?" a voice asked me, presumably the doctor's. "Do you smoke crack? The X-rays show that your stomach has completely burned through. It looks like you swallowed Drano. This kind of burning in the esophagus only happens when people smoke crack or do a lot of drugs."

And for this I got out of my own bed.

"I don't do drugs and I don't smoke crack," I informed Dr. Curly groggily. "I've been under some stress lately."

That was putting it mildly. About three years of unrelenting stress.

"I'm putting you on an IV," Dr. Curly advised me. "You won't be able to eat any solid food for a few weeks at least."

"How long will I have to be in the hospital?" I asked, thinking, How long will I be looking at your toupee?

"About two weeks. Ten days, if you're lucky."

Lucky? I was lucky that I'd be acting in a film in three weeks. I didn't need to be knocked down before I even got started. The next day I called Albert Brooks to say that I was in the hospital but should be out in a few days. Even though he told me not to worry, just to get well, I could sense that he was concerned.

Lillian Sidney agreed to come to the hospital to coach me. Anne Russell read the script with me every day too. I had to memorize the material before filming started, and I needed to develop the character. As we said in El Paso, *Oy!*

For the next week Lillian and Anne stayed by my bedside at St. Joseph's, reading and rereading the script with me. My IV was the only way to get nourishment; once I was done with the IV, I would be switched to liquids. Lillian and I discussed the motivation for each scene, and she recorded my line readings on a portable cassette player, for reference.

The hospital let me out early, and a week later I was at home, with the IV in place. The day after that I met with Albert at Paramount to work on the script. I wore a long-sleeved jacket, to cover the IV tube and my arms—still bruised from all the blood tests. Albert told me he wanted my character to be tougher and crisper, and underplayed. He read the lines with me. I was nervous because there was so much dialogue and Albert's writing is very quick and precise.

Carrie was right: Albert is brilliant. He'd written a story that was funny and touching, a remarkable examination of the relationship between a difficult mother and her troubled yet talented son. Albert himself plays my son. I wish I had been stronger during filming, but with Anne's help I pushed through. She went with me to the studio and was there every day of shooting, keeping me on track. Annie and I would visit the set on my weekends off, to rehearse the following week's scenes and work out shtick for my character. I wanted my scenes to feel natural. A number of them took place in the kitchen. I spent one Sunday memorizing the set, so I would feel as comfortable as if I were in my own kitchen when we shot the scene. Such touches add so much to a performance, and I wanted to be as good as I could be.

The decision to do *Mother* was a hard one for me. The hotel was in so much trouble that I felt it would certainly go under if I took time off to do the film. I thought I might be able to save it by staying there and working. This was a terrible conflict for me and caused me more anxiety in addition to learning my part.

Albert had written a great script, and he didn't need me to mess it up. Making movies had changed a lot since the time when I was doing them every day. The filming was quicker because of the hand-held cameras; lighting took less time. Everything moved swiftly, and I had to keep up. Albert took a chance with me. I was thrilled that he gave me the opportunity to play the role.

I have no idea how I got through it. I know I couldn't have done it without Albert's patience and Anne's daily assistance. Toward the end of the filming, I was in overdrive. My brain had become totally convulsed with dialogue. The stress of the hotel and the hard work of making the picture took their toll. I finally buckled under the pressure. Albert was under a lot of stress himself, since he was involved in every detail of making the movie. He shot around me for two days so I could rest and learn my lines. He was so kind to me, even though he didn't know all the trouble I was having.

I'm really proud of the work we did in *Mother*. It remains one of the best movies in my body of work. I appreciated Albert's kindness and his willingness to work so closely with me. Jack Haley Jr. took me to the Los Angeles premiere, and after the screening the audience gave the cast a standing ovation. I was so moved.

When it came time to promote the finished movie in England, I couldn't leave the hotel in Vegas to go on the press junket. This upset me, and I'm sure it upset Albert too. But I was watching my hotel slip away, taking my life's savings (and then some) with it, and I just couldn't leave, even though promoting the film was so important.

Renowned film critic Andrew Sarris named *Mother* the best film of 1996, and it was well received by the other critics. Albert's script went on to win awards from the National Society of Film Critics and the New York Film Critics Circle. I'll always be grateful to him for this role and his wonderful heart. I wouldn't be surprised to learn that he wanted to kill me at some point. But Albert was always a gentleman and has never spoken a bad word about me. He is indeed a very special man.

With the super-talented Albert Brooks.
I'm proud of the work we did in *Mother.*

The best reason to see *Mother* is the deliciously off-kilter performance of Debbie Reynolds, who speaks in pure honey-sweet tones yet keeps planting tiny seeds of disapproval, using her maternal "concern" as an invisible form of warfare. You never quite catch her doing it; the character doesn't even know she's doing it. She just is who she is, and by the end you realize that that's her glory.

—*Entertainment Weekly,* January 17, 1997

Chapter 12
Looking for Mr. Wrong

There's a line in *The Sound of Music* when the nuns are singing about Maria that goes "How do you pin a wave upon the sand?" Pinning something on Mr. Hamlett was going to be almost that difficult.

My lawyers were diligently working to untangle the mess that Richard had left behind him. This involved my assets before our marriage, my loans to him, and money that he had taken as "management fees" without telling me. In addition, there were all the folks making claims that Richard had signed notes on my behalf to raise money for the hotel—money that probably went to poker games at Caesars.

Preparing for court was not without intrigue. "Someone" who lived in a beach community in California contacted my accountant, saying he had "knowledge of Richard Hamlett's business dealings." One of my attorneys went to this person's home for a meeting, only to be informed when she arrived that he was not going to show her any of the documents.

"All right," my lawyer responded and got up to leave.

As her mysterious host walked her to the door, he handed her an orange Hermès bag, warning, "You can't copy any of the papers in this bag."

"What bag?" she said coyly, taking the parcel from her host.

A week or so later the bag and its contents were returned to their owner with no copies having been made.

That Hermès bag turned out to be a gold mine disguised in orange leather. The information it contained helped my legal team dispute many of the claims against the hotel and me. Between the Raid on Roanoke and the Person with the Hermès Bag, we were able to prove that Richard had taken my money and property without my knowledge or consent. My ego was almost as wounded as my bank account.

When Richard finally appeared in court, he was well prepared but ineffective. His own colleagues testified against him. This didn't prevent him from being confrontational with my attorney. Richard did not even try to hide his contempt for her. As they were leaving the courtroom after one of many tense sessions, Richard looked down at her and said, "People like you pay taxes so people like me don't have to."

My lovely attorney was no shrinking violet. She stood up to Richard at every turn. This blatant statement stunned her into silence.

As part of the divorce decree, the court awarded me my hotel and my share of the properties I'd bought in Virginia. Richard was ordered to return the monies from my pension fund that he'd "borrowed" and also to pay my attorneys' fees. The total was almost $9 million.

On May 14, 1996, our divorce was final, and I was single again. The minute Richard was freed from the bonds of matrimony, he filed an appeal to deny me the money he owed me. He also managed to get the appeal moved to a Virginia court, to accommodate his busy schedule. By 1997 I was paying legal teams to fly to Staunton, Virginia, to collect from my ex-husband. This touched off a bit of a firestorm in the east.

One night Richard called me in an agitated mood.

"You can chase me forever, but you will never find anything," he snarled. "You'll never collect on these judgments."

He raved on about how sorry I would be if I continued to pursue him.

Finally he threatened, "If you keep trying to get this money, I'll do whatever it takes to bring down the people around you."

I hung up before he could say another vile word. Hadn't he done enough to hurt me already? Ever since our separation, I had been afraid of Richard. I was sorry I'd ever loved him. His behavior now just made me more determined to recover what was mine. It wouldn't be easy, but at least I knew that he was digging in for a fight on his own turf.

Shortly after that conversation, Richard declared bankruptcy.

In almost every divorce, emotions run high. Members of Richard's family and a woman who worked in his office took my side. They flew to Las Vegas to testify in the divorce trial on my behalf because they were appalled by the way Richard had treated me. I believe he never spoke to them again. I know that he cut off his mother and didn't go to her funeral. Perhaps this damage was unavoidable, but it pained me deeply to cause a further rift in his family.

While Richard continued his war on me from afar, I was surprised to receive an offer from Scott Rudin, one of the producers of *Mother*. He'd recommended me for a role in his new film, to be called *In & Out*. The movie is about a high school drama teacher, played by Kevin

Kline, whose life is turned upside down when a former student wins an Academy Award and thanks him in his acceptance speech, telling the audience that his teacher is gay. This comes as a shock to the entire town, including the teacher, whose wedding (to a character played by Joan Cusack) is scheduled to happen soon. In the course of the story, the teacher discovers that he is, in fact, gay.

George Burns told me never to turn down a job because you don't know when they'll stop coming along. The part was wonderful, but doing it would be a mixed bag. The movie was being shot in New York, which meant I would have to leave Vegas to go on location. I couldn't help thinking, Here I go again, splitting my time between my hotel and my career.

I was hired to play Kevin Kline's mother. I didn't know Kevin before we worked together. He turned out to be the most amazing actor, a pleasant discovery for me. Our director, Frank Oz, liked doing lots of takes. It felt like my days on *Singin' in the Rain,* when Gene Kelly would do dozens of takes of a musical number and then use the first one. Kevin managed to give Frank something different each time. It was difficult for me because, after performing a scene a dozen ways, I ran out of ideas about how to do it. I also disagreed with Frank on my character's point of view. He wanted me to play her as a nasty, pushy person who does not accept

At the premiere of *In & Out*. Kevin Kline is an
amazing actor. I loved working with him.
Time & Life Pictures/Getty Images

her son's homosexuality. I wanted to play her more
softly, with humor. I also was convinced that my character and her husband accept their son, no matter what.

I spent a lot of time at the Essex House on Central
Park South. On days when I wasn't working, I would go
to the set somewhere in New Jersey to watch Kevin work.

The scene where he dances to "I Will Survive" is one of the funniest things I've ever seen, absolutely brilliant. I have the greatest admiration for Kevin and his talent, but I think he got a little tired of being stalked by his pretend mother; after he was done with his thirty takes, he always made a quick exit. Everyone in the cast was truly talented. Joan Cusack ripped through the film like a champ, beautifully playing every nuance of her character's emotions. I was thrilled to be in that company.

I returned to Las Vegas to find that the trustee of the bankruptcy court in Virginia wasn't helping matters. This old boys' network extended to old ladies too. At 4:45 P.M. on a Friday, my lawyer got a phone call from the trustee, saying that she had allowed Richard to transfer one of his assets to his brother's name. It took the trustee the whole weekend to realize that she'd permitted the transfer of the one property Richard still owned that actually was worth something. Her mistake cost me a few million dollars. I wonder who owns that building now.

When that happened, I had to make a decision. Either I could keep spending money I didn't have to pursue Richard and wind up with a bunch of properties worth very little that I would have to hire someone local to manage—then worry if that person was honest—or I could settle with Richard for a fixed amount. Richard's lawyer called my attorney and offered to pay me

$300,000, telling her that it was every cent we would be able to find. This was a bit more than the $270,000 I'd paid Richard for his share in the hotel. Reluctantly, I accepted it. I'm sure he was pleased with himself. He probably believes he was being generous.

Meanwhile, my legal troubles were heating up again in Las Vegas. As I left the stage after my show one night to greet the audience, I was approached by a man with an envelope.

He handed it to me, asking, "Are you Miss Debbie Reynolds?" as I began to autograph it.

Wasn't it obvious, considering the circumstances?

"I am," I said, flashing him a friendly smile. "What's your name?"

"This is a summons," he responded flatly.

I was stunned. Obviously one of my creditors had decided to embarrass me publicly. They could have served me or Todd, my CEO, at any time of the day or night at the hotel, but they'd chosen this awkward moment. Nobody ever said show business is boring. This particular lawsuit was settled easily when we proved that the plaintiff had already helped himself to money from the hotel while he was working for us.

It seemed that just as I put out one fire, another would ignite in some other corner of my life. Apparently I was still parked under the elephant's tail.

Chapter 13
Divorce American Style

AMOUNT I WAS AWARDED BY DIVORCE
   COURT: $8.9 MILLION

TOTAL OF LEGAL BILLS TO CHASE MY EX: $1.4 MILLION

MONEY COLLECTED FROM HUSBAND
   NUMBER THREE: NEXT TO NOTHING

FEELING I HAD GETTING RID OF
   THAT PHILANDERING DEVIL WITH
   THE KILLER BLUE EYES: *PRICELESS*

Chapter 14
Hail Mary Deal

With my miserable divorce chase over, I was free to concentrate on the hotel, which was sinking right before my eyes.

In July 1996, one of the board members had written to the shareholders saying that I should be removed. In the same letter, he said I had no talent and wasn't worth the $25,000 a week I was being paid to perform in my own hotel. At another time, the hotel's attorney, Ed Coleman, told the press that I had never earned that much a week in my life. Little did he know that in 1962 I signed a $1 million contract with the Riviera for a month of shows. I had cut my rate to a minimum to make the hotel a success.

Even though I put all the money I made back into the company, when we hired other entertainers to cover for me on my days off we paid them more than the board thought I should receive. The Smothers Brothers, Johnny Carson, Rip Taylor, and many other performers were paid well when they subbed for me.

I made many mistakes while I owned the hotel, and keeping any of these vultures on after Richard left may have been the worst. In 1996 the hotel had a negative cash flow of $6.4 million—which was an improvement over the previous year, when we were $8.6 million in the red. The only thing that could save us would be investors who could get us out of this hole.

This was a desperate time for me. In 1994 I had done a guest spot on the television program *Wings*, playing Crystal Bernard's mother. Crystal and I became friends. We'd sit at my house and visit, drinking champagne and talking. I became very fond of her. When I was hitting bottom with the hotel, she agreed to lend me $100,000, to be paid back when I could. I gave her a lot of my antiques as collateral. She was so good to do that for me. It took years for me to get far enough ahead to repay her, but I did. It was embarrassing to have to borrow money from my friends, and I was thankful that Crystal and others were so kind to me at this difficult time.

By 1997 we had finally cleared up a lot of the trouble—but not all of it. ILX, a time-share company in Phoenix, Arizona, helped us with short-term loans. Todd did business plans and presentations for any possible partners. He met with everyone who might help us stay afloat long enough to become self-sufficient, including a worm farmer outside Las Vegas who was interested in investing. Meanwhile, I heard that when some of the board members were in town for meetings—and God knows what else—they kept the local hookers busy, partying in their suites on the top floor of the hotel. Never mind that their *business* efforts, if they ever existed, had not made our stock attractive. They still hadn't gotten us a gaming license. Jackpot Enterprises, who'd been running the hotel's gaming operation, left in March 1996, taking their 182 slot machines and 2 blackjack tables with them. We'd filled the space with items from my memorabilia collection, except for 25 slots owned by an independent contractor. The hotel was losing money, and the gaming commission wouldn't give us a license until we put up $2 million and our financial situation improved.

While I was doing everything in my power to keep the hotel in business—and these guys in their positions—they treated me dismissively. I was sure that they were plotting to get rid of me.

When Joe Kowal came onto the board, he'd been given 250,000 shares of stock. At a board meeting after the offensive letter went out, Kowal shouted at me. He sang a familiar tune—that I was just an entertainer, that I didn't own anything, that I worked for them.

You can imagine that these statements didn't sit well with me, and that's putting it mildly. I was eating an apple and decided to share it with Mr. Hockey Player Koo Koo Roo Mogul.

Joe Kowal is a very big guy. Picture Miss Burbank standing up at the table and launching the apple at the Hulk, standing a few feet in front of her. It hit him smack on his left lapel, exactly where I meant it to. (My aim was still as good as when I landed a cake on Jean Hagen in one take in *Singin' in the Rain*.) I didn't want to hit him in the head, just juice his designer suit and shut him up.

And then I wanted to wipe the grin off his face. Move over, Joan Crawford, warning her Pepsi boardroom, "Don't fuck with me, fellas."

I lunged at Joe Kowal in a rage—no matter that he towered over me—and pounded his waist with my little fists.

Kowal flicked at me as if I were a flea leaping at him from the floor, while Todd and the other board members pulled my squirming body away.

Needless to say, I didn't attend any more board meetings after that.

By June 1997, I was out of money. My apartment in Las Vegas and the house in Los Angeles I shared with my brother were both mortgaged to the hilt. My dance studio had been used as collateral. Our last hope was a deal with ILX, but they couldn't justify buying the hotel because of all its encumbrances. To protect myself, it was necessary to declare bankruptcy—for myself and for the hotel. This in turn forced me to lay off forty-four employees, leaving me with a total staff of ninety-five. I also had to resign as company chairman.

Todd worked for more than a year to find backers who might be able to bail us out. Early in 1997, he'd found a very successful time-share developer from Florida named David Siegel, who, after negotiations and an unforeseen delay, offered to buy 92.5 percent of the hotel stock for $15.6 million. That would have paid off the creditors and stockholders and given the hotel enough money to stay in operation. Siegel planned to add 1,000 time-share rooms to the property. He would have managed the hotel while giving Todd and me the gaming and entertainment. It was the Hail Mary deal of the century and sounded too good to be true.

And it was.

The unsecured creditors weren't content with recouping their investments. They thought they could do better with an auction. Led by one of my former employees, they took me to court to block the Siegel offer.

The hearing was held in June 1998. By then, the hotel was down to twenty employees.

Unfortunately, the judge sided with the creditors. He rejected David Siegel's guarantee, saying, "I'm a poker player."

"A poker player with *our* money," Todd leaned over and muttered to our attorney.

Now everyone's fate rested on the auction.

Chapter 15
Black Wednesday

A ugust 5, 1998, arrived. Black Wednesday.
I felt like I was in a barrel at the top of Niagara Falls: I knew I was going over. I just didn't know how the journey would end. I couldn't believe I was attending another hotel auction in the same building. Only now it was *my* hotel on the block.

I was anxious as I got ready to leave, but in these situations it's better to appear happy than to look somber. I dressed in a bright apricot-colored jacket with brass buttons and put on a cheerful face. I didn't know yet which earrings I wanted to wear, so I took along several pairs in my jacket pocket. In another pocket I had the statement I'd prepared to read.

Everything hinged on this auction. When we'd heard that David Siegel might be attending, Todd quickly arranged with financier Greg Orman to give Siegel the $1 million guarantee he would need if he wanted to bid. It was almost as simple as me giving my paddle to Ralph Engelstad at the Paddlewheel auction.

I arrived at the casino to find the room crowded with bidders, onlookers, and press. Todd told me that David Siegel was in the room. He was our last chance to save the hotel and make good on all the outstanding debts. I went over and hugged him, saying, "Thank you for coming today. I'm so glad to see you."

As I went to the side of the stage to wait for the cue to make my announcement, I heard whispers that my ex-husband was in the room. Thank God I couldn't see him. I thought it was incredibly bad taste that he would show up on this day. After all, it was his treachery that had caused me to default in the first place. If he had just paid the divorce judgment, I wouldn't have needed to sell the hotel.

I breathed deeply, to calm myself, and thought of the Wicked Witch of the East, telling myself, "He has no power here. Maybe I'll get lucky and one of the 'debt collectors' from the casinos will drop a house on him." A reporter from the Las Vegas Sun came over to me while I was digging in my pocket to find my earrings. "I didn't know which pair to wear, so I brought them all," I explained.

It was time. I walked to the front of the room and took the stage, smiling at the crowd. You could have heard a pin drop.

"Thank you all for coming today," I began. "Life has always been an adventure, and I have never been afraid of walking down a new path. When I bought this property in 1992, there was no thought in my mind of any difficulties such as the ones existing today. This property is wonderful to me, and I would love to have been able to remain here for the rest of my performing years—which should be about noon today."

People laughed uneasily. Trying not to be distracted, I went back to my notes.

"I truly have called this my home and have worked here for six years, often with no salary. I continued to perform in the showroom without pay to keep the doors open. I believed we could make it. We could not. Not without a proper financial picture."

Gazing around the room, I saw David Siegel and tried to smile at him.

"We had a buyer from Florida who would have enabled us all to remain here and work happily in Las Vegas, where I have been a resident for over twenty years, but because of others' greed, we lost that buyer and are now forced to auction to the highest bidder."

Black Wednesday, August 5, 1998. This tops the list as one of the saddest days of my life. *Photo by Jeff Scheid. Courtesy AP Photos*

I looked around. Some people were crying, people I didn't even know. Crying for me. Tears welled in my own eyes; I could hear my voice cracking as I continued to speak.

"I will miss the beautiful Star Theater and the fabulous Motion Picture Museum that since 1972 has searched for a permanent home. Todd Fisher, my son, designed and built the showroom and the museum, and I want to thank him for standing by me and the hotel through all of these difficult times. I want to thank him for giving up his career to help me. He's the only man who has never left me. I will move on, but I will miss my second home—this property.

"Thank you all for coming today. Tomorrow is a new day. I will be touring and entertaining forever."

Everyone applauded as I left the stage, and Todd helped me to a seat where we could observe the proceedings. Everything depended on David Siegel now; if he bid, we could be saved.

But David Siegel wasn't one of the bidders. I guess he'd been through enough with all the legal wrangling of the last few months. The auction started, and the bidding didn't last long. The World Wrestling Federation bought my hotel for $11 million. Now only the people with secured loans would benefit. The greedy creditors who thought they could do better in a general auction and blocked David Siegel's offer wouldn't be paid at all. It was small comfort to me, if any.

A few days later, David Siegel called me. He said that he'd gone home to Florida and watched my movie *Tammy and the Bachelor.* Overcome with regret, he made a multimillion-dollar offer that would settle all the debts and keep the hotel in operation.

But it was too late. The bankruptcy court upheld the sale to the World Wrestling Federation.

This was one time when I didn't feel unsinkable.

Chapter 16
Bottoming Out in Beverly Hills

There's a scene in Carrie's first *Star Wars* movie where she is trapped in a container filled with space debris, and "something alive" in the water, with huge tentacles and one big slimy eye, comes after her looking for dinner. Suddenly the walls of the trash compactor begin to close in. That would have been a step up for me.

Sometimes you have to run for your life, and sometimes you have to fight for it. I didn't feel like I was able to do either now that I had hit bottom again. I took some time for reflection.

Carrie had moved to a large house in Beverly Hills with a lot of property, including a tennis court. It was usually pretty quiet there in the daytime. I would drive there and sit on a bench and stare into space, going over everything that had taken place in the past few years and wondering how in hell I'd let this happen to me again. I passed the time crying and thinking about so many things.

First I thought I was in love and in a happy marriage. I was partly right. I was in love in a happy marriage while my husband was in love outside our happy marriage. Oh well, that had happened to me once before. Then I thought about how my husband had mangled our finances so badly that I was forced into bankruptcy, losing everything but my memorabilia collection. That had happened to me before too. What do you do when your heart says one thing and your head—and your lawyer—says another? I was a romantic. I put my whole heart on the line when I loved someone.

It never ceases to amaze me that people feel free to help themselves to my money and property. There is a mentality at work that says, "It's okay to rob Debbie blind, I work for her." Or, "She's my wife, everything she has is mine." I don't think like a thief, so I never see this quality in others until it's too late.

I thought about how so many people in the arts have been destroyed by people around them who either mismanage them or steal everything they own. Doris Day's husband and her lawyer took all her money and hid it somewhere. Her husband died before anyone knew it was missing or could do anything about it. My depression kept taking me back to all the people I'd known who had gone through tragic events and didn't make it.

Perhaps the most tragic story of all was Pier Angeli's. Pier was my dear friend, and her last name suited her perfectly. She was an angel, a beautiful, innocent-looking girl who was loved by almost everyone who knew her. She was also sexy. What a hot combination. Pier had a relationship with James Dean. She was engaged to Kirk Douglas briefly, but they broke up.

The first time Eddie Fisher asked me out was as his guest for his opening night at the Cocoanut Grove in Hollywood. Pier was seated at the table next to mine. She left right after the show, when she saw all the photographers taking pictures of Eddie and me together. I didn't learn until much later that he'd also invited her. I'll bet he went to her house right after he dropped me off in Burbank.

Although many handsome men courted Pier, she decided to marry Vic Damone, another singer, which shocked all of her friends. The rumor was that her mother had insisted on it. Vic had a bad reputation around town. I remember telling Pier that she could call off the wedding and I would drive her to Palm Springs to hide. But Pier refused. "The invitations have already gone out," she said. "My mother wouldn't allow it." She was afraid of her mother, with good cause.

On Pier's wedding day at St. Timothy's Catholic Church, we all watched this beautiful young girl walk down the aisle. When she passed my row, I saw tears in her eyes. My heart sank. I wasn't the only one who was upset that day. Outside, James Dean sat on his motorcycle across the street from the church. He rode off when the wedding party emerged after the ceremony. I never saw him again. He died ten months later.

Pier's tears didn't stop after the wedding. Shortly after she and Vic were married, she became pregnant with their son, Perry (named after Perry Como, one of Vic's friends). Pier was thrilled about becoming a mother. During this time, I went to her house for a visit. When I knocked, Pier wouldn't let me in. I told her through the door that I wasn't going to leave until she opened it. Pier knew how stubborn I am, and slowly opened the door, hiding behind it.

When I saw her face, I knew why. It was swollen, and she had a black eye.

I was outraged. I tried to convince Pier to leave Vic. She wouldn't do it. She was too embarrassed, and afraid of him.

Predictably, Pier's marriage to Vic ended badly, and they fought bitterly over the custody of their little boy. Pier moved back to Italy to live with her family. Her twin sister, Marisa, was wonderful to Pier, but their domineering mother was difficult as ever. She had Pier committed to a mental facility near Rome, where Pier suffered hell on earth, including sexual abuse by the caretakers, both male and female. Her sister eventually got her released, and Pier returned to Los Angeles to resume her acting career.

But things had changed in the few years she'd been gone, and Pier had trouble finding roles. She studied with an MGM coach, then made the mistake of contacting Vic for aid. He promised to help her get a role in a film if she visited him in Vegas.

She returned from that trip crushed and despondent. She told me that Vic's promise of help had been empty. She was ashamed and shattered. I invited her to move in with Harry Karl and me, and she slept on our couch until she found herself a little apartment in Beverly Hills.

After she moved, she asked her doctor for a strong shot of something to relieve some kind of pain she was suffering. She didn't say that she'd already taken a lot of pills. The shot he gave her combined with her other medications to kill her. She just couldn't face the world anymore. I didn't know how she could do this to her child, but I understood the feeling of desperation that led to her ending it all.

Pier couldn't overcome her tragedy, but I couldn't see myself taking her way out, no matter how wretched I felt now. It would destroy my family, the most important people in my life.

Thinking about Pier and my own situation, I realized how different people's lives would be if we made different choices. Staring into space outside my daughter's house, I wondered: What is my third act going to be? How am I going to overcome this grief?

When Eddie and I were divorcing, I was in my late twenties. I had to be strong for my children, who were both under three years old. I remember packing up the kids to go for a ride in the car. But the front yard was filled with reporters waiting to get a statement or a picture. I understood why my friend Frank Sinatra would explode whenever a photographer or reporter invaded his privacy. Finally I put down the diaper bag and car keys, went outside, and asked everyone to please leave me and my family alone. They took some pictures, wrote a few lines, and eventually left. I could handle the stress when I was young and protecting Carrie and Todd.

Fifteen years later, when I left Harry Karl, I was at rock bottom in a different way. As Mrs. Karl, I drove

Car keys in one hand and diaper bag in the other, I'm ready to take the kids out. But the reporters are crowding my front lawn. The beginning of experiencing real-life heartbreak. *Photofest*

a Rolls-Royce convertible. Right after the divorce, I was sleeping in my old Cadillac because I didn't have anyplace to live. By then I was in my forties. Hard as it was, recovery was still easier than it would be now. Or so I feared.

Sitting in Carrie's yard, thinking back over the years, I remembered how hard Daddy had worked to make a home for us in California, saving all his money for a year until he could buy a lot and build our family a house while Mother worked just as hard in Texas until we could join him. "Work never killed anybody," she used to say. "Would you rather be digging ditches?" My parents believed that *can't* is never an option. We all have to make sacrifices for the people we love. The people I loved needed me now, and I could not give up.

At some point, as I reviewed everything in solitude in Carrie's quiet yard, my depression turned to resolve. I thought about all the hard fights I'd had in my life and career and remembered that I love to work. I love to perform and make audiences happy. They make me happy, and it's all joy. As my character Molly Brown says, "Nobody wants me down as much as I want me *up!* I ain't down yet."

Thank God.

Chapter 17
On the Road Again

If there's one thing I know, it's the road.

My second picture for MGM, in 1950, was *Two Weeks With Love.* The movie was not that successful, but a song from it was. "Aba Daba Honeymoon," a novelty tune about a monkey and a chimp in love, became a very big monkey of a hit. So the studio sent the two kids who sang it in the film—Carleton Carpenter and me—out on the road to capitalize on its popularity. Roger Edens, MGM's brilliant songwriter and lyricist, was assigned to write special material for our little act, which would be part of a larger revue.

That was my first experience as a live performer. I was only seventeen years old at the time, which meant that an adult had to come along as my guardian. Needless to say, it was my mother. In those days MGM owned the Loews theater chain. The studio booked our revue in Loews in cities all over the country. We began the tour in Washington, DC.

Carleton and I were specialty performers in a lineup that included the Weire Brothers—the funniest men I've ever known in my life—and three or four other acts, including someone performing with a bird of some kind. Altogether there were five or six acts that made up this revue. A twenty-four-piece orchestra accompanied our five shows a day, which we did between screenings of the film. In addition to caring for me, my mother was in charge of the wardrobe for the show. We stayed in hotels where everybody shared a bathroom. The Weire Brothers didn't have very good aim when it came to the facilities, which perturbed Mother and me a little.

Our revue was part of the last wave of vaudeville, the wonderful circuit that launched the careers of such legendary performers as W. C. Fields, the Marx Brothers, and Bob Hope. It was thrilling playing to packed houses with teenagers screaming for Carleton and me as we did our two numbers from the movie, "Aba Daba Honeymoon" and "Row, Row, Row (Way Up the River)."

Carleton had so much more experience than I did. He'd been a professional magician and acted on

Broadway before coming to Hollywood to be in movies. He thought I didn't know what I was doing and he was right. I may have been a novice, but I was a quick study and a natural performer. Carleton got upset when I ad-libbed onstage, perhaps because the audience laughed at everything I did. He used to call me his "little crea-ture," which I took as a term of endearment. Once he misjudged the distance to the orchestra and tumbled into it doing a choreographed high kick. I found this very funny, but Carleton was not amused. Carleton sang the melody to our songs while I did the harmony. One day he was down with the flu and I had to go on alone. Unafraid, I sang the entire song in the harmony. The reviewers called me "a little girl on a big stage," not only because of my size—I'm five-foot-one—but because Carleton towered over me, he was so tall. Doing that tour hooked me on performing live; until then I wasn't sure I wanted to stay in show business. I was lucky to see so many great performers doing their nightclub acts—Frank Sinatra, Dean Martin and Jerry Lewis, and of course, Judy Garland, whom I'd become friends with at MGM. Judy sang tunes from her movies for me when I visited her at home after work at the studio. What a beautiful friend she was.

That was the last year for vaudeville; soon after our tour ended, shows like ours quit running in those big theaters. The same thing happened when I was at MGM. I caught the last gasp of the studio system. TV came into vogue in the 1950s, and by the end of the 1960s the era of big movie musicals was just about over. The writing was on the wall for all of us who had worked in films for years.

In 1963 I made the transition to nightclubs when I put together my first act for Vegas, shortly before I got the part in *The Unsinkable Molly Brown*. As it became more difficult to get good film roles, I was happy to appear live for audiences around the world, and fortunate to have Roger Edens to help stage my act. Roger was the genius who wrote "Dear Mr. Gable" and "Born in a Trunk" for Judy Garland and "Moses Supposes" for *Singin' in the Rain*. He'd also worked on Judy's live shows.

In July 1974, I was booked to play the Palladium in London, where Mama Cass Elliot had just finished a sold-out two-week engagement. I packed up my kids, Mother, and Daddy, and we all left for England.

It was a great time for us. The promoters gave us an entire floor at the Savoy Hotel. Daddy wound up with his picture on the front page of the paper after photographers found him in a park near the hotel, dressed in a cardigan sweater and a baseball cap, feeding the pigeons. Bianca Jagger attended my opening night.

Instead of my picture with Bianca, the papers featured Daddy standing next to her, his glance fixed downward. Let's just say he wasn't looking in her eyes.

Carrie and Todd were then in their midteens. When they heard that Mick Jagger had invited me to a party, they were keen for me to go so they could tag along.

The party was in full swing when we arrived at Mick's town house in central London, crammed with people from the British social scene as well as friends of the Rolling Stones. As we began to mingle, Mick pulled me aside and cautioned, "Keep the kiddies down here. There's lots of adult activities up the stairs you don't want them to see."

Happily, there was a great band playing downstairs, so I didn't have to worry about the huge bowls filled with cocaine spread out like a buffet on the second floor and any other adult behavior "not for teenies," as Mick had described it. We found lots of folks to talk to.

As the evening wore on we began to see the effects as the upstairs crowd stumbled through the first floor to exit the party. Keith Richards was carried out on a stretcher. Cass Elliot left in the wee hours and, tragically, died that night at Harry Nilsson's London apartment, where she was staying. I've always thought it a shame that she went home alone. She might have been saved.

Sometime during the party Todd met a woman in her late twenties or early thirties named Elizabeth (a popular name among the men in the Fisher family). Elizabeth owned restaurants in London, and Todd was about to become her main course. Todd was only sixteen, but he was eager to learn the facts of life. I was thrilled that he would have such a lovely teacher. I wished I'd had someone other than his dad to show me the ropes.

Todd's Elizabeth moved back to the Savoy with us for the duration of our stay in London. He was quite pale for the next few days, but very happy. Not so my mother, who was outraged when Elizabeth moved in with us. Daddy went back to feeding the pigeons while daydreaming about Bianca's bosom.

Somewhere between Todd's joy and Mother's disapproval, we all managed to have a jolly good time.

Working is how I handle crisis. When my marriage to Harry Karl was in trouble, I took on *Irene.* Now I would have to tap-dance as fast as I could to dig myself out of the huge hole caused by the loss of the hotel. It was time to go on the road again. Of course, my 1999 show would have to be very different from the ones I'd done in earlier years. I couldn't afford to hire dancers or tour with a lot of musicians. I'd have to cut down on travel expenses as best I could. My agents booked me

My son, Todd, and me at Heathrow airport for my engagement at the London Palladium in 1974. Todd's holding my
cane. I had fractured my ankle during a show. *Photofest*

gigs in Atlantic City, on cruises, and in the usual nightclubs. I was grateful for every engagement. And then I
got a very nice surprise.

At the beginning of the year, I received an offer
to play Debra Messing's mother on *Will & Grace,*
then in the second season of what turned out to be an

eight-year run. My character's name is Bobbi Adler; Debra plays Grace Adler on the show. The first episode I taped was called "The Unsinkable Mommy Adler"—a tremendous ego booster for me because it indicated that the producers believed the reference to my movie, and therefore my name, might attract my audience if they weren't already watching the show. My first entrance was mugging as Ethel Merman singing a riff on "Everything's Coming Up Roses" from *Gypsy*. In another scene, I got to sing a chorus of "Good Morning" from *Singin' in the Rain* with Megan Mullally. The writers had tailored my part just for me.

Doing *Will & Grace* was so much fun. The cast was a spectacular group of actors. Sean Hayes is a wonderful musician who is now a successful producer. Eric McCormack was also a stitch. He went to New York and took on the very difficult job of playing the lead in *The Music Man*. Megan was lovely to me. She and Carrie are good friends now. Everyone in the cast was lovely to me. We spent a lot of very good times together. I adored them all. They worked very hard, as did Jim Burrows, the director. I had to move quickly to keep up with everyone, but I've been a tap dancer for decades. My only regret is that I was working so hard on the road every week that I always seemed to be rushing into a rehearsal or taping, and when I finally got to the set I was exhausted. Truthfully, I've been exhausted ever since I was sixteen!

Grace's relationship with her mother on the show is confrontational, just to the point of real conflict, which is the basis of the show's comedy. When Debra and I were in character, our interactions were supposed to be a bit edgy. That's what they wanted, and that's what we gave them. On one of the taping days, we had a scene where Bobbi wins the moment by saying to Grace, "Gotcha again"—meaning "You told me a lie, you told me a lie." I swooped in just in time for the taping. Debra gave me the hand gestures I use, which tag the scene and get big laughs. She was very generous to share that "business" she had created. It really helped me with the scene. And Jim Burrows let me have a cue card to refer to if I needed it. We had to do two shows that day, so I was very appreciative of their kindness.

I went on to do nine more episodes before the show ended its long run in 2006. The experience was terrific. *Will & Grace* was a combination of skilled actors and writers led by one of the best directors in television. They worked together like a well-oiled machine. Even though I was devastated emotionally by my latest divorce, the loss of the hotel, and financial ruin, I threw myself into the work, just as I had done on *Mother.*

Everywhere I go, people tell me how much they enjoyed the show. It appealed to a large audience, straight and gay, because it was funny and well done. I'll always be grateful for being given the opportunity to be a part of *Will & Grace*.

With Debra Messing in *Will & Grace*. I played Debra's mother, Bobbi Adler. The show was hard work, but I enjoyed being part of the great ensemble cast. *Photofest*

Chapter 18
Family and Faith

E arly in 1999, Carrie called to tell me that the "gardener's house" next door to the gate to her property was for sale. Now that I was finished with Las Vegas for the moment, she thought it would be good for me to be closer to her and my granddaughter, Billie. This small cottage had been the residence of the original estate's caretaker and at some point the lot was broken off from the acreage. Before Carrie bought it, several Hollywood celebrities had owned the estate, including Cary Grant. Between husbands, Elizabeth Taylor stayed in one of the guest rooms when costume designer Edith Head had it. Carrie's news was great and I welcomed it. I wanted to be a bigger part of her life and Billie's.

So I bought it. I had been working as much as I could after the hotel auction and had started to repay my friends who'd lent me money. Fortunately, the owners of the property were willing to take a small down payment and carry the mortgage for me. The house needed work, of course, and my brother, Bill, began refurbishing it so I could move in. He worked on it every day for a year while I was off doing my act.

But first, Carrie, Billie, and I decided to take a vacation to Hawaii together. One day while I was sitting by the water, Billie came running out to tell me that Uncle Bill was on the phone.

"Uncle Bill" is my brother, but everybody calls him by this nickname. At that time he was living with and caring for our ill mother. I wasn't really worried, but I knew that he is not the type to call just to chat.

"Hi, Uncle Bill," I said. "What's wrong?"

He came right to the point.

"Mother's not doing well. You should come home. I'm going to take her to the hospital."

My brother isn't one for drama, so I immediately made arrangements to leave for Los Angeles.

My mother had been ill with heart disease and colon cancer for some time. Her doctors had given her a choice: either she could have major surgery that she might not survive and that would only extend her life for a short time, or she could do nothing. She chose to do nothing. She believed she would be blessed with Heaven because she had lived by the Golden Rule of "Do unto others as you would have them do unto you."

Daddy had had the same attitude about dying when his time came.

When I arrived at the hospital, Mother was in a coma. Her eyes were glazed, and her face shone—there wasn't a line on it. I sat by her side, singing and talking to her softly. Sometime later a nurse came in to take her vital signs, but I knew that Mother had gone.

It had been the same with Daddy, fifteen years before: I got to the hospital just in time; I put my mother's hands and mine in his; he sighed deeply and went on his way to a glorious baseball game in Heaven. Both my parents chose not to take extraordinary measures to prolong their lives, preferring to let nature take its course and to move on to their new world. I'll never forget the total peace on their faces. It makes me believe they were secure in their faith.

We kept the funeral for my mother very simple. Carrie and Todd read passages from the Bible. Two of the boys from my nightclub act, Steve Lane and Shelby Grimm, sang "Nearer My God to Thee."

When Daddy died, Carrie wrote a tribute to him that captured so many of his wonderful qualities.

RECIPE FOR RAY

take one small stubborn Texan
preferably lean

add a big busted gal from
               thereabouts
that answers to Maxene
fold in some railroad work,
               a depression
two kids and a move to LA
beat in a bunch of baseball
(and) you've begun your recipe
               for Ray

take your small stubborn
               Texan
and gently remove all his
               hair
build him a shop
outside any house he's got
and stick a radio there
sift in some well chosen
               words
a kind heart beneath
               leathery skin
stir in some peanuts and
               coke
a tendency to smoke
sprinkle in some "Dear Lord
               Help us jump in." [Daddy's
               version of Grace]

add a dash of the sweetest
                    smile
some Palm Springs and a
                    little Ouray
fold in a favorite chair
the funny walk that gets him there
add "and the farmer hauled
                    another load of hay" [Daddy's
                    phrase for B.S.]:

This recipe for Ray
can be cooked up anytime
it simmers in our hearts
it fills us up real fine.

My family was always close. I was born in El Paso, Texas, during the Great Depression of the 1930s. We lived with my grandparents in a small house that had no shower—we used the bathroom at the gas station next door. I shared a bed with my brother and three uncles, who were close to us in age. My brother and I slept with our heads at the top of the bed, my uncles with theirs at the foot. I woke up every morning with toes in my nose. I never slept alone until I got married.

Daddy worked for the railroad. Believing that we would have a better life in the West, he took the train to Los Angeles and for a year slept on the ground in MacArthur Park in all kinds of weather. He worked and saved his money, making a lot of sacrifices. When he'd saved enough to buy a small lot in Burbank where he could build us a house, he sent for us. I was seven years old.

Although life in California was better and held more promise, we still lived very modestly. Mother made all my clothes or bought them from the Salvation Army. As soon as I was old enough to mow lawns or babysit, I worked around the neighborhood to earn a few extra dollars.

Daddy and Mother gave Bill and me security and a firm sense of the value of family in our lives that has sustained me through the years. Even though my children were raised without a father, they still had my parents and brother, who were always there for them.

My parents also taught me about hard work, sticking to a job until it's done, and downright stubbornness. My mother was a tough lady when it came to discipline. To be fair, I know I was a willful child. When I was about six years old, she locked me in her closet as punishment. After about an hour in solitary, I called to my mother, asking for a glass of water.

"Why do you need water?" Mother said through the closed door.

"Because I spit in all of your shoes and I'm out of spit," I answered.

In spite of her harsh punishments, Mother was wonderful at taking care of us. She was always making dinner for our friends, even though we lived on very little. She let me join the Girl Scouts at an early age. I loved the Scouts. I learned leadership and many skills and earned forty-seven of one hundred merit badges. Those qualities stay with me today. At heart, I think I'll always be a Girl Scout.

Mixed in with his gentle soul, Daddy had definite ideas about everyone's role in the family. When I started making money as a movie actress, one of my great joys was doing things for my family. I bought Mother a fur stole with some of my early earnings. I bought Daddy a new car and a set of golf clubs. Soon I had enough money saved to pay off their mortgage, which thrilled me.

Every summer Daddy would hitchhike to Texas to visit his family. Now that he had his red MG, he put his new golf clubs in the back and left for Texas. One summer I had a new closet built in my bedroom while he was away. During another summer visit, I thought I would surprise Daddy with something he would never buy for himself. My "Aba Daba Honeymoon" duet with Carleton Carpenter was then a hit single that paid a lot in residuals. With that money, I installed a swimming pool in the backyard, which was so small that the pool completely filled the space. On the top step of the pool stairs, I had the words ABA DABA HONEYMOON spelled out in beautiful colored tiles.

When Daddy returned from Texas, he wasn't happy about the pool that took up his whole yard. Due to ear problems, Daddy wasn't a swimmer. He didn't like the idea of his little girl making improvements to the house without his knowledge or permission. The minute I left home to marry Eddie Fisher in 1955, Daddy had the pool filled in with dirt. It wasn't seen again until about five years later, when the people who bought the house from my parents looked under the topsoil in the yard and found it. At least someone finally got to enjoy it.

Conflicts with my mother continued for most of my life. We clashed over our differences in spite of loving each other dearly. Mother traveled on the road with me all the time. When the children were small, she came along to help care for them. When they were grown, she came along for the fun of being part of my entourage. At one of my Vegas engagements, we were enjoying a Sunday night off with my dancers and musicians and other road crew, who in addition to working for me were my friends. We were in my hotel suite, watching a movie. Around midnight, my mother pulled me aside and told me it was time to go to bed. Shocked, I told her that we were going to stay up and watch TV and have some fun on our day off. Mother became insistent and tried to bully me into going to bed. My temper flared, and we actually got into a fight. It started out small but somehow escalated, to the point where we were punching each other, actually brawling, only a few feet from our friends.

Suddenly the whole thing just seemed so ridiculous that we started to laugh. It was a turning point in our relationship. Although I would always be my mother's little girl, she never tried to discipline me again.

Now I was moving into a house that would let me be near my own little girl and her daughter, Billie Catherine. We were all thrilled when Carrie got pregnant. Not wanting to have drugs in her blood that could affect her baby, Carrie went off her antidepressants. It was a very brave and difficult thing for her to do. Having a baby is hard enough without all the mental changes that Carrie went through.

When it was time for Billie to be born, I went with Carrie to Cedars-Sinai hospital for the delivery. Billie's father, Bryan Lourd, was there too. When Billie arrived, he took her and bathed her with such love and tenderness that I never forgot it. No matter what Carrie went through with Billie's father after that, I'll always cherish the memory of him taking care of our little Billie so beautifully. The first time I saw Billie I was reminded of the Stevie Wonder song "You Are the Sunshine of My Life." Billie is our sunshine girl, and even though she's grown up now, I still call her "baby."

Whenever I've faced difficult times and wondered how I was going to get through them, my family and my faith have sustained me. Faith is a powerful thing to have in your repertory. When Eddie Fisher left us, I sat quietly with a tablet of paper and waited for some words to come to tell me what to do. I did the same thing in Carrie's backyard when I lost my third marriage, my hotel, and all my money yet again. Words come to me from God—or Jesus or whatever you choose to call the most powerful force in the universe. Certainly I've felt despair, sometimes so much that I thought it would be easier to die. But my family and my faith have sustained me until, when I least expected it, life picked me up again.

My favorite picture of me with Daddy, at my first wedding in 1955.

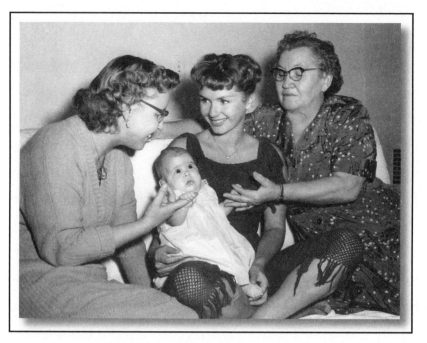

With Mother and Grandma Harman when
Carrie was a newly born baby.

Carrie; my mother, Maxene; Carrie's daughter,
Billie Catherine; and me.

Chapter 19
These Old Broads

C arrie was busy writing. In addition to working on the Academy Awards and other specials, she'd been hired to doctor scripts and was trying her hand at original screenplays. One of her TV scripts was a sitcom pilot for CBS called *Esme's Little Nap* about a girl in a coma. Andrea Martin played Esme. She spent the whole half hour in a hospital bed; all her lines were voice-over narration. I played the mother who moved in to take care of the family. I think Carrie was a little ahead of her time with that one. The pilot was not picked up.

Carrie wrote a campy and fun "Movie of the Week" that aired in February 2001, featuring Elizabeth Taylor as a high-powered Hollywood agent and Shirley MacLaine, Joan Collins, and me as aging film actresses. Naturally she called it *These Old Broads*.

If the title fits . . .

Elizabeth was in very poor health, and her doctors didn't want her to do the role. She had arthritis in her spine, which caused her constant pain and made it very difficult for her to walk. But Elizabeth agreed to do the movie for Carrie. She had to be helped onto the set, and you'll notice that there are few scenes in which she is walking. I was a bit surprised that she would do this. I felt it was an attempt to make amends to Carrie and me for her part in my first divorce decades before. She and Carrie had become good friends over the years, and it was very sweet of Elizabeth to do this for her.

"Can you believe the way we look?" Shirley said when she arrived on the set the first day.

"You look great," I responded. "All things considered, I think we all look pretty good."

Shirley sniffed. "We're so old."

Shirley always was the beautiful vixen, but her looks had matured. Joan Collins just showed up and did a hundred sit-ups every day. We all had a lot of miles on us—half of them on our faces.

Elizabeth's trailer was near mine, and during breaks we would visit. I usually went to her rooms because of her health difficulties. Being on the lot together reminded us of our MGM days. We'd never worked together at the studio, but we'd both gone to the MGM high school, which was one room with a tiny bathroom where Elizabeth would hide to avoid lessons. The teacher would wait about fifteen minutes and then knock on the door and ask if Elizabeth was all right. Elizabeth always had some excuse for why she needed to be locked in the little girls' room. She'd been a star at MGM since she was a youngster. She was growing from a beautiful child into a beautiful woman who didn't think she needed to spend time on lessons. I was only seventeen and still planned to be a gym teacher when I finished college, so I did my best to learn.

Elizabeth got married to Nicky Hilton when she was very young, just eighteen. She and Nicky spent their honeymoon on a cruise. Nicky was an alcoholic who loved to gamble. He behaved terribly when he was drunk, treating Elizabeth roughly, in a disrespectful way. When they returned from their honeymoon, Elizabeth was still bruised from Nicky's abuse.

After Elizabeth's marriage to Nicky Hilton inevitably ended, she married a British actor named Michael Wilding. Michael was charming and funny and sweet and kind—and he adored Elizabeth. They had two sons together, which made them both very happy. But their marriage was doomed to fail. When you've been hurt by a man as Elizabeth had been by Nicky Hilton, you can find other men too placid. This was true of Elizabeth with Michael.

Elizabeth invited me to a dinner party at her house on Beverly Estates Drive, which is a winding road above Beverly Hills. The house had been designed by architect George MacLean and had an indoor swimming pool. After dinner, Elizabeth and Montgomery Clift went for a swim. They laughed and giggled while making out in the water in front of us all. They were having a great time. Even though Monty had boyfriends as well as girlfriends, it was obvious that he and Elizabeth had been intimate. Elizabeth could seduce any man, gay or straight. She and Monty were great pals and very dear friends. After I left the party, there was a horrible accident. Monty's car crashed into a utility pole as he drove down the winding road outside Elizabeth and Michael's home. His face was smashed through the windshield. Everyone at the house heard the crash. Elizabeth ran down the dark street to Monty's car and got into the wreck to be with him. When he signaled that he was having trouble with his throat, Elizabeth stuck her hand in his mouth, felt the back of his throat where some of his teeth had become lodged after being knocked out, and pulled them out to prevent him from choking. He might have died if she hadn't come to his aid.

Monty was never the same after that accident. His handsome face remained disfigured in spite of plastic surgery. Elizabeth always stood by him. When she loved you, she was a steadfast friend.

One night sometime later Elizabeth went to visit Evelyn Keyes and her lover, Mike Todd. Evelyn was best known for playing the role of Scarlett O'Hara's sister Suellen in *Gone with the Wind*. She believed that she and Mike would get married someday. But destiny had other plans. Mike left Evelyn immediately for Elizabeth, breaking Evelyn's heart.

Mike and Elizabeth were a great match. They both were strong and very passionate and had no compunctions about showing it. Eddie Fisher was Mike Todd's best friend, so we spent a lot of time with the Todds. When Elizabeth and Mike got married in Acapulco on March 8, 1957, Eddie was Mike's best man, and I was Elizabeth's matron of honor.

Their wedding was comparatively modest. In addition to Eddie and me it was attended by Elizabeth's mother and Cantinflas, a leading Mexican actor who costarred in Mike's hit film *Around the World in 80 Days*.

The night before the service I washed Elizabeth's hair for her. Elizabeth had gotten pregnant by Mike while she was still married to Wilding. To settle her divorce quickly, she sold a very expensive painting and gave the proceeds and all her savings to Wilding.

One night Elizabeth and Mike came for dinner at Eddie's and my house on Conway Drive in Beverly Hills. At some point, Elizabeth said something to Mike that caused him to haul off and hit her, knocking her to the floor. They got into a big argument and began screaming at each other. This upset me terribly. I went after Mike, jumping on his back and pummeling him so he would stop fighting with Elizabeth.

Suddenly everyone turned on me. Eddie accused me of being naive. Mike told me that Elizabeth could "take it." I honestly thought he was hurting her, but Elizabeth told me to stop being a Girl Scout. How did this turn into something *I* did wrong?

I didn't know that this was foreplay for Mike and Elizabeth. At the time Eddie was my first and only lover, and needless to say, we didn't carry on like that. Elizabeth liked it rough. Maybe that was caused by her relationship with Nicky Hilton, or maybe that's just how she'd learned to make love. Other girls at MGM liked rough sex. Lana Turner often came to the makeup room with bruises or a black eye. Sometimes they would have to reshoot things after she'd been knocked around.

Frank Sinatra was strong with women. It really was "my way" with him. Ava Gardner told me that they often hit each other when they were married, but I had never witnessed it. Ava shot Frank once, and lucky for Frank, her aim was lousy. She only hit him in the leg.

My lack of experience in this department made it difficult for me to please Eddie. He wasn't a very good teacher, even though he'd been around a lot before we were married. Carrie was only an infant when things became strained between America's Sweethearts. Eddie was spending a lot of time away from home. He was clearly unhappy. I wasn't happy either. I sensed that our marriage was in trouble and that pretty soon I'd be alone with our new baby.

More than anything, I wanted another baby so that Carrie could have someone to grow up with and share her life, as I'd had with my brother, Bill. The problem was, Eddie and I hardly ever had sex after Carrie was born. There were plenty of other men I could have had sex with, but I wasn't that kind of girl—and besides, I wanted my kids to have the same father.

Time was running out and I had to do something. I was on a mission to get pregnant.

It was May 1957. Eddie and I were visiting Elizabeth and Mike in Italy, where Mike was promoting *Around the World in 80 Days*. Elizabeth was pregnant with their first child, and their happiness was contagious. Eddie was in a great mood. We all stayed in a charming villa. At dinner one night I saw my chance. Opportunity was knocking, and I planned to get knocked up.

Elizabeth and Mike were up to their usual antics. She was on the second floor of the villa, yelling over the balcony to Mike to come upstairs. He yelled back in his normal profane way. When Mike finally climbed the stairs to satisfy Elizabeth, he did the job well. We could hear their raised voices as their fight continued, followed by the equally loud sounds of their lovemaking. I decided to make a move of my own.

I ordered Eddie a beer, and he drank it, even though he preferred the highs provided by his friendly physician, whom I called Dr. Needles. Then I asked the server for another beer for my sperm bank—uh, husband. Eddie being a nondrinker, it was enough to put him in the mood.

After dinner Eddie and I went up to bed. Sure that I was fertile, I was excited about getting my hands on Eddie. I soon got Eddie excited too, even though he was half asleep. I was swift, and so was Eddie. When the deed was done, I used the beautiful headboard on our bed to prop up my legs all night, determined to keep every molecule of baby ingredients inside me until the last possible moment. I stayed that way until I left for the airport the next morning.

Eddie remained in Italy while I flew home with my friend Jeannette, who'd accompanied us on the trip. When Eddie returned to LA, he was distant once more. He was stunned when he found out he was going to be a father again, but he became a good husband as we waited for our new baby. Nine months later, Carrie had a brother and my wish came true. Two beers, in and out—I got Todd. Todd Emmanuel Fisher, named after Mike Todd.

Mission accomplished.

It was February 1958, and Eddie was actually thrilled to have a son. Mike and Elizabeth's daughter, Lisa, had been born in August, and Elizabeth's two sons from her marriage to Michael Wilding were also living with them. Early one morning in March I was at my dressing table combing my hair when my housekeeper knocked on the bedroom door. I had gotten up before seven to take care of the children. Eddie, who was then a major singing star with many hits, was working out of town.

"Did you hear what happened?" Mary asked. "Mr. Mike Todd was killed in a plane crash. I just heard it on the radio."

My heart sank. No one was as full of life as Mike Todd, and now he was gone. What a tragedy for Elizabeth. I left immediately to go to her.

When I arrived, there were reporters and police everywhere. Michael Wilding and a doctor had been called. I sat quietly downstairs, where I could hear the police giving Elizabeth the horrible news upstairs. Elizabeth screamed. She appeared at the top of the stairs, wailing, "No! No! It's not true! It's not true!" It broke my heart. The doctor tried to calm her, but she was hysterical.

Elizabeth's babies shouldn't be around all this commotion, I thought. Our house was set up for kids. Carrie entertained her friends on a toy carousel that I'd installed in the living room. The addition of three more children wouldn't faze us. So I packed up Elizabeth's three- and five-year-old sons, little baby Lisa, and two nurses for the short trip back to our house.

Michael Wilding came too. He spent his time sitting at the bar in the living room, drinking everything we had in the house. Eddie and I weren't drinkers then, so I had to keep calling the liquor store to deliver more bottles of whiskey. Eddie flew back to Los Angeles and went to Elizabeth with my blessing. The four of us were so close, I was sure he could comfort her. Eddie would come home every few days to get clean clothes, and then return to Elizabeth.

If things weren't intense enough, I'd already agreed to sing "Tammy" at the Academy Awards show, to be held only a few days after Mike Todd was killed.

On the afternoon of the Oscars, I went to the Pantages Theater for rehearsal. I told the conductor to follow me as I sang my popular hit song. I knew it would be so difficult for me to get through this during the show. When the moment arrived, it was all I could do to keep from crying as I sang the romantic and innocent lyrics. Offstage, my life was filled with grief and loss. I did my best not to let it show. The moment the song was over, I left the stage and got into the car to go home. There was no time to think about anything other than my friends and all the children at home.

Michael Wilding spent the next two weeks on our couch, still upset about his divorce from Elizabeth. I got the feeling that he thought he might be able to reconcile with her now that she was a widow. He loved her completely. Elizabeth had that effect on people. It didn't bother him that she had been unfaithful to him with Mike Todd. To love Elizabeth was to love her forever.

After two weeks, I asked Wilding to go home. He wasn't much trouble, but I felt we all needed to get back to normal. Shortly after that, Elizabeth was able to take her children home, and then she took a trip to New York.

Eddie decided to follow her. The rest, as they say, is history.

Performing "Tammy" at the Academy Awards a few days after Mike Todd was killed in a horrible plane crash. It was so sad for everyone concerned. *Photofest*

Even though Eddie and Elizabeth and I shared headlines for a year, I knew that their marriage wouldn't last. Eddie wasn't her type. He wasn't strong enough to keep up with Elizabeth. She was so devastated by Mike Todd's death that she looked for comfort in a convenient person who also was Mike's best friend. That connection made her grab on to Eddie in an attempt to get over the loss of her true love.

When Elizabeth met Richard Burton while they were on location in Italy filming *Cleopatra,* it was Eddie's turn to be left behind. At that point, Eddie was drinking heavily. He went into a rage when he discovered that all the gossip he heard about Elizabeth and Burton was true. Maybe that was because Elizabeth had found someone as charming, intelligent, and fiery as she was.

Elizabeth, Eddie, and I were a love triangle that became one of the biggest scandals of its day. In my heart, I hoped that Eddie would come home to his children once Elizabeth got tired of him. As much as I had loved him, I hated the way he abandoned Carrie and Todd.

Several years after all of our divorces and remarriages, I was in New York City with my second husband, Harry Karl, about to sail to Europe for a vacation. As the bellboy took our few suitcases through the lobby, I saw a dozen bellmen taking care of countless trunks, suitcases, birdcages, and animal carriers—all matching and all headed for limousines in front of the hotel. I asked someone what group they belonged to and was told, "The Burtons." They were crossing the Atlantic on the *Queen Elizabeth.*

I told myself this couldn't be happening. Harry and I were booked on the same ship. There would be no way to avoid the press. There were six first-class suites on the top deck of the luxury liner. Elizabeth and Richard had booked five of them; Harry and I were in the one remaining suite.

We both decided to contact the other at the same moment, each of us sending notes to the other's cabin. Elizabeth and Richard came to our suite for cocktails. Once Elizabeth and I saw each other, we were back to being girlfriends again. I don't think we even mentioned Eddie Fisher more than in passing. We drank champagne and had a lovely time. Richard Burton was a delight. We all decided to go down to the dining room for dinner, which caused quite a sensation. Photographers hiding behind potted plants were waiting to grab a shot of us. It was a wonderful reunion that led to many fun evenings together.

In 1967 Elizabeth and Richard were my guests at the annual ball given by the Thalians, a charity that Jack Haley Jr., Hugh O'Brian, and I, along with some other then-young stars, had founded in 1955. The Thalians' mission is to educate and enlighten the world about mental illness in order to eliminate the stigma attached to it. Each year, to raise money, the Thalians honor someone extraordinary from the Hollywood community with their "Goofy" award, designed by Walt Disney in the shape of one of his cartoon characters.

This particular year it was Peter Ustinov, who was making a film called *The Comedians* with Elizabeth and Richard. After the ceremony, everyone came back to the Karl house on Greenway to finish off the evening. Elizabeth and Richard got into a fight, carrying on as if they were doing a scene from *Who's Afraid of Virginia Woolf?* By now I knew what this meant.

"Just drag her off to one of the bedrooms, Richard," I yelled at them. "And don't wake the kids!"

Elizabeth and I had shared so many happy times since then, and it was good to be working on Carrie's movie together. One day Elizabeth asked to see me. There was a scene in the script about her character stealing my character's husband while in an alcoholic blackout.

"I'm so sorry for what I did to you with Eddie," she said.

Elizabeth sounded very emotional. It seemed clear to me that she'd been thinking about what she wanted to say.

"That was another lifetime," I assured her. "You and I made up years ago."

"I know, I know," she said. "I just feel so awful when I think of how I hurt you and your children."

We spoke often, sometimes spending time together. One night I went to her house to watch a movie with her and took along a pumpkin pie for us to eat. The movie was *The Last Samurai,* starring Tom Cruise. It features a lot of sword fights, which really didn't interest us. We sat in Elizabeth's bed, eating pie and chatting, while Elizabeth's nurse sat quietly beside us.

During our visit, a man dropped by with a diamond tennis bracelet for Elizabeth, asking to see her as he handed the trinket to her friend and assistant, Tim Mendelson. When Tim brought the bracelet to the bedroom and conveyed the message, Elizabeth instructed him to tell the man to come back another time.

"I don't really like him much," she explained to me as she put on the bracelet.

It was a bit tight.

"You may have to add a diamond or two to that, so it fits better," I said.

"That won't be necessary," she said. "I'll just wear it early in the day, when I'm not so swollen."

Elizabeth had jewels for every occasion—and every stage of water retention.

The last time I spoke to Elizabeth, she was close to death.

"Getting old is really shitty," I said.

Elizabeth laughed that wonderful full laugh.

"It certainly is, Debbie. This is really tough."

I told her to be strong and just hang in there. Elizabeth liked kidding about being ill, but she hated all that pain.

Elizabeth and me on the set of *These Old Broads*. It was
like the old days when we were girlfriends on the lot
together, young and happy.

"I'm really trying," Elizabeth said softly.

When she finally died, I knew she was at peace. She
had suffered for so long, yet she still grabbed life by the
balls. Even with her failing health in her later years,

she would go off to Hawaii to swim with sharks. There was no one like her.

My dear friend remembered me in her will. She left me a beautiful set of sapphire earrings with a matching bracelet and necklace. Her gesture touched me deeply, not just because of her great taste in jewelry and her endless generosity, but because she'd thought to acknowledge our friendship. Elizabeth had always been generous with me. Many years ago, one of Richard Burton's costumes from *Cleopatra* went up for auction. I didn't have any money to bid on it, so I called Elizabeth and asked if she could help.

"Of course," she answered.

"It's a beautiful costume, Elizabeth. I'd like to have it."

Elizabeth said she'd also like me to have it, and asked, "How much is it?"

I told her I wouldn't know until I bid. Without hesitation, she told me to buy it.

Richard's costume ended up costing $16,000. When the auction was over, I called Elizabeth with the total. She sent me a check and never even saw what she'd bought.

Many people asked me for my thoughts when Elizabeth passed. I was happy she was out of pain, yet sorry that I wouldn't see her again. I released this statement to the newspapers:

Elizabeth had a long, productive career. She was the most glamorous star and sexual star of our generation. No one else could equal Elizabeth's beauty and sexuality. Women liked her, and men adored her, including my husband. Her love for her children is enduring. She was a symbol of stardom. Her legacy will last.

Chapter 20
I'm Princess Leia's Mother

In December 2000, about seven weeks before *These Old Broads* first aired, Carrie did an interview on ABC's *Prime Time* in which she told Diane Sawyer—and an audience of millions of viewers—that she had a mental condition that, in its most extreme state, would lead her to need hospitalization. This was not exactly news to anyone who'd read or seen *Postcards from the Edge.* Carrie's best-selling book and hit movie were at least a decade old by then. But I have to admit, it was a little strange to watch Carrie chat with Diane as if she were talking to a doctor, openly discussing her mishaps and hospital stays. Not every parent with an addict in the family gets to turn on the TV and see her child telling a newscaster how she took thirty Percodan a day to regulate her moods.

Carrie described how she'd named these moods "Rollicking Roy" and "Sediment Pam." Roy takes her on incredible highs during which her mind races so much that she can't sleep, sometimes for days. Pam stands for "piss and moan." Pam stands on the shore and sobs. She's in charge of Carrie's low moods. As Carrie explains it, Roy is the meal and Pam is the check, and anyone who has stayed awake for days is likely to wind up psychotic. Which is what happened to my daughter.

But that's Carrie's story to tell, which she went on to do in her hit show and book *Wishful Drinking*, in the process not only entertaining audiences and readers but finding humor in her devastating experiences and demonstrating her belief that "if you claim something, it has less power over you."

I don't think many people these days need me to explain manic depression, or bipolar disorder, to them. Those readers who do can find it in Carrie's brilliant book or watch the DVD of her show. She's done so much to educate people on the subject. Instead, I want to tell you what it's been like for me to have a child I love completely who has a biological condition that cannot be cured, only recognized and treated. To do that I need to go back about forty years, to when Carrie was thirteen or fourteen and her personality changed.

She became reclusive. One day she'd be friendly with someone, and the next day she didn't want to see that person anymore. Around this time, all our lives were changing due to the breakup of my second marriage, to Harry Karl. It was difficult to keep track of the emotions the family was experiencing, and I thought some of Carrie's conflicts with me were just natural teenage rebellion. There are different kinds of mental conditions, and some people who have them are more affected than others. I'd worked with the Thalians for years, raising millions of dollars for mental health treatment and research—it's ironic that this was my charity. But it didn't occur to me that my daughter might need professional help at that time.

When I was hired to star in the Broadway show *Irene* in 1973, I decided to take Carrie with me to New York. She was then sixteen. Todd was in junior high school; he stayed behind with my soon-to-be-ex-husband and joined Carrie and me after the show opened. Carrie smoked pot with the kids in the chorus of *Irene.* This didn't seem to be something I needed to control. Then Carrie went to London for eighteen months to study at the Central School of Speech and Drama. While she was there, she made it clear that she did not want to be in contact with me. I felt rejected and hurt, but since I was the one who had insisted she go in the first place, ultimately I had to do it her way. After she moved back to Los Angeles, Warren Beatty cast her in his film *Shampoo,* which was a huge hit and for which Carrie received glowing notices. Then she was cast in *Star Wars* and returned to London to make the film.

Carrie was only twenty when *Star Wars* was released in May 1977 and made her an international star. I was the same age in 1952 when *Singin' in the Rain* made me a celebrity. The similarities ended there. When I was twenty, I lived with my parents, and alcohol was never allowed in the house. Two and a half decades later, the culture was sex, drugs, and rock and roll. I don't know many young people who didn't join the fun in those seemingly carefree days before AIDS, crack, and punk rock. Carrie partied all the time with the likes of Dan Aykroyd and John Belushi and the *Saturday Night Live* crowd. She met her husband Paul Simon through them.

In 1981 I was working at Warner Brothers, on the TV series *Aloha Paradise,* when I received a phone call informing me, "Your daughter is in the hospital at Century City. We don't know how serious it is." No mother ever wants to get such a call. When it happens, the world stops. Your heart pounds so fast, you think you'll faint, even as your adrenaline rises to meet the crisis. Someone you love is in trouble, and you might not be able to help. It's out of your control. All you can do is pray.

Carrie had been working on a movie called *Under the Rainbow.* I knew she was very unhappy, but not that she was in trouble. Without changing my clothes, makeup, or hair, I put on a scarf and rushed out of the studio into a rainstorm. Between my tears and the screaming rain, it was impossible to see the road. I drove across town afraid I wouldn't make it to the hospital.

I finally arrived at Century City to find Carrie being taken somewhere on a gurney. She was still in her *Under the Rainbow* wig and costume, curled up on that table, so still and small. Terrified that she was dead, I asked one of the doctors in attendance if my daughter was going to be all right.

"We hope so," he said.

Then they wheeled my little girl away.

I can't remember much about the waiting room except my anguish. I believe that every mother who thinks she might lose her child has the same feeling. You don't know what the outcome will be. They don't tell you that she's dead, but they don't know if she will live. It's horrible. I was frustrated and afraid. Helpless. (I went through something similar when I couldn't reach Carrie the day I married Richard Hamlett, until Ava Gardner came to the rescue.)

Somehow I didn't cry. After an eternity, one of the doctors came to tell me that my daughter's condition was stable and that she'd been lucky. I shook with overwhelming gratitude that Carrie was going to be all right.

Several years later, Carrie was admitted to Century City Rehab. She didn't want me to come to the hospital with her because I was so recognizable that her anonymity would be gone immediately. Instead, her brother was her companion, constantly by her side. Carrie and I are so fortunate that our Todd is always there for us. Our housekeeper, Mary, would go to the hospital with fresh linens, quilts, and anything else I could think of that might make Carrie more comfortable. I did whatever she wanted. When the lows hit, we all rally around Carrie, to buoy her up and assure her that she is loved.

This was the episode that triggered her writing *Postcards from the Edge*. Carrie came out of it finally learning to live a sober life—one day at a time—and used her experience and sense of humor creatively to become a successful writer.

Carrie's bipolar disorder wasn't properly identified for a long time after I first noticed a change in her; it wasn't a common diagnosis in the '70s and '80s, as it is now. Mood swings that I felt were normal in a young girl later became known as symptoms of a serious condition. Even though I had access to the best doctors in the mental health field through my work with the Thalians, none of them could tell me anything conclusive about Carrie's behavior. And none of us could imagine that she would be on this journey for decades.

Sometimes it takes a while before medical knowledge catches up with reality. I remember when the Thalians honored Rita Hayworth as "Miss Wonderful" in 1977. Most recipients made elaborate acceptance speeches. After Gene Kelly handed her the award, beautiful Rita just stood onstage staring at the audience.

"Say thank you," I whispered in her ear.

"Thank you," she repeated mechanically.

The fact is, Rita had Alzheimer's. She used to sing in the street near her house with no clothes on, going over to see Glenn Ford, who was her neighbor and friend. This was before Alzheimer's was commonly diagnosed. The tabloids accused Rita of being a drunk. My father later developed Alzheimer's. We now know millions of people have it, and there still isn't any cure.

Bipolar disorder isn't new, but its diagnosis and treatment have only become common in the past thirty years. Rosemary Clooney admitted in the late 1970s that she struggled with manic depression. Several scientists connect the condition to the creative part of the brain, which explains why a higher percentage of performers, writers, and other creative types seem to suffer from it. In *Wishful Drinking,* Carrie lists many famous people who were bipolar. Women are also more likely to be bipolar than men. It is difficult for everyone it touches.

Originally Carrie believed she was just a drug addict, but finally she came to understand that her body has a chemical imbalance that cannot be dealt with solely by abstaining. It can be controlled with the help of psychiatrists and medicine, and Carrie has been fortunate to have great doctors. Bipolar disorder is progressive: as time passes, depressions can become increasingly severe. It's a constant battle. A few years ago, Carrie experienced a deep depression that made her (as she put it) not necessarily feel like *dying,* but feeling a lot like not being alive. This can be normal for some bipolar sufferers, but it was new to Carrie, and it scared her. Carrie has so much courage. She always ventures forward to seek the newest treatment, refusing to give up. So a few years ago, she decided to try electroconvulsive therapy, or ECT.

ECT is not the horrifying shock treatments inflicted on Jack Nicholson in *One Flew Over the*

Cuckoo's Nest and Rock Hudson in *Seconds* and Ellen Burstyn in *Requiem for a Dream* and, going all the way back, Olivia de Havilland in *The Snake Pit.* ECT is a new frontier in the treatment of bipolar disorder, done under light anesthesia so Carrie can recover as soon as she comes home, the same day as the procedure. Now when the lows become intolerable, Carrie gets ECT. She has written about all this in her book *Shockaholic.*

There are no long-range studies on ECT yet. We have to trust that the doctors administering these brain treatments are doing what's best. It's new territory for them as well as for my daughter. Todd and I have spoken to the doctors about the effects of this treatment. Carrie works every day to fight her demons. No one else can do it for her, but we support every step that Carrie takes. We try to do everything we can to help her not get depressed and to remain strong. It's hard for everyone, but it's hardest for Carrie.

Still, it's heartbreaking to watch someone you love struggle so. As a mother, I find the hardest thing for me is to love my daughter and not to intervene in her life. I want to do everything humanly possible to keep my girl out of pain, to pick her up when she's down. If I could, I would suffer for her.

Over the years, many professionals have told me to practice "tough love" with my daughter—to reassure Carrie that she is loved and then cut her off. I can't do this. So many of my friends had children in similar situations and did what the doctors instructed. George C. Scott lost his son to drugs, as did Carroll O'Connor. Their tough love didn't matter once their children were dead. It's not natural to outlive your child. This has always been my greatest fear. Like countless others, celebrity families are touched by substance abuse. Being famous doesn't protect you. Every family has to decide how they will handle their child who needs help, even when that child has grown up. Carrie is my child, and I love her with every ounce of strength I possess. If love alone could cure our children, they would always be well. Since it can't, I will do whatever I can to make her life less difficult. Too many mothers have lost their children, for thousands of different reasons. I don't know if I could survive that. I'm so grateful to Carrie for working so hard to stay well when sometimes it might seem easier to give up.

Every day I worry about my children. When I wake up, I wonder where Carrie is and how she's faring. Todd has these concerns too, but I do the lion's share of worrying. I'm sure that's normal for most mothers. Carrie is blessed to have her daughter. Billie loves her and needs her, and Billie's love anchors Carrie. It gives her strength. She and Billie work through everything and are in a great place.

We all have to find strength wherever we can. The AA program has worked well for many people with alcoholism. They also have programs for people on narcotics, and people with food issues or sex addiction. There is help if you seek it. Luckily, I've been able to find help in my faith and in my son and daughter, who make my life worth living.

God has given me many gifts. When I count my blessings, which is often, strength is one of the gifts I'm most grateful for, as well as the fact that the things I've needed to be strong for have all been outward circumstances and situations. I haven't had to deal with inner demons as Carrie has, and continues to do every day. When you have someone in your family who suffers from these severe mood swings, you think that someday you'll be able to handle them. Not true. All you can do is pray and hang on.

At the end of *Wishful Drinking,* Carrie states, "At times, being bipolar can be an all-consuming challenge, requiring a lot of stamina and even more courage, so if you're living with this illness and functioning at all, it's something to be proud of."

I'll end this chapter with a fervent *Amen to that.*

With my beautiful daughter, Carrie.

Chapter 21
Hollywood & Highland

After the hotel was sold and my third divorce was final, my life became more settled.

Temporarily.

My dream of a museum for my collection had been put on hold by the sale of the Vegas property. Now, creating a permanent home to preserve all these magnificent pieces became my priority.

After Todd moved the pieces from the Vegas museum to the warehouse on his ranch in Northern California in 1998, he was concerned about maintaining everything properly. So he visited the Victoria and Albert Museum in London to learn how they archive their costumes. The Victoria and Albert curators informed Todd that their collection, which includes clothing that was worn by Henry VIII four hundred years ago, is not costumes but "textiles." Todd learned that all the labels MGM and 20th Century Fox had used contained acid that could burn through the fabric. All the hangers were wrong. (This explained why some of my things were falling apart on their hangers.) Everything had to be laid flat, wrapped in acid-free tissue, and kept at a consistent temperature.

When Todd built the museum at the hotel, he began a database to keep track of all the costumes and props in the collection, as well as the films they appeared in, the actors who'd worn them, and other pertinent information. It took him years to complete the database. Before the Vegas museum was built, most of my collection had been stored at my North Hollywood dance studio. We now knew that to preserve the costumes properly for future generations, we needed to store everything at a controlled temperature, so the electric bill at our new storage space was four times what it had been at the studio. Todd removed all the acid labels and bought thousands of boxes and miles of tissue paper. It took a lot of manpower and many years of work. The studios had thought of the costumes and props as objects to be used, reused, and then thrown away—which may be why people used to make fun of me for buying all those "rags."

Now that the museum in Vegas was closed, people approached me about putting a new museum in the theater and shopping complex being built at the corner of Hollywood and Highland in the heart of Hollywood. The initial call came from a company called TrizecHahn, which was developing the space. They were excited about creating a Hollywood memorabilia museum so close to Grauman's Chinese Theatre and many other entertainment industry attractions. They put us in touch with the Community Redevelopment Agency for the City of Los Angeles, which had agreed to issue bonds to cover the development of the complex. The CRA had already put up a lot of money through fund-raising and issuing bonds.

In 2001 I signed a lease with TrizecHahn for a large space on the fourth floor of what came to be known as the Hollywood & Highland Center. Todd hired architect Dianna Wong to design the space, and I continued to pay for the monthly maintenance at Todd's ranch.

In June 2001, there was a groundbreaking ceremony for the Hollywood Motion Picture Museum at Hollywood & Highland. Todd, Carrie, and my brother, Bill, came to the ceremony, where Johnny Grant, the honorary mayor of Hollywood, presented me with a check in the amount of $50,000.

The TrizecHahn developers set the opening of the complex for mid-September—a deadline we were expected to meet. Meanwhile, the construction from other Hollywood & Highland tenants began invading our space. Ventilation shafts from the restaurant underneath us on the third floor came up in the middle of our proposed theater, where we planned to run the film clips from the movies in which the costumes originally appeared. Pipes and columns appeared out of nowhere. It was devastating. When it became clear that this situation could not be changed, the president of

On top of the world at Hollywood & Highland. Todd, Carrie, and I celebrate the announcement of the new Hollywood museum plans. This turned out to be another disappointment. *Getty Images*

TrizecHahn suggested that the museum could occupy the "nose" of the building—a glass-enclosed area with several floors that overlooked all of Hollywood, including the HOLLYWOOD sign.

We signed a new lease in December. Our space was increased to ten thousand square feet. Our expenses went up too. Dianna Wong prepared plans for this expanded, multilevel space. Since everything we had done already had to be moved or redesigned, we were no longer expected to finish in time for the opening of the complex, so I took the opportunity to go to New York City to attend a special event.

Chapter 22
September 10, 2001

It was September 10, 2001. Michael Jackson was giving a concert at Madison Square Garden to celebrate his thirtieth anniversary in show business and, belatedly, his birthday in August. I was looking forward to seeing Michael perform live onstage. Although I'd known him for many years, I usually only saw Michael when he was rehearsing at my dance studio, where he'd worked on his *Thriller* and *Beat It* videos. I was glad that he felt at home there. The concert was being taped for a television special, and Elizabeth would be giving a speech to honor Michael. Before leaving LA, I'd called Elizabeth's assistant, Tim Mendelson, to ask about getting a ticket.

I went to Madison Square Garden by myself and was seated close to Elizabeth's party. Michael escorted Elizabeth to her seat; after she sat down, I waved to

Elizabeth from mine. Macaulay Culkin was in the audience, as well as many of Michael's other friends.

The concert was magnificent. I love live performing, so it was a real thrill for me. Michael and his family performed, as did other artists. There wasn't an empty seat in the house—except when the crowd was on its feet, which was just about every moment. It was an exhilarating evening. I was so glad that I had taken the opportunity to be there.

After the concert I went back to my midtown hotel. I was so wound up from Michael's brilliant performance that I stayed awake watching TV and reading magazines like the *Enquirer.*

I woke up to the horrible smell of something burning. My first thought was that the hotel was on fire. I called down to the front desk and was told that there had been a crash downtown and that I should stay in my room until further notice.

I turned on the television and saw footage of the planes crashing into the World Trade Center and the Twin Towers collapsing. There was only one channel; the destruction had knocked out the transmitters for the other networks. I couldn't believe what I was seeing. I watched in horror as the nightmare unfolded in an endless loop on the screen. When the third plane hit the Pentagon, I was sure we were all in danger.

Michael, Elizabeth, Joe Jackson, and Macaulay
Culkin on the red carpet at Madison Square Garden,
September 10, 2001. *Kevin Kane/Getty Images*

The reporting wasn't clear on what happened, but the
footage was upsetting. I looked out the hotel window,
now covered in ashes. The devastation in the city was
overwhelming. People jammed the streets trying to get
safely home.

The phone rang in my room. It was Elizabeth's
assistant. "Elizabeth heard that you were here alone
and asked me to check on you," Tim said.

"This is so horrible," I responded numbly. "How's
Elizabeth? I'm very frightened."

"Elizabeth would like you to come to the Pierre and stay with us," Tim responded. "Her children left the hotel immediately after the concert and are back in Los Angeles by now. You can have their room. Michael and his family left last night by bus." (The media later reported incorrectly that they'd flown out.)

I packed my things and called the front desk for a bellman. The elevator operator was crying as the bellman helped me with my luggage. Everyone I saw had tears in their eyes. I couldn't keep from crying myself.

I finally let go once I got to Elizabeth's suite, where I hugged her and we cried together. There was news footage of people with no hope of being saved jumping out of the towers. A fourth plane had crashed in a field in Pennsylvania after heroic passengers overwhelmed the terrorists who'd hijacked it and were heading to the White House. Every minute was consumed with stories of the people on the planes and in the towers; there were also stories of miraculous escapes before the buildings collapsed. So many people were suffering. Our world would never be the same.

Elizabeth was a gracious hostess in spite of being in a great deal of pain with her back. Her doctor was with her, as well as José Eber, her hairstylist. Elizabeth's masseur and his little girl were also staying in the large suite. Her French butler took very good care of us as we watched the TV in disbelief, all of us sitting and crying together. When it became too much, we'd go to our rooms and try to rest.

September 11 was a Tuesday. I had a concert scheduled in California that Saturday. By Thursday I realized that I was going to miss it; by government order, no planes were allowed to fly. We didn't know how long we'd be stranded in New York.

I really hate not fulfilling my obligations and disappointing people. On Friday I told Elizabeth, "I have a show to do tomorrow in Escondido."

"Where's that?" she asked.

I wasn't surprised. I knew that Elizabeth lived in her own world.

"It's near San Diego," I said. "My engagement has been sold out for months. I hate to cancel, but I don't think there's any way we'll get out in time."

"I'll phone John," she said. "Maybe he can help." Sometime later Elizabeth called to me from another room, "Debbie, we have a plane. We're leaving in the morning."

"Nobody is getting out, Elizabeth," I responded.

"I know," she said. "But I was married to John. He was happy to help us."

Of course you were, I thought. And of course he was.

John was Senator John Warner of Virginia. It must be nice to have an ex-husband who can actually be your friend and be useful too.

Even so, I was skeptical that it would actually happen. In the best of circumstances, Elizabeth was famous for her tardiness. She wasn't feeling well. Her eyes were red and swollen from crying all week. Her doctor was worried about her heart palpitations.

But when morning arrived, Elizabeth was up and ready to go. We all went downstairs to cars that were waiting to take us to Teterboro Airport, where a private plane would fly us home. There was no traffic as we left Manhattan and no other planes in sight at the airport. The sky was empty, although in the distance we could see smoke in the direction of the city. As we flew over the crash site we saw the heartbreaking devastation below us.

It was an eerie flight. Everyone was exhausted and relieved to be leaving New York. It was so strange to be the only ones in the air.

When we landed in Van Nuys, a helicopter owned by my friend Bob Petersen was there to meet me. Bob owned Petersen Publishing and *Hot Rod* magazine—if you're not rich yourself, it sure helps to have rich friends. I thanked Elizabeth and waved good-bye to everyone as I climbed out of the plane and into Bob's helicopter. For security reasons, we had to fly in designated airspace.

My curtain was at 2:00 P.M.; I got there at 1:35. My assistant, Donald Light, was waiting for me in the red vest that he always wears to my shows, his arms filled with programs. A trailer dressing room had been set up for me. I dashed into it, taking a few minutes to put on a little stage makeup and change my clothes. There was no time for vocalizing or going over my lines—just a touch of lipstick and I hit the stage.

When the audience saw me, they all stood up and cheered. They'd been told that I might not make it. It was very emotional for all of us; we were all crying. The audience was particularly wonderful that day. I couldn't tell jokes or do half the material in my show, so I told them about spending the past few days with Elizabeth and her friends in New York. They all laughed when I said that since Elizabeth had gotten me there on time, I guess that made up for the Eddie thing. I spoke about going to Korea during the war there. The whole audience was sad, yet they showed up to see my show. We all felt better being together.

I ended the show an hour later with "God Bless America." Everyone stood up and sang with me. The horror of New York seemed so far away. I was exhausted. The turmoil of the last week was nothing for me compared to what so many had suffered. I felt heartsick for all those who'd lost loved ones. We were united by this senseless attack on our country, drawn together by something terrible.

God bless the USA.

Chapter 23
Museum, Interrupted

Horrible as the events of September 11, 2001, were, we had to keep on living. Once I was safely back in California, things began to change at the Hollywood & Highland Center. Construction slowed down at the new site. Although the opening of the complex was postponed until November, even then our space wasn't completed. The move there required a lot more work, which I was having trouble underwriting. We now projected that the museum would be completed in February 2002.

Soon it became apparent that the bond issue was not going to move quickly enough for us to finish the plans and complete the museum. February came and went.

In the summer, Todd contacted Greg Orman, who had lent us money for the hotel in Vegas and was our angel on the day of the auction by guaranteeing $1 million for David Siegel if he wanted to bid on the hotel. Greg flew from Las Vegas to Los Angeles to survey the site. Todd and I walked with him through our space in the nose of the complex, and Greg agreed to put up a million dollars as an unsecured bridge loan, at 10 percent interest, the going rate at that time. This made it possible for us to hire more people to work to meet the new deadlines. It was understood that this loan would be for the short term, just until the bond money came through.

We received the loan on September 4, 2002.

Then the CRA changed their minds. In a meeting with all the lawyers and players, a CRA representative announced that the bond issue would be done, but with a cover letter stating that the bonds were not backed by the city. Our banker from the Royal Bank of Canada couldn't believe the news. He had presold the bonds with the city's assurance that they were valid. In one minute, the bonds became worthless. The City of Los Angeles had money troubles after 9/11 that changed things for everyone at Hollywood & Highland, and they were taking me along with them.

Todd and I were stunned. We'd spent more than $1 million over the years on plans, construction, and rent. It was obvious we had to abandon the hope of having a museum in Hollywood. With a heavy heart, I relinquished my lease at Hollywood & Highland.

In February 2003, the Hollywood Chamber of Commerce honored me with a Lifetime Achievement Award. The ceremony was held at the Hollywood Roosevelt Hotel. Carrie introduced me, rattling off all the events of the past few years, including how the CRA had defaulted on their promise to underwrite the financing of the Hollywood & Highland museum. The honorary mayor of Hollywood, Johnny Grant, had been trying to work things out among the politicians, but it was beyond his control. Carrie wasn't the only one living at the edge.

To make things more insane, TrizecHahn sued Todd and me for breaking the lease. The suit was later dismissed, but once again I had to spend time and money to fight it.

By March 2003, it was clear that there was no way I could quickly recoup all the money that I'd already lost on this project. And we needed money to keep fighting the people who had originally been our allies. I realized that I would have to auction part of my collection to keep going. I decided, with great reluctance, to sell about three hundred pieces of my memorabilia, in the hope that the money I got would pay to preserve the rest.

The auction was scheduled for December 6, 2003. Todd and I chose the items to sell. These included costumes that had been worn by Jimmy Cagney in *Yankee Doodle Dandy* and by Judy Garland in *Ziegfeld Follies*. It broke my heart to part with any of them while I still thought I could create a museum somewhere. There was a pastel portrait of Jean Harlow I loved, that I'd bought at the Fox auction in 1971. I told Todd to pull it. He said it was already listed, but somehow he managed to save it for me.

Everything was set up in a big conference room at the Le Meridien Hotel on La Cienega Boulevard in West Hollywood. Julien, the auctioneer, had invited his entire family to the auction to meet me. Someone came up to me and said how sorry she was that I had to sell my beautiful things. I burst into tears and looked away, overwhelmed, and avoided anyone else who tried to approach me.

I made enough from the auction to keep my family and me afloat. Even though I sold only what I had to, it still cost me a piece of my heart. And I was still in debt.

Chapter 24
On to Pigeon Forge

And then, in a galaxy far, far away called Tennessee, it seemed that someone was interested in my collection. A company called BIV Retail sent Todd and me a proposal to build the museum in Pigeon Forge, Tennessee, the home of Dolly Parton's Dollywood.

We were skeptical at first, but we decided to see what they had to offer. Todd flew to Tennessee, where he found a wonderful community and a major tourist destination. Every year more tourists go to Pigeon Forge than to Branson, Missouri, a huge entertainment center. The area around Dollywood has dozens of other attractions, including theaters, theme park rides, and summer festivals. The developer showed Todd Belle Island, a beautiful spot where the museum would be built.

While we considered BIV's proposal, Todd and I also pursued other possibilities, still hoping to find a home for the collection in Hollywood, where everything in it had been created.

I met with Roger Mayer, the treasurer of the Academy of Motion Picture Arts and Sciences. Years before, my friend Jack Haley Jr. had taken me to see all the land that the Academy had bought for a museum. Over dinner at Trader Vic's in Beverly Hills, Roger confirmed that they were putting together big money to build one. Roger explained that the decision was up to the Academy's board of directors, and that they weren't interested in my collection. How ironic that the people of Tennessee cared more about a Hollywood museum than the masters of Hollywood did.

This was a great disappointment to me, but I continued to hope that they might change their minds.

Todd did several presentations for Steven Spielberg and his associate Andy Spahn when we first ran into trouble at Hollywood & Highland. They passed on our project. We tried again a few years later, with the same result. Carrie called her friend David Geffen, who has always been supportive of Carrie in every way. When I followed up with David, he told me that he wasn't interested. "Why don't you just sell that stuff?" he asked me. How many times had I heard that before?

I approached George Lucas. George has his own vast collection of everything you can imagine related to his films (except, as it happened, some of the items in my collection, including one of the cameras he'd used to shoot the first *Star Wars* movie). He appreciates the value of saving film artifacts. Surely he could see the value in what I was offering. But George wasn't interested in my collection either.

Even though he didn't offer to help, I appreciated his kindness in seeing me.

Tennessee was looking better and better. The people there couldn't have been nicer or more open to our ideas. Their proposal showed us the value of building in Pigeon Forge. The town has a highway with six lanes of traffic to handle all the tourists. Belle Island Village was designed as a family-themed attraction that would include my museum, the Darrell Waltrip Racing Experience, and Otter Cove (produced in collaboration with the Knoxville Zoo). There were retail shops, restaurants, and rides for children.

They proposed building a structure that would have ample room to display my memorabilia, including three theaters measuring almost two thousand square feet each.

In March 2004, I announced the relocation of my collection to Pigeon Forge.

Todd designed a miniature of Hollywood Boulevard in the 1940s. A tableau featuring Frederick's of Hollywood would be displayed in front of the ladies' rooms. Our plans included a Fashion Pavilion, a Western Pavilion, and an Egyptian palace to display the costumes and props from *Cleopatra* and *Ben-Hur*. Items from epic films like *Lawrence of Arabia* and *Mutiny on the Bounty* would be displayed in yet another room. The museum was similar to the one in Vegas, but much larger in scale. Todd incorporated the carousel screens to run film clips of the featured movies. I did a voice-over introduction. One of our movie theaters would be able to seat 125 people. As we had done with the museum in my hotel, the entrance was designed to evoke memories of old movie palaces like the Pantages and Egyptian movie palaces in Hollywood. The exterior of the building was designed to look like the riverboat from the classic MGM musical *Show Boat*.

There were some hiccups along the way, but we were very pleased as the building was constructed. The developers put up a $12 million loan to cover all the costs. The Greg Orman loan could be reduced and the balance renegotiated at a more favorable interest rate. The Tennessee developers projected that the numbers supported the expense, as the potential income for the first year forecasted a profit in the millions.

Once the shell of the building was completed, I flew to Tennessee for what they called a "topping-off" ceremony. There was a party on May 27, 2008. We all watched as a giant crane placed the final steel beam on top of the six-story, forty-thousand-plus-square-foot building. Todd and I had signed the beam, along with Darrell Waltrip's partner, NASCAR star Jeff Hammond. The whole town turned out. I had my picture taken with a local man dressed like an otter, from the Otter Cove attraction.

This was my dream. Movie fans would have a place to visit the costumes worn by the most famous stars in film history. After more than forty years, it was finally happening.

But God had other plans. The Bush economy of 2007 and 2008 collapsed, taking a lot of people with it. Countrywide Financial had underwritten our museum. Down went Countrywide, and Debbie right along with them. Regions Bank took over the Countrywide loans and planned to foreclose on the Belle Island Village project. The funding for the developers' loan was canceled, in spite of its merit. The banks didn't want to lend money to anyone.

The City of Pigeon Forge had guaranteed the project with municipal bonds. Just as we'd completed the building's shell, they pulled out. A city planner sent

My next attempt at a museum, a beautiful complex
in Tennessee. Yet *another* disappointment,
with much time and money lost. This drawing of the
proposed site was part of a promotional brochure.

us word that the city had decided to go with another project. I never understood the reasoning. Aside from shattering my dream of building a museum for what would be the last time, this decision also deprived the Pigeon Forge area of some wonderful attractions that would have continued to employ many people in the area. Our museum would have been only a few miles from Dollywood, and right next door to the NASCAR building. That alone would have made us a success. Todd and I both called the office of the governor of Tennessee, but we never got a response.

Once again, my troubles were just beginning. When Pigeon Forge backed out, I buried myself in work to keep all of us going. Meanwhile, the $1.5 million loan Todd had arranged with Greg Orman was in default. The loan had gone on for more than five years, and when we didn't repay the loan or the interest, the interest rate kept rising. Todd knew about this, but had kept the details from me. So I was unprepared for the lawsuit that Orman filed against us.

Still, the worst was yet to come.

Chapter 25
Another Day in Court

Todd and I decided to make one more effort to save the collection. In June 2008, I filed for Chapter 7 bankruptcy protection for the Hollywood Motion Picture Museum, to buy us some time to find other backers.

Carrie called Paul Allen, a friend of hers who was one of the founders of Microsoft and is known for his philanthropy. His Paul G. Allen Family Foundation gives millions to charity and education every year. Paul had created the EMP Museum in Seattle, which celebrates the history of popular music and includes the Science Fiction Museum and Hall of Fame. Because of this, we all thought that Paul might be interested in helping establish a motion picture museum.

Todd met with Paul and his sister, Jo Lynn Allen, and presented them with the possibilities, suggesting that they merge my collection with their music and science fiction museums. The Allens do so much for many causes, but they passed on our proposal.

In April 2006, I'd performed with the Omaha Symphony in Nebraska. Warren Buffett came backstage to meet me with a group of his friends. He loved my show and told me that my Barbra Streisand impression was a scream. He invited me to his home for a dinner party with him and his then-girlfriend and two other couples. Warren asked me to sign a picture for him, which I did gladly. Then I asked him to sign one of him for me. He sent me a picture of himself on a camel and another of him kissing me.

Warren is just a stunning man. He's funny. He played the ukulele for me and sang. On the off chance that the Oracle of Omaha might be interested, Todd and I flew to Nebraska, and Warren took time out of his busy schedule to hear our proposal for a museum.

After listening to stories of what I wanted to do, he said to me, "Debbie, don't sell the farm."

"What do you mean?" I asked, confused.

"You mustn't indebt yourself, and you mustn't sell the farm."

I took Warren to mean that my dream was clouding my judgment and could cost me everything. By raising money for a museum to house the collection, I was risking the security I had after a lifetime of work. The collection was my only real savings to carry me through to the end of my life. I might wind up spending all of my money for a building that would house it, but never earn back what I'd spent.

But I didn't want to give up until I had exhausted every possibility.

There were four meetings with the Motion Picture Academy. They weren't interested in helping me save any of the costumes, but they were willing to let me donate my posters to the Academy. Todd made several attempts to negotiate a repayment with Greg Orman. We were far apart on what we thought would be fair. Orman was asking for $9 million as a payoff on his loan of $1.5 million. I thought that was excessive. We offered $3 million, which would have doubled his investment. He refused.

A court date was set for September 8, 2010.

During the run-up to the trial, I continued to work on the road, taking every job I could find. In the spring of 2010, I was booked for a tour of the United Kingdom that would take me all over England and Wales, ending with a two-week engagement at the Apollo Theatre in London's West End. The tour was called "Debbie Reynolds: Alive and Fabulous!" We arrived a few days before a volcano erupted in Iceland, stopping air travel to and from Europe for almost three weeks.

On April 1, I spent my seventy-eighth birthday at a press conference in the lobby of the Sofitel Hotel in London. As I posed for the cameras and answered questions, I prepared to spend the next three weeks traveling the country on a double-decker tour bus. This wasn't as much fun as you might think. We left London for our first date in Norwich, followed by stops in Liverpool, Manchester, Bristol, Cardiff, Malvern, and several other cities. I performed at a beautifully restored opera house in Leeds. What a lovely setting. I didn't know how my material would play in England, but the audiences were wonderfully receptive. They laughed in all the right places when I did my impressions of Katharine Hepburn and Bette Davis. I've always loved doing impressions. My most difficult one is Barbra Streisand. It took me a long time to learn, as her singing voice is placed so differently from her speaking voice. Audiences burst into applause when I appeared in my Streisand wig, fake nose, and *Yentl* overcoat. I sang "The Way He Makes Me Feel," then joked about how I wrote, directed, produced, and starred in the movie. "When the movie was over, I threw a wrap party," I said in Barbra's speaking voice. "I ordered one pizza." Then, in my own voice, "I'm sure the only reason I'm alive after doing this impression is because Barbra hasn't seen it." That got big laughs. The British especially loved my impression of Irish character actor Barry Fitzgerald, who played my uncle in *The Catered Affair* in 1956. After two hours of singing my favorite songs, joking with the audience, and dancing along to clips from my movies, it was time to close with "Tammy."

As much as I love performing, playing fifteen cities in three weeks was exhausting. We would do a show every evening and immediately strike the set, pack everything up, and get back on the bus. We were usually on the road to the next destination by midnight or 1:00 A.M., with bus rides sometimes lasting four hours or more. We'd roll into a new city around 3:00 or 4:00 A.M., check into our hotel, unpack, and try to sleep. Then up again a few hours later for breakfast, followed by an afternoon sound check, a break before the show to vocalize and go over my lines, and then another performance. And then we'd start over. I was, as the Brits say, knackered. That means tired, for those of us in America who don't speak English. I never saw the beautiful countryside because we traveled at night. I missed so much that I wanted to see.

By the time we got to London for the last two weeks of shows, it seemed like a vacation to stay in the same place every night. I love England; everything there is at least five hundred years older than I am. It was amazing that I got through it.

When it was time to go home, the Iceland volcano had settled down, so I just had to face the latest volcanic activity in the Orman case.

I had a tough decision to make. We'd exhausted every possible avenue we could think of to find backers for the museum. After the loss of my hotel, I couldn't ask my friends for financial help again. Todd and Carrie encouraged me to sell the collection.

In any case, the fate of the collection was out of my hands, resting with a judge in Santa Barbara.

The night before the trial, my friend and assistant Donald Light drove me from Los Angeles to Santa Barbara. We stayed at a small hotel called the Canary, which was within walking distance of the courthouse. We got up early the next morning and made our way over.

Todd was in front of the building, conferring with his lawyer. As the trial proceeded, Orman's side called many witnesses. Julien, who had handled my small auction in 2003, testified that I was undervaluing the worth of the collection, even though we said it was worth between $20 million and $30 million.

Todd and I had been considering asking him to handle the auction if the trial didn't go our way. Now he'd made that decision for us.

Todd and I hoped for a settlement. We hoped that the judge would find our offer of $3 million to be fair. She went right down the middle, denying Orman's request for $9 million but awarding him $5.3 million, to be paid within the next few months.

Tears came to my eyes as the devastating news sank in. This was it. The end of this vision I had worked for since the early 1960s. There I was, seventy-eight years old and facing yet another disappointment. I truly believed that the value of my collection remained to be seen. I had spent many years going to auctions where beautiful items sold for pennies on the dollar.

I will always regret not being able to build a museum, but I know that I did everything I could to make it happen. No one shared my belief that our Hollywood history should be preserved in one place for movie fans everywhere, even though individual items like Judy Garland's ruby slippers regularly made news when some collector bought them. I guess this could be expected from an industry that trashes everything after it's served its purpose—from actors to movie sets. The studios reused what they could, even if that meant burning down sets from *King Kong* for the destruction of Atlanta scene in *Gone with the Wind*. Letting go of my collection was one of the hardest things I ever had to do.

On top of that, another constant in my life was disappearing. Right around the time I had to appear in court to fight Greg Orman's lawsuit, I'd received a letter from Cedars-Sinai Medical Center saying that the Thalians' help was no longer wanted.

I'd been involved with the Thalians since 1955, when many of my friends in the entertainment business and I had founded the charity to give back to our community by supporting children's mental health. Over the years our coverage expanded to people of all ages with autism, Alzheimer's, depression, addiction, and other mental conditions. When Mount Sinai and Cedars of Lebanon merged to form Cedars-Sinai Medical Center in the late '50s, the Thalians gave the hospital $1 million to build the Thalians Mental Health Center. All told we'd raised more than $30 million for them. Without consulting us, Cedars had been slowly taking over the space in the Thalians' building to treat other ailments besides mental disorders, and then the new management asked us to relocate. They changed the building's name to the Thalians Health Center. There was endless back-and-forth and unpleasantness.

It was too much for me to bear when I was losing my collection. How many times could my heart be broken? I just couldn't face it. I put it aside and let my dear friend Ruta Lee and other Thalians deal with it.

Although the hurt was still there along with the feeling of rejection, it was time to prepare for yet another auction.

There was so much work to do. Todd and I were in contact with Christie's in New York. They are truly the gold standard for this kind of sale. One of their requirements was that we hold the auction in New York, which I didn't think would be possible in such a short amount of time. We settled on a relatively new auction company, Profiles in History, whose CEO, Joe Maddalena, had been trying to interest me in working with him for many years. He once bid $5,000 to have lunch with me so he could pitch his company. In December 2010, we signed agreements with Profiles to hold the auction on June 18, 2011.

The next six months were a whirlwind of activity, travel, publicity, and heartache—for me and for everyone near me. My assistants, Jenny and Donald, went up to Todd's ranch to help prepare for the auction. Everything had to be taken out of storage. Two volunteers from Profiles, Lisa Urban and Dan Stebin, put the costumes on mannequins to be photographed for the catalog and the website. The art director for the catalog, Lou Bustamante, took the pictures. Todd built a soundstage with a turnstile, so the costumes could be shot at 360-degree angles. Profiles set up an area nearby with computers to run the films and verify every costume and prop. (Some of them had been used in more than one film.) Then Lisa, Dan, Donald, and Jenny took the costumes to another area and packed them carefully in boxes with acid-free tissue paper for their journey to Los Angeles. For weeks Jenny ran into town every morning before 7:00 A.M. to get coffee and snacks for the crew; then everyone worked until eleven or twelve at night. I helped identify things, but I don't think I was any good to anyone because I was an emotional wreck.

Profiles in History had a wonderful press agent working for them, a woman named Nancy Seltzer. She arranged for me to do interviews and appearances all over the country. My first big appearance was on Oprah Winfrey's show, in February 2011. Carrie was also booked, and she did a segment with Oprah before I came out. We all sat and talked for a few more minutes before we debuted some of the costumes to be auctioned. The most famous piece was the "subway dress" that Marilyn Monroe wears in *The Seven Year Itch* as she stands over the sidewalk grating and her skirt billows around her. I told Oprah that I remembered how upset Marilyn's husband at the time, Joe DiMaggio, was about that scene in the film. He didn't want everyone seeing her panties as the skirt rose up in the gust of air created as the train sped by beneath her. Carrie and I even sang together for the first time on television. Oprah stood in the wings watching our moment. She seemed to enjoy our number. It was very touching.

I took to the talk show circuit to tell people about the auction and raise awareness of the collection. When I appeared on *The View,* I took Harpo Marx's hat with his curly wig peeking out from beneath the brim. My rounds included the *Today* show, *Extra,* and interviews with every major news outlet. The *Wall Street Journal* did a cover feature on the collection a few weeks prior to the sale. When I came back from the press tour, we were ready to install the collection for its Los Angeles debut.

The Paley Center for Media in Beverly Hills agreed to let us use their space for the auction and an exhibit that would run for two weeks prior to the sale, beginning on Saturday, June 4. It's a beautiful building, three stories of elegant glass and white stone with a huge rooftop garden. How kind and generous they were to let me use their facility. I felt so fortunate to have such a special place to present my collection.

As soon as the doors opened, masses of people crowded in to see the costumes that had been worn by their favorite stars. Attendance was overwhelming: thousands of people thronged to the Paley Center. I went many times during those fourteen days preceding the auction, to talk to reporters and chat with fans, somehow managing to put on a pleasant face. The question on everyone's lips was "Why didn't you get someone in Hollywood to help with the museum?" No one realized the journey I had taken to find a home for the collection I'd saved since the early '70s. Little did they know that I was praying that a big investor would buy everything so my treasures wouldn't be scattered all over the world.

By the day of the auction, I was in a daze.

Chapter 26
June 18, 2011

I went to bed early on Friday night, but didn't get much sleep. Carrie called at 1:00 A.M. to say that she and Billie were stranded at the Los Angeles airport. They were going to London for a holiday, but United Airlines was having trouble with their computer system. The planes were grounded, and there was no way to rebook the trip until Sunday. So Carrie and Billie would be coming to the auction instead. I was sorry their trip was delayed, but happy that they would be there with Todd and me.

The dreaded day finally arrived. I couldn't believe I was about to auction off my precious collection. The past year had been a whirl of insanity surrounding the lawsuit that triggered this sale as well as my efforts to promote it. I'd been on the road since February, done dozens of TV appearances, print interviews, and radio shows. Everyone expected the sale of Marilyn Monroe's subway dress from *The Seven Year Itch* to set a record. I'd be thrilled if it made enough money to settle Greg Orman's judgment.

My favorite suit hung ready for me in my closet. My assistant Jenny was scheduled to pick me up at 11:00 A.M. to get us to the Paley Center in time for the noon start of the auction; the doors opened at 10:00, and it would take at least an hour for everyone to be seated and settled. I put on my white suit and a dark green jewel-tone silk blouse with a bow sash at the neck. My hair and makeup didn't take much time at all. I wrapped the pain pill I knew I would need for my back in a tissue and secured it in my bra, a trick I learned from my mother. Some fresh lipstick and a spray of L'Air du Temps and I was ready to go.

When we pulled into the reserved parking space behind the Paley Center, Todd's camera crew met us to capture every moment. I reminded myself to breathe. We entered the building at the back and walked a hundred feet or so down a hallway, to seven steps leading up to a door, where Todd, his girlfriend, Catherine, and his dog, Yippee, were waiting. Carrie, her friend Beverly D'Angelo, Billie, and a friend of hers were already inside the auditorium. Todd told me that people had been lined up around the block by 9:00 A.M. in hopes of securing places; the 150-seat auditorium was packed, as was an overflow seating area in the lobby where part of the exhibition was on display.

We opened the door.

There were crowds of press, fans, and friends everywhere. The folks from Profiles in History were fluttering around attending to last-minute details. The auctioneer looked ready to take the stage and his gavel. The air was electric with anticipation.

I felt like I was in a dream—or a nightmare— sleepwalking through my own life as it was about to unfold in this tiny, unattractive theater. The bright lights dispelled any mystery or excitement I might have felt if I had been there to buy. This was not where I wanted to be, forced to participate in something I'd prayed would never happen.

The stage in the Paley Center auditorium is at the bottom of the room. DEBBIE REYNOLDS—THE AUCTION was projected in light on two curved panels on either side of a large screen spread across the far wall. Now I was an auction. Well, I'd been just about everything else at one time or another. To get to my seat at the front, I had to walk down a set of stairs, past the audience. All eyes were on me as I made my way along the left side of the auditorium to join Carrie and her party in the second row. Heads turned and people applauded. I waved acknowledgment and sat beside my daughter.

After everything settled down, Joe Maddalena from Profiles in History went to the Plexiglas podium and thanked everyone for coming. I got up and went to the side of the stage, putting a spring in my step that really wasn't there, to be ready when he introduced me.

"This is a good day and a sad day," Joe said. "But we're happy you're here. Ladies and gentlemen, Miss Debbie Reynolds."

Somehow my feet carried me to the microphone as the crowd cheered and yelled "Bravo." I hope I made sense as I talked about my collection for the last time from the notes I'd prepared.

"First of all, thank you all for being here."

I blew kisses to the overflow crowd in other rooms throughout the Paley Center.

"I know that you all feel sad, as I do, because it all means a lot. We really don't want to let any of this go because it's in our hearts. I feel very good that you're here because this will soon be in your hearts.

"I do thank you, and I thank you for caring about preserving our golden age of costuming and props.

"I've been collecting these for forty-five years—and I'm only forty."

The audience laughed and cheered.

"These precious items, really, I just pray that you who obtain these pieces will love and care for them as much as we do for our future generations."

My voice cracked and my eyes filled with tears.

In a choked voice, I said, "Now . . . I never cry. Only when I love everything."

Getting my strength back, I continued.

"So, on behalf of Profiles in History and Joe Maddalena . . . isn't that a silly name? Todd, my son, who did all this work. Without Todd all these years, I never would have been able to do it. And my daughter Carrie's here too. And my granddaughter, we even have another child. Her name is Billie Catherine, she's right over there."

As I waved to Billie, my friend Rose Marie waved to me from her wheelchair in the first row, right in front of my family.

"Rose Marie, stop that. You're not my granddaughter!"

The audience laughed. Rose Marie is famous for having been a regular on *The Dick Van Dyke Show* and *Hollywood Squares* for years.

"I want to say something to Phillip Hoffman, who's standing back there. He decorated everything . . ."

I had to wrap this up.

"I know you love everything as much as I do. I'm so thrilled that I was around to save it because I was so stubborn, I wouldn't give it up. Thanks for being here."

There was no way I could get through that speech without emotion. My knees were weak from it. More than forty years of collecting and preserving my memorabilia was about to end in the next few hours. How many auctions had I been through in my life? Selling the hotel had been painful, but afterward I still had my collection, and all the hopes I'd invested in it. After tonight, it would belong to someone else. No words can accurately describe what I was feeling at that moment; the fact is, I don't remember. I couldn't believe it was really happening.

The auctioneer was middle-aged, stocky, and bald, wearing a dark brown bowling shirt with wide beige vertical stripes running down the front. He went to the podium as the slide for the first item appeared on the screen: a Bell & Howell movie camera from 1915. Two younger-looking men seated at a table to his right handled Internet bids. The reserve opening price had been set at $10,000; after a few moments, it sold for $30,000—a good start.

The second item up was the "Suit of Lights" matador outfit Rudolph Valentino wore in *Blood and Sand*. The reserve for this was $60,000. Before I knew it, the suit had sold for $210,000. Excitement rippled through the room as everyone, including me, realized that this was going to be a serious sale. I told myself not to get my hopes up. The subway dress was lot 354. There were still 351 items to be sold before then.

As the auction continued, I noticed that every time I heard the word "sold" after a high amount, it was followed by "to bidder 249." We later discovered that bidder 249 was a buyer from Korea who'd come to the auction to purchase as many items as possible. He wasn't the only one. Buyers had come from around the world, and like bidder 249, most of them insisted on remaining anonymous.

The auction had been going on for about two hours when I had to use the ladies' room. As Jen and I made our way there, I realized I wouldn't last until Marilyn's dress came up unless I had something to eat. We decided to go to the Cheesecake Factory, just two blocks away. But first we stopped by the greenroom, where friends of mine were tracking the sales.

Leaving the ladies' room, Jen and I walked down the hallway behind the Paley Center reception area. As we turned right to go into the greenroom, I could see the crowd in the overflow area of the lobby. The display with Marilyn's subway dress revolved in its case in front of us as we went to meet our friends.

Judy Garland enjoying my first
speech at the Jewish Home for the
Aged. I was so nervous. Judy would
have said, "You're doing great,
Debbie. Just keep talking, kid. You'll
get 'em." Ida Mayer Cummings,
the mother of MGM producer Jack
Cummings, asked all the MGM stars
to help raise funds for the Jewish
Home, her favorite charity.

What a beautiful daughter. How blessed am I?

My favorite picture of Todd and me.

Dancing with the extremely talented Harve Presnell in
The Unsinkable Molly Brown (1964).

The "Belly Up to the Bar, Boys" number from
The Unsinkable Molly Brown (1964).
Licensed by Warner Bros. Entertainment Inc. All rights reserved

With the wonderful Don Rickles in *The Rat Race* (1960). I gave
Don a teddy bear to help him with his nerves during filming.
Though normally a comedic actor, he was playing a dramatic role
in *The Rat Race* and wanted to do a great job. *Photofest*

Some of the MGM girls get together for lunch:
(back row, left to right) Katherine Grayson, Ann
Miller, Esther Williams, Ann Rutherford;
(kneeling in front) Margaret O'Brian and me.

With some of the treasures from my collection, among them Elizabeth Taylor's headdress and Richard Burton's costume from *Cleopatra* (1963) and Claudette Colbert's costume from *Cleopatra* (1934).

Clockwise: Jean Hagen's gown from *Singin' in the Rain* (1952); the detail on Marlon Brando's cape from *Désireé* (1954); hand-painted suits from the "Fit as a Fiddle" number in *Singin' in the Rain*; Audrey Hepburn's ascot gown from *My Fair Lady* (1964).

Photos by Carol Hannaway

With Jerry Wunderlich, my dear friend and the most brilliant set designer.
He helped me so much at my hotel in Vegas.

With Sydney Guilaroff, the famous MGM hair designer
and my special friend. I called him "Father."

With Margie Duncan.
Margie is like a sister to me
and looks like my twin.

With Rudy Render, who served in the army with
my brother, Bill. He was my pianist for twenty-
five years. Rudy came to live with us in Burbank,
and he never left our home or our hearts.

With my brother, who always has my back.
Everyone calls him "Uncle Bill."

My two favorite girls: my daughter, Carrie, with her daughter,
Billie, at Billie's high school graduation.

With Todd, Catherine, and Carrie on Todd and Catherine's
wedding day, December 22, 2012. *Photo by Amie Preston*

With Carrie and Billie at the Paley Center for Media for the Turner Classic Movies party celebrating my memorabilia collection, June 7, 2011. This is one of the few pictures I have of the three of us together.

Photo by Juan Rico/ Juan Rico Images

The greenroom had been set up with monitors, a couch, and eight chairs. Everyone was excited. My friend Margie Duncan and Donald, my other assistant, were following along in the catalog and making a record of the numbers.

"The *Wizard of Oz* dress and the ruby slippers are up next," Margie said. "Sit down for a few minutes to see what happens."

She was talking about legendary designer Adrian's original costumes for Judy Garland, before Victor Fleming decided he wanted something more contemporary-looking (for 1939). The ruby slippers that I sold were closer in design to the description of Dorothy's shoes in the book, in the style of Arabian shoes, with pointed toes and accents. Judy wore these in the wardrobe tests for the film. They were her favorite. The reserve for the blue cotton dress was $60,000. I felt a pang as this treasure appeared on the screen. Judy had been my dear friend. I loved every role she played. How could I let this dress go?

But I had no choice.

The bidding went fast. In a matter of minutes, the price rose in $10,000 increments to more than half a million dollars.

"Now we're cooking," I commented to my friends in the greenroom.

Everyone was quiet as I slumped on the couch to take the pressure off my aching back.

"Eight hundred thousand," the auctioneer announced.

"Nine hundred thousand . . .

"Nine hundred and ten thousand. Do I hear nine hundred twenty?"

His eyes searched the auditorium for another bid.

"Aaaaaaaand *sold* for nine hundred and ten thousand dollars!"

I sat up on the couch, relieved that someone else valued this jewel of Hollywood history as much as I did. For that price, I'd gratefully let it go.

The next item, lot 111, was the ruby slippers. Before I could rearrange myself in the couch cushions, they'd sold for $510,000.

In the fifteen minutes between the auditorium, the ladies' room, and the greenroom couch, I'd made $1,420,000.

Before I left for lunch, I returned to the auditorium. Facing the crowd from the front of the house, I asked, "Did anything happen while I was in the ladies' room?"

Everyone burst into laughter and applause.

"I'll be back in a little while," I announced, waving to the audience. "Let me know what happens next."

As Jen drove us to the Cheesecake Factory, I felt distracted and a bit relieved, but I was still in a daze. Delicious as my fried zucchini tasted, I wasn't in the mood to eat after all. But we were in no rush to get back to the auction. With many of the famous items already gone, there was still a long time to go and lots of lesser-known pieces to be sold before another major piece came up for bids. So we took our time. When we finally left, I tried to retrieve the pain pill from my bra. I made a few swipes at it; the pill had shifted in the few hours since I'd left the house. We were standing in the hallway leading out of the restaurant. Anyone seeing me clutch at my blouse might have thought I was having some kind of spell. I felt a little better once I'd taken the medication.

Back at the Paley Center, things were moving along. Carrie and I chatted as the bidding continued. Lot 188 came up: the red silk velvet Santa Claus suit Edmund Gwenn wore in *Miracle on 34th Street.* Gwenn won the Academy Award for Best Supporting Actor for his portrayal of Kris Kringle in this classic holiday movie.

In my early days at MGM, I had seen Mr. Gwenn around the lot. I thought he was so cute. Several years later, one of the trade magazines ran a notice that he was in poor health and would appreciate visitors. I visited him often at the Motion Picture Home in Calabasas. I knew that he loved the caramels from See's, the popular San Francisco candy maker. So I always brought a box with me, and he'd eat the whole thing.

"Hello, Debbie. Thank you for coming to see me," he'd greet me in that wonderful British accent, his mind still sharp. Not only was he a good character actor, he was a darling man. I just loved him.

Mr. Gwenn's Kris Kringle outfit meant a lot to me. So many memories and experiences were wrapped up in it. This was true of my collection in general. The pieces in it weren't only historical artifacts, they had personal associations for me. If I weren't numb, my heart would be breaking.

At around seven-thirty, it was time for lot 354. By then, I'd made enough to settle the judgment, pay the taxes, and have some money left over so that I wouldn't have to work in every honky-tonk in the world. But I was still in a fog and hadn't really taken it all in.

This was the moment everyone had been waiting for. People whooped and applauded when Marilyn's iconic dress appeared on the screen. Then the room quieted down. Through much of the earlier bidding the auctioneer had perched himself on a bar stool behind the Plexiglas podium, hardly seeming to refer to the pages on the clipboard listing the items. He'd gone through so many that the pages were spilling over the front edge of the podium. For lot 354 he was standing.

He checked with the phone banks in the back to confirm that they were ready.

"Let me know when we can start," he told the men at the computers, one of whom said, "I have an opening bid of . . ."

"I'm not ready for you," the auctioneer said cheerfully.

The audience laughed.

The auctioneer announced what everyone already knew: "Three fifty-four is the Marilyn Monroe ivory pleated subway dress from *The Seven Year Itch*. Let's start the bidding at . . ."

He extended his right arm to the table.

". . . one million dollars," the man with the Internet bid responded.

Hoots and cheers and applause from the crowd.

I felt like I was wrapped in cotton, the tension in the air was so thick around me; insulated against the world as I listened to the bidding go up in increments of $100,000.

At $2,300,000, the auctioneer announced "Going once," only to be greeted with another bid. At $2,800,000, he said, "Two hundred eight million," then corrected himself with a smile.

"Three million."

Each time it reached another million the crowd loudly expressed its approval and delight.

"Four million."

No costume had ever sold for this much money.

Only two bidders were left. Somehow the bidding continued.

A phone bid came in.

"Four million, one hundred thousand," the auctioneer announced.

The next few seconds felt like an hour.

"Four million, two hundred thousand.

"Four million, three hundred thousand."

The bidding slowed down.

"Do I hear four million, five hundred thousand?"

The auctioneer's eyes scanned the room.

"Yes, four million, five hundred thousand. Do I hear four million, six hundred thousand?"

A pause that lasted forever.

"Yes! Four million, six hundred thousand. Four million, seven hundred thousand?"

Silence.

I stood up to see who had bid, then sat back down.

The auctioneer repeated the bid, then repeated it again. "We have a couple of seconds," he said, adding, to the crowd's amusement, "It's not your everyday dress."

That was when I realized I'd stopped breathing.

"Anybody else? At four million, six hundred thousand, aaaaaaa- and . . ."

Exhale.

". . . *sold!*"

Whoops burst through the room. Tears filled my eyes as Carrie leaned over in her seat and took me in her arms. People were standing up and applauding loudly as the realization sank in that in the last five and a half minutes we'd all just witnessed history being made. As I rose to join them the crowd cheered. Everyone was on their feet. I could hardly see it through my tear-filled eyes. With the addition of the auction-house premium of 20 percent, the total cost to the bidder came to $5,520,000.

The rest of the auction was a blur. Now that I'd made enough money, I started bidding on my favorite items, to keep from losing them. I decided not to sell Harpo Marx's hat that I'd shown on Oprah. It's in my home today. (Todd kept an Indiana Jones hat.) A friend tells me that at one point I turned to a woman in front of me and ordered her to stop bidding on something I wanted. Apparently she obeyed, and I won the bid.

I stayed for another hour or so, until some inner voice told me it was time to get out of there. I knew that Audrey Hepburn's Ascot dress from *My Fair Lady* might do well, but I didn't have the strength to wait until it came up.

Jenny drove me home and set up the computer so we could watch the rest of the auction in my living room. I called Carrie, and she and Beverly rushed over to join us. Jen and I drank my cheap white zinfandel, and Beverly had a glass of red wine. Carrie sipped a Diet Coke. Feet up, we watched the thirteen-inch computer screen, leaning in to hear the results.

When Audrey Hepburn's Ascot costume, designed by Cecil Beaton, sold for $3.8 million, I was done in. When Todd sent me a text message, I answered him (with help from Carrie):

"Holy shit."

I'd been right about the value of my collection. Everyone who'd rejected it or told me I was crazy to want to preserve it—for all those many, many years— had been proved wrong. Closing my eyes, I said a prayer of thanks that my efforts had been worth it.

I had saved the collection, and now the collection had saved me.

Marilyn Monroe's subway dress, which sold for
$5,520,000, breaking all records for the sale of a
motion picture costume.
Photo by Lou Bustamante/Profiles in History

Part II

Debbie Does Eighty

My phone rang at 9:00 A.M. on the morning of April 1, 2012. It was Carleton Carpenter, calling to wish me a happy eightieth birthday. I've known Carleton since I was seventeen years old and we acted and toured together for MGM. He was so excited and sweet that I couldn't be upset that he woke me out of a sound sleep.

For me, the hardest part of getting older is that I think I'm thirty. Then I look in the mirror and see somebody else looking back. It still startles me.

But then I think of my friendships and the loves of my life. I was blessed with so many wonderful friends that I couldn't possibly mention them all, but my family means the most to me, and among my family was my other "mother," Lillian Burns Sidney. Lillian raised me during my MGM years and remained my friend and teacher until the end of her life.

When Lillian died in August 1998, she left me in charge of her estate. Her wish was to be cremated and to have her ashes placed in the Sidney family section of the mausoleum in Beverly Hills. Lillian had been married to George Sidney for thirty years, until he dumped her for a younger woman, but the Sidney family had bought a slot for Lillian's ashes. So I took them down to the cemetery, where they were interred near her father-in-law and mother-in-law, who'd been so close to Lillian when they were alive. Lillian had taken care of them both when they were elderly. They loved her so much.

Some months later, I got a call from the director of the cemetery, telling me that Lillian had been evicted from the Sidney slot on the orders of George's widow. The widow either didn't know how close Lillian was to the Sidney family or just didn't care. George wasn't there—he's buried in Hillside Memorial Park Cemetery in Culver City. So what was the big deal?

I drove down to the cemetery to collect Lillian, this time to try to fulfill her alternate wish, which was to have her ashes scattered in the rose garden of her beautiful home on Tower Road in Beverly Hills, where she had lived with George. The only problem was that

Lillian hadn't lived in that house for more than twenty years—and I didn't know the people who owned it now. Which didn't stop me from going there.

I wrapped the bag with Lillian's ashes in a Chanel scarf and drove to her former home without knowing what I was going to do or say when I got there. I pulled into the driveway, walked up to the front door with Lillian under my arm, and rang the bell. A lovely young woman answered. (I later learned that her name was Mrs. Peterson. She was a daughter of a prominent Chicago family and married to a fitness guru named Gunnar Peterson.)

I could tell she was surprised to find Debbie Reynolds on her doorstep. She was very gracious as I explained that my friend had lived in the house many years ago and wanted to be scattered among the roses in the backyard. She told me that they had taken out the rosebushes, but I was welcome to look around. As we walked to the garden, I asked her for a spoon. She went inside the house and brought me back a wooden mixing spoon. Then she left me alone in the garden with my dear friend's ashes.

I unwrapped the scarf, opened the bag, and spread Lillian's ashes all around where the rose garden once stood. I kept some of the ashes, which I now have in a beautiful Chinese vase of Lillian's that I keep in my bedroom. When I'm buried, part of her will go with me. The kids can keep the vase.

When one gets to be my age, it's easy to have regrets. As Frank Sinatra sang, "Regrets, I've had a few—but then again, too few to mention." Well, I must mention a few.

I can't regret Eddie Fisher. When we first married, I loved him dearly, and we had two beautiful children who are the joys of my life. And he's given me a source of jokes for the past fifty years. Thanks, Eddie.

Even though Harry Karl took us to the depths of despair with his gambling and cheating, he was the best husband he knew how to be.

My third marriage was regrettable, but it's over, and I thank God for giving me the strength to get through that ordeal.

My biggest disappointment in this life has been not being able to create a museum for the collection that I built and loved and protected for fifty years. I know that I gave it everything I possibly could. I spent decades and lots of money gathering and trying to preserve our entertainment history. But it didn't happen. Hopefully my efforts gave value to the pieces I sold to collectors and fans. The motion picture memorabilia I owned were always treasures to me; now others will have to protect them. I held a second auction in December 2011, but it wasn't as successful as the first one. Lightning never strikes twice, so I wasn't surprised that there wasn't as much excitement for the second sale as the first one created. It was hard to part with all the costumes and props, as I had such a personal connection to each piece. Every costume I bought over the years had been worn by someone who was either my friend or an actor I admire. I have trouble watching old movies now because it pains me to see "my" costumes onscreen, knowing that they belong to someone else and aren't in a Hollywood museum. I hope someday it feels better. It was time to let go.

My home is filled with mementos of my friends and family, things that bring back happy memories. Pictures of the great friends I've worked with through the years. I have Harold Lloyd's piano in my living room, right near chairs that belonged to Ann Miller. Agnes Moorehead's lamps are on either side of my sofa. The Maltese Falcon sits on my mantelpiece, next to Eva Gabor's blackamoor lamps from her living room. Phyllis Diller gave me several of the oil paintings she'd done, as well as a turban with earrings attached to it and a lot of silly pairs of slippers. Everything around me has a story of someone I love that makes me feel their presence. I like ghosts and I like stories. I feel surrounded by their love and happy with the friendships that we shared.

There's an Irish proverb that says, "May the road always rise up to meet you. May the wind always be at your back."

I wish that for you—and to be sure that the wind at your back isn't your own, here's my recipe for beans, which has been in my family for generations.

Growing up in El Paso, beans were the staple of our diet. We were so poor that we were all crammed in a small house together. This bean recipe makes them digestible without giving you gas, so you can spend quality time with your family.

Reynolds Family Bean Recipe

2 cups dried pinto beans

1 Tbsp baking soda

pinch of seasoned salt

1 Tbsp castor oil

1 half onion, chopped (optional)

chili powder to taste

small can of baby chili peppers

Soak the pinto beans overnight in water with the baking soda, seasoned salt, and castor oil. The next day, drain the beans and rinse with clear water. Cover the beans with water and put them in a slow cooker. If you like, you can add chopped white onion for flavor. I like to add some chili powder and diced baby chili peppers. It's very simple. The baking soda and castor oil keep you from tooting your own horn.

When I'm not around the house eating my favorite Mexican foods, I'm usually on the road. But last September, when I was finishing this book, I was almost finished myself.

I was performing in Branson, Missouri, when a new pill I was taking caused a reaction with my other medications. Suddenly my feet became very swollen. I couldn't fit into my stage shoes, so I borrowed a pair from one of the Lennon Sisters, who happened to be playing in the same hotel.

Once I got home, I was in real trouble. My feet were still swollen and I had difficulty breathing. I was exhausted. It was really scary.

I was admitted to the hospital, where I found out my kidneys had almost failed. After about a week there, I was allowed to go home, provided that I cancel all appearances for the rest of the year. I settled in and obeyed the doctor's orders, hoping to regain my health. One day I was minding my own business when I started talking to people in jibberish. I knew what I wanted to say but it didn't come out right. I could understand everyone but I couldn't say what I meant. I'd had incidents like this before that frightened me. They seemed to be connected, but this one felt different.

Back to the hospital to find out what was wrong.

P.S. I'd had a TIA. That stands for transient ischemic attack—a kind of mini-stroke—brought on in my case by high blood pressure.

Thankfully, it passed. After a few months' rest, I'm on the mend, taking good care of myself and looking forward to doing my show again.

Work is important to me. I love performing for audiences. Their warmth and applause make everything worthwhile. I thank all of you who have come to see me over the years. We've had some fun, and I plan on entertaining you as long as I can—which, looking at my watch, could be another twenty minutes.

I've been an actress for most of the past sixty-five years. Thanks to the studio system, I got to play many wonderful roles while I studied with the best teachers in the world. So many people nurtured my talent and made me look good on film. As I learned and grew as an actress, I appreciated this education. My love of film started when I was very young. I used my babysitting money to go to the movies when they cost less than fifty cents for a Saturday matinee.

Now I'd like to take you back to the days when I was a teenager who was lucky enough to be signed by the great Warner Brothers studio. If we were sitting together, sharing a glass of wine or four and having a good chat, you might like to ask me about the movies I've made. The following stories let you see what it was like for me to make more than fifty films. I've shared the stage with so many terrific people. And some not-so-terrific people too.

Let's start when I was a young girl in Burbank, California. . . .

Miss Burbank 1948

Right around my sixteenth birthday, I heard about a contest for Miss Burbank. You had to be sixteen to enter, and every contestant received a free blouse and a scarf. Wow! That was a big deal.

So I signed up, intending not to compete. I just wanted the blouse and scarf, and I knew I wouldn't win because I was too short. Aren't all beauty contest winners tall? My mother told me that if I was going to take the blouse and scarf, I had to earn them—and that meant showing up. Daddy agreed.

I wore a secondhand Cole bathing suit with a hole in the seat to the contest. Jerry Odens, a friend of mine from school, drove me to the Olive Recreation Center in Burbank and lent me his record player. I dragged it onstage and then lip-synced to "I'm Just a Square in the Social Circle," that Betty Hutton sings in the 1945 movie *The Stork Club,* dancing and mugging just like when I did it in the Girl Scouts. My brother and his buddies sat in the back and laughed and laughed, sure that I would never win. When I did, I fooled them and myself—but not Jerry. What a friend.

In those days the studios were looking everywhere for talent. Solly Baiano, the talent scout from Warner Brothers, and Al Trescone from MGM were in the audience. They were both interested in me and flipped a coin. Solly won. The contest was in May. The following July the *Los Angeles Times* ran an article with the headline GIRL WANTS BLOUSE—GETS FILM CONTRACT. Jack Warner had seen my screen test and told Solly to sign me for seven years at $60 a week, with a raise to $75 after six months. That was more than my father made! The article talked about my plans to continue high school and get dramatic training at Warner Brothers. Because I was a minor, the court in Los Angeles ordered that 20 percent of my earnings had to be invested in government savings bonds.

The road to Warner Brothers was not easy. My family were members of the Church of the Nazarene and very religious. Our minister didn't approve of the movies or the sinners who worked in them. Daddy and

Mother made a trip to Warner's so they could decide for themselves whether to let me work there. When they saw all the carpenters, truck drivers, painters, and other "regular" folks doing the many jobs it took to make a film and run Warner's, they were satisfied that more than the Devil's work was being done at the studio.

So there I was, riding my bike the few blocks from our house to the studio and then, after work, taking the bus between Warner Brothers and my high school. Pretty amazing stuff for a sixteen-year-old kid.

Warner Brothers was always buzzing with activity. Burt Lancaster, Kirk Douglas, Bette Davis, and Olivia

On the lot at Warner Brothers. This was the first day of my new life—new name, new career. *Photofest*

de Havilland were the big stars on the lot. I loved seeing Jimmy Cagney because we were about the same height. Humphrey Bogart and Errol Flynn made their classic films there.

My classroom at Warner's was right next to the gym where Mushy Callahan was training Douglas to play a prizefighter in *The Champion*. I used to sneak in to watch the real, retired champion teach the actor how to box. It was very exciting. Boy, did they have great bodies. Mae West would have loved their pecs.

Jack Warner was the head of the studio. He was ever so dapper, with a thin, perfectly trimmed mustache. A small white fence surrounded the circular driveway outside his office. I'd wait there every day to see him arrive in his big Rolls-Royce, hiding behind the fence and watching all the activity as Mr. Warner got out of his car. Two guards were always there to walk him into his building.

One day Mr. Warner spotted me.

"Who's that?" he asked.

"Hi, Mr. Warner," I greeted him. "I'm your new contract player."

"Really? What's your name?"

"I'm not sure yet," I said.

He looked down at me quizzically. "What does that mean?"

"Well, my name is Mary Frances Reynolds. But they think Mary's too plain, and Frances is a talking mule."

William Orr, one of Mr. Warner's executives and his son-in-law, takes credit for renaming me Debbie. Delmer Daves, a writer-producer at the studio, had a new baby named Debbie. Mr. Orr thought this was a cute name that suited me. For years afterward, I only answered to "Frannie" or "Mary Frances" because I didn't identify with my new name. Mr. Warner usually referred to me as "the kid." I put up a fight when they wanted to change my last name. Reynolds was Daddy's name, and I insisted on keeping it.

The next three pages are from my assignment at John Burroughs High School in Burbank, California, in 1948. It's my essay on what it's like to be a movie starlet.

The Life of a Movie Starlet

"Oh Boy! Am I tired" you think as you stagger into makeup at
6:30 in the morning. Oh No! What is it? Don't be alarmed its just
you looking in a mirror before you get on your make-up or before you
wake up.

In comes your make-up man and you slump in his chair which has a
round cushion that you keep rolling around on. Pretty soon you are a
"Dead End Kid" but you don't dare say anything. "Hold Still says he
just as you slipped forward on that darn seat. You'd like to tell
him what you think about that chair but naturally you don't because
that isn't lady like. Nuts! Then its his turn to slip and the powder
goes in your eye. "Oh! Is something in your eye?" He stuppidly asks
as you sit there getting a more and more bloodshot eye. He then says
" You should hold still." You just can't win.

Forty-five minutes later he has finished and as you go out he
reminds you not to scratch your face, so if you have a itchy nose,
Too bad! It will just have to itch. Got to blow? Tough! Just snuff
all day. Sounds awful you say? NO! Its not so bad once you get use
to it.

You then rush to the hair dresser because you have to meet the
dead line which is 9:00. She pulls like crazy and you feel like crab-
bing a little but you don't dare because she could fix you so you
would look like the devil on the screen. So you smile and say "Thank-
You" Even though there are about 20 hair pins, sticking you in every
direction.

Contued on page 2

"Hurry up" you hear as you run madly on the set. You feel like saying "Shut up I'ammhurring" but instead you smile and say "Good - Morning"!

Now for the dressing room routine. You rush in and three hands grab you. You could get dressed faster by youself. Oh Well!!(Blankety Blank) So on goes the dress, which is too tight and then the long cotton stockings which feel so good especially since it is only 100 degrees outside.

Eventually you are ready for the shot. "Relax!" says the assistant director you have another hour before we get to you shots. Controlling your temper you go back to your dressing room and there you are greeted with a book to study. Its given to you by your favorite teacher but that does'nt help, you still have to study.

At long last they are ready to shoot. They line up the shot when in runs the hair-dresser and startes combing and the make-up man starts powdering and finally the shot. You do the scene well but they yell "Cut" Because someone has dropped something. So you do the scene over and on the 5th shot after everyone has dropped everything, and all the lights have popped you get a good scene on film without mishap.

Now its back to school to get in that three hours.

You think "Boy am I hungry" and when you hear them call lunch you and your teacher rush to the cafeteria. After waiting 20 minutes to order and 10 minutes to get your food half the lunch hour is gone. The food isn't very good and you go back disgusted and still hungry.

While doing a scene the other fellow gives you the wrong cue so you falter a little and the director bawls you out for not knowing your lines. You don't dare say "It was his fault" So you say "I'm sorry I'll get it right the next time".

Cont

At the end of the day, having just barely gotten in your three hours of schooling, you are ready to drop. You rush home, eat, do the dishes and go to bed, after rolling up your hair and spending an hour and a half getting offf all that gooey makeup. You then cream your face, study lines for the next day's work and by then its 9:00 or 10:00 o'clock so you fall asleep exhausted.

The alarm awakens you and then you are off again in that whirl wind that never stops.

P.S. On your one day off during the whole picture publicity calls up and says "Could we come over for one shot?" Thinking No! you say "Yes", for one shot. Three hours later they leave with about 30 shots. Nuts Is It worth it? Yes! Its Fun.

June Bride

(WARNER BROTHERS, 1948)

My debut was a bit part in this romantic comedy starring Bette Davis and Robert Montgomery. I play the girlfriend of one of the characters in attendance at the wedding at the end of the movie. The most thrilling thing for me was that I got to meet Bette Davis during the filming of that scene.

I have trouble finding myself in this film today. I didn't get a credit, which was fine because they hadn't changed my name yet.

One day I climbed up into the rafters of the soundstage to watch Bette Davis and Robert Montgomery film a love scene in front of a fireplace. She was lying down as he leaned over to kiss her. Suddenly Davis's eyes opened and looked right into mine. She stopped kissing and screamed, "Who the hell is that? What's that up there?"

"Beat it, kid," the lighting man next to me muttered.

Terrified, I scrambled down the ladder and ran to my ballet classroom, behind the stage where they were shooting the scene, and hid there until I was sure that things had quieted down.

My dance teacher, Buddy, came in and found me hiding. Buddy was a sweet man—underline *sweet* (he wore pink ballet slippers while he taught me)—and told me that I wasn't supposed to be on a closed set.

I was just grateful that Bette Davis wasn't armed.

The Daughter of Rosie O'Grady

(WARNER BROTHERS, 1950)

Months passed after I made *June Bride*, and it seemed that Warner's didn't know what to do with me. Then they put me on hiatus, which was fine with me. I was still planning to become a gym teacher. I got a job at J. C. Penney selling girls' blouses during the Christmas season. One day Warner's called my home to say I was wanted at a luncheon for their starlets. Mother told them I was at work. So they scoured the studio and called her back when they couldn't find me. She told them about my job, and they were furious. They sent a car to pick me up at the store.

Not long after that, one of the studio's acting coaches, Sophie Rosenstein, told me that they'd written a part for me into *The Daughter of Rosie O'Grady*, a musical set in 1898. My guess is it was because I was under contract and the movie was already scheduled. I play June Haver's little sister. June plays the daughter who wants to be in vaudeville against her father's wishes.

June Haver was then dating a very successful young dentist, who died suddenly. It was a great tragedy for her. At the end of filming, she decided to enter a convent. Sister June was all set to take her vows when she met an actor named Fred MacMurray at an event. Fred fell for her in a big way and informed June that the only vow she was going to take was a marriage vow with him. Fred was a widower at that time with young children. When they married, they adopted beautiful twin girls.

Gordon MacRae plays legendary vaudeville producer Tony Pastor. One day Gordon came into my little dressing room on the set while I was in the middle of a class with my studio tutor, Lois Horne, and put his arm around me. I didn't think anything about it.

But Miss Horne did. "Don't you touch her," she shouted. "You don't talk to sixteen-year-olds in a dressing room. Certainly not alone. Not without a chaperone. Now get back to your singing."

And she threw Gordon out on his ass.

Gordon was stunned. I'm sure he had no intention of doing anything inappropriate, certainly not in the middle of a studio set. And I was embarrassed. Gordon was a favorite with the ladies, but he knew better than to make a move on this little Girl Scout. And if he had tried anything, I knew that I could easily have slugged him myself. I didn't need Miss Horne to take care of him.

Our director, David Butler, treated me well. A heavyset, happy man, he took a liking to me. He wrote me into scenes and spent time teaching me film techniques.

Sophie Rosenstein taught me how to be as natural as possible on film. That meant acting naturally—in this case, simple and sweet, as that was my age. They put me in a lot of flowered period frocks. Sophie was a small woman who dressed impeccably. I thought she was rather plain, but everyone loved her. She later married the handsome actor Gig Young. Nice work, Sophie.

S. Z. Sakall plays a friend of the O'Grady family, and he was my favorite on this shoot. We had such a good time. From him I learned how to grab both sides of my face in shock or surprise. Doris Day also copied this move, as did Sandra Bullock, decades later. No one would look at the three of us and think we were all influenced by "Cuddles" Sakall.

Lois Horne taught me about setting a table, as I had no experience in social graces. Lois was from a wealthy Oklahoma family. She taught me an appreciation for antiques, that ornamental carvings on the side of an end table are works of art. I had a lot to learn.

A few years later, when I was filming *Singin' in the Rain,* I stayed at Lois's place in Culver City, a short distance from the MGM studio, when I was too tired to make the trip home to Burbank.

The Daughter of Rosie O'Grady was shot in the beginning of 1949. After two films at Warner Brothers, it was obvious that the studio would be cutting back on the production of musicxals. Warner's had closed the music and dance departments. It became clear that my contract wouldn't be renewed. Solly Baiano, the scout who'd won me in a coin toss, continued to look after me. He drove me to audition for producers at MGM.

I'll never forget riding to MGM Studios in Solly's new Cadillac. I felt like a movie star. I was to audition for the Helen Kane role in the upcoming film *Three Little Words.* Solly drove me to Jack Cummings's office, where four important men proceeded to stare at me. I had never been in a room with that many older and very important men before. Jack Cummings stood by the fireplace and asked me if I could sing a song for him.

"No," I said, "but I can play you one of Betty Hutton's"—and I put on my record of "I'm Just a Square in the Social Circle" and repeated the routine I'd done for the Miss Burbank contest.

They laughed and applauded! They loved this little "kid" Warner's had sent to them and hired me for $300 a week.

What a day! About to be dropped by Jack Warner but hired by Louis B. Mayer. Solly drove me back to the Warner's lot. I jumped out of his shiny Cadillac, climbed on my bicycle, rode home to Mommy and Daddy on Evergreen Avenue in Burbank, and went happily to bed—safe, sound, and a newly signed contract player at MGM.

MGM: "More Stars Than There Are in Heaven"

I magine walking onto the lot at MGM for the first time as a teenager. In 1949 that happened to me. MGM was a magical world that created movies almost everyone in America saw. In the days before television, movies were the only game in town. People listened to radio at home and then went to the movies for entertainment. To this day, I feel privileged to have been there.

MGM had a completely different feel than Warner's. Both lots were collections of office buildings, soundstages, bungalows, and buildings that housed wardrobe, sets, props, and all the support people crucial to making films. But MGM still made musicals—brilliant, wonderful musicals. Music floated in the air near rehearsal halls. You heard the sound of music as it was being written, and the lyrics being fit to the music. MGM also had a lot of younger people under contract. Peter Lawford drove his Cadillac convertible down the studio's streets with his surfboard in the backseat. Mickey Rooney was on the prowl, as usual flirting with everyone. Grips and electrical workers walked around the lot beside stars like Spencer Tracy, Judy Garland, and Greer Garson. It was like your life itself was a movie and you were part of one big creative family.

Louis B. Mayer had a big office in the Thalberg Building. Mr. Mayer's office was decorated all in white. His desk was on a riser so that he sat above people who came to visit him. Benny Thau, MGM's top casting person, also had a large office. There were floors full of writers, producers, and creative people of every kind, all in small offices. Director Richard Brooks would be in an office right next to a scriptwriter like Sidney Sheldon, who later became a television writer and producer before going on to write many best-selling books, such as *The Other Side of Midnight*. Drama writers mixed with comedy writers. There were writers who wrote only for Joe Pasternak's light musical comedies, and five rows of desks with writers working on the Andy Hardy series. Another row worked on Lassie's films. Westerns had their own group. The studio created entertainment for every class and style of people in the USA.

Johnny Green was a songwriter, composer, musical arranger, and conductor. He was in charge of all the talent in the music division. Johnny was a little man. He looked like he'd stepped out of *The Wizard of Oz*. He was married to a very tall, beautiful lady from Texas who loved him dearly. Johnny worked with the great composers and arrangers Roger Edens and Conrad Salinger and the legendary producer Arthur Freed, who had his own unit named after him that was responsible for such great musicals as *The Wizard of Oz, The Band Wagon, Gigi, An American in Paris,* and *Singin' in the Rain.* Roger Edens wrote special material for Judy Garland, including "Dear Mr. Gable" and "Born in a Trunk." His work on Judy's one-woman act showcased her talents brilliantly. He was the genius behind many of the performers at MGM. These men were all incredibly talented and funny.

Gene Kelly, Fred Astaire, and choreographer Hermes Pan also worked in the music building. There was constant, exhilarating hubbub, with doors opening and closing as people came and went, everyone busy doing something. Music for Westerns, musicals, romances, and comedies—for every type of movie that MGM made—was created there. A huge soundstage included a recording studio for orchestras that could number over one hundred musicians. Johnny Green was right down in front, conducting. It was very energizing, very exciting. When you grew up in that atmosphere, it was no wonder you believed that there's no business like show business. I still do.

André Previn was another genius who worked in the music department. I'd go to his apartment some evenings to hear André and his friends jam. Knowing what a chatterbox I could be, André warned me, "You can come to my house, but just sit and be quiet. If you start talking, you'll have to leave." So I kept still while he and his friends improvised the most wonderful jazz.

Life at the studio was an education. In addition to the time I spent at John Burroughs High School after work, the studio was required to provide three hours of academic lessons so I could graduate. As part of my professional training, I was taught the basics of the film trade. These included acting, dancing, singing, makeup and hair design, lighting, sound, vocal technique, wardrobe, and sewing! A woman named Adrienne Fazan in the editing department was allowed to teach me how to edit, because I was interested and wanted to learn. At that time, most department heads at MGM were men. Adrienne was one of the few women editors there. She was also one of the best. In a career that spanned thirty-seven years, the films she edited included *An American in Paris* (1951), *Kismet* (1955), *Lust for Life* (1956), *Gigi* (1958), *Some Came Running* (1958), and *Bells Are Ringing* (1960), in addition to *Singin' in the Rain* (1952) and my fourth film, *Give a Girl a Break* (1953). She retired in 1970. I was grateful that she had the time and patience to work with a teenager who got into everything.

I spent most of my free time wandering around the lot looking at each department. I adored the antique furniture in the props department. Daddy was a carpenter, so I spent a lot of time watching the men in the carpentry department working with their big saws and lathes and thinking how much Daddy would love that.

Helen Rose was one of the best costume designers in Hollywood. She designed the dress for my first wedding. She did the gown for Elizabeth Taylor's marriage to Mike Todd. When Kate Middleton married Prince William in April 2011, the future Queen of England's dress was an updated version of Helen's gown for Princess Grace's marriage to Prince Rainier of Monaco in 1956. We actresses kept Helen busy with all our weddings.

MGM graciously allowed my mother to come to the wardrobe department and learn from the craftspeople there. She became a kind of unofficial apprentice.

Mother worked on the second floor with the seam-
stresses who made MGM's costumes. Helen Rose
would make sketches and help Mother with drafting
patterns. It was a big thrill—for Mother and for me.

In the early 1950s, the studios ran Hollywood.
In 1951 I was told that I was to be a presenter at the
Academy Awards. I was scared to death. For some
reason, the studio didn't dress me for the evening. Off
I went to Lerner's to buy a gown for the awards show.
I chose a strapless evening gown with a tight, beaded
bodice and a full skirt covered with multicolored net.
I wore a ribbon around my neck. Having a tiny waist
was important to me, so I had the dress altered accord-
ingly. Then I could barely fit into it. Daddy had to put
his foot on my rib cage so we could get the side zipper
closed when I was getting ready for the Oscars ceremony. That dress only cost me $11, but it was beautiful.

Backstage I kept going over the index cards with my
prepared remarks—there were no TelePrompters for this
show in those days. Just my luck that my category was
cinematography. I couldn't pronounce the word. Fred
Astaire was one of the hosts that night. Prior to announc-
ing me, he introduced a contract player from 20th
Century Fox by the name of Marilyn Monroe. Marilyn
appeared in a huge ball gown with a ruffled collar. Fox
probably helped her with that outfit. When Fred Astaire

introduced me, he said, "Please welcome the most talented and most delightful Miss Debbie Reynolds."

As I walked onstage, the orchestra played "Younger Than Springtime" from Rodgers and Hammerstein's musical *South Pacific,* then in its third year on Broadway. I read the cards and rushed through the nominees. I believe I said "cinematographer" instead of "cinematography," but I kept reading and announced the winners, my head down and my eyes fixed on the cards, a nerve-racked teenager in a tight dress.

At MGM, there was magic around every corner. Noël Coward and Clifton Webb became my good friends. They even talked my mother into letting me go with them to Jamaica for a vacation. Noël played the piano while I sang, and Clifton would enjoy the show. The three of us walked on the beach together. Clifton and Noël held hands, but I didn't think anything of it. I felt their friendship and I thank them for including me. I know that one may wonder why they invited me, so much younger than they were and a girl. They loved youth and innocence, and I was funny. We entertained one another. We did the same at parties in Los Angeles. How lucky I was to have such extraordinary friends.

One of my favorite moments at MGM was meeting Clark Gable. When I was a young girl, he was the greatest movie star. One day when I was walking around the lot, I saw Howard Strickling, the head of

With W. M. Guthrie and Robert Surtees backstage
at the Academy Awards show in 1951. This was
the only time I can recall being nervous in my
career. Even though I had trouble pronouncing
"cinematography," these gentlemen still looked happy.
Academy of Motion Picture Arts and Sciences

publicity, coming out the commissary door. As we
passed he grabbed my arm and introduced me to the
man behind him.

"I want you to meet the new star on the lot, Clark,"
he said. "Here's Debbie Reynolds."

He was so handsome that I was stunned. I think my mouth may have dropped open.

"Well, kid, you'll find it an interesting life," he told me.

For once, I was speechless. I'm sure I thanked him and said hello, but I was stopped in my tracks by the experience.

In May 1954, Gable left MGM without any fanfare. The decision was made in the boardroom not to renew his contract. That was it. When a decision was made, it was law. A letter was sent to every department on the lot. If a person was fired that day, they left that day. Their clothes and personal effects were removed from their dressing room. Clark Gable didn't tell any of the people who worked with him that he was leaving. He was escorted off the lot like a prisoner getting out of jail. After more than twenty years as one of the greatest movie stars in history, Gable ended his days at MGM by driving himself out the gate, never to return. Afterward, everyone on the lot was so sad. A small article in the paper later stated that Clark Gable was leaving MGM to pursue other opportunities. All because a decision was made in the boardroom that one of the greatest stars of all time wasn't worth the money the studio was paying him.

When I met Spencer Tracy, I was reminded of my introduction to Mr. Gable.

"So you're the new kid," Mr. Tracy said.

Everyone called me "kid." I was one of the two youngest contract players on the lot. Russ Tamblyn was the other, and we became friends. Russ went on to become famous for his roles in the films *Seven Brides for Seven Brothers*, *Peyton Place*, and *West Side Story*.

Mr. Tracy advised me, "Well, you want to be a good actress, so remember to be real. Got that?"

"Yes, sir," I replied.

Soon afterward, I was seated next to the remarkable Ethel Merman at a special studio luncheon in the MGM commissary. My ear for imitation is keen, and it was on overload around Ethel. Remembering Spencer Tracy's advice, I decided to be real. Real *loud.* Ethel inspired me. I created my impression of her immediately and continue to do it to this day.

MGM was my university. I majored in musical comedy with a minor in drama. The studio educated me, chose my escorts for premieres, managed my press, and advanced my career by having me make special appearances. They even sent me on a press tour to the White House, where I met President Truman, the first of several presidents I was to meet over the coming decades. I worked hard to keep up with all the great talent.

It was a time like no other—the most magical time you could imagine.

On October 8, 1951, in Washington, DC,
President Truman greeted motion picture industry
representatives as part of the fiftieth anniversary of the
American Movie Theater at the White House. *Front
row, left to right:* Elizabeth Taylor; Adolph Zukor,
Chairman of the Board of Paramount Pictures; President
Truman; Mrs. Randolph Scott; Joyce O'Hara, Acting
President, Motion Picture Association; and Debbie
Reynolds. *Second row, left to right:* Louise Allbritton,
Arthur Mayer, Arthur Arthur, Julian Brylanski,
Virginia Kellogg, and Randolph Scott. From Burbank
to the White House in just a few short years! Notice
Elizabeth with her gloves. Etiquette, always etiquette.
MGM taught us to be movie stars, but always with good
manners. The studio lent me the suit for the occasion.
President Truman played the piano for us. (Many
years later, Warren Buffett played his ukulele for me.)
Harry S. Truman Library and Museum. Photofest

Three Little Words

(MGM, 1950)

After my audition with Jack Cummings, I went to work in this musical comedy. A street scene has me with Red Skelton, one of the funniest men I've ever known, and Fred Astaire, one of the most elegant. As they play the piano on the sidewalk, I walk into the frame wearing a dark brunette wig and lip-syncing "Boop-Boop-a-Doop" to Helen Kane's voice. Kane was a popular singer in the late 1920s whose high-pitched voice was used for the animated character Betty Boop. My years of mouthing songs in the Girl Scouts served me well. Then Carleton Carpenter and I filmed a scene where I pantomimed Helen Kane's voice in the entire song "I Wanna Be Loved by You." I'm told that when Mr. Mayer saw the dailies, he said, "I like the way her eyes light up. Sign her."

Two Weeks With Love

(MGM, 1950)

This was my first real role for MGM. It was a fun shoot. Every day my mother would pack my lunch. I usually ate sandwiches made with bologna ground up with pickle juice. Louis Calhern was one of MGM's great stars and had a fancy lunch prepared for him by the studio. Even though he was on a special diet, he usually traded me for my bologna sandwiches.

Once again I was paired with Carleton Carpenter. We sing "Aba Daba Honeymoon." When the song became a big hit after the film was released, MGM sent the two of us on a multicity tour to capitalize on our success. We played all the Loews theaters, beginning in Washington, DC.

Busby Berkeley did the choreography for this film. Dear Busby liked to drink. He was famous for his brilliant overhead shots that featured dozens of dancers in elaborate settings and patterns. Because he was usually tipsy during the afternoons, the crew used to strap him to the boom camera, where he sat high above the action. Whenever there was a halt to filming, we used to sing, "Somewhere there's Busby, how high the boom?" to the tune of "How High the Moon." To this day, when there is a glitch on a movie set, I sing that tune to recall that brilliant director and choreographer.

Dorothy Kingsley was one of the writers on this movie. Dorothy was part of the famous Freed Unit, hired by our producer Arthur Freed himself. She was always being called down to the set of his musicals to rewrite scenes while they were being shot. Often she wasn't credited on films where she contributed dialogue

or helped with problems. This is my brief tribute to
that talented lady.

Our director, Roy Rowland, was a wonderful man
who gave the best parties. He'd hire a pianist, and people
like Lena Horne and Judy Garland would sing. We all
did. It was heaven. Lena and I would chat about being

Onstage with Carleton Carpenter during our Loews
tour—my first time on the road. *Licensed by Warner
Bros. Entertainment Inc. All rights reserved*

Having a gay old time with Farley Granger *(front row left);* Jack Larson, who played Jimmy Olsen on *Superman* in the 1950s *(standing next to Farley);* Carleton Carpenter *(towering over everyone, as usual);* Shelley Winters *(front row right, kneeling);* and other pals who came to enjoy the new pool I had built at my family's home in Burbank.

contract players on the lot. Lena told me that she found her job very lonely. She was having a hard time making friends at the studio. I was much younger than she, and thrilled that she would talk to me. Whenever I saw her on the lot, which was almost daily, we would sit together. One day I asked her, "Why don't we have lunch in the commissary?" She told me that she never went into the commissary unless it was for a press event. There was an unspoken rule, or strong request, that she not eat in the dining room. I was shocked to learn this. So we continued to bring our lunches in paper bags, sometimes eating together in Lena's pretty dressing room.

Mr. Imperium

(MGM, 1951)

In this film, Marjorie Main plays the owner of a small hotel in Palm Springs. I play her niece who helps with the guests. It's a very small part, but it was fun working with Marjorie and the movie's star, Lana Turner.

At the time we were filming, Lana was pregnant and looking forward to being a mother. She was married to a man from Texas named Bob Topping, who claimed to be rich. Lana later found out that he was rich all right—rich with her money. Although he'd had millions, he lost it all. And then he took her money. Many years later, Doris Day and I would join the ranks of women who trusted our husbands too much with the money we worked so hard to earn.

Lana wasn't very happy while making this film. Her costar, Ezio Pinza, was a wonderful bass singer who enjoyed a second career on Broadway after retiring from the Metropolitan Opera. He loved to eat garlic. When he had romantic scenes with Lana, he would try to make them as realistic as possible, which infuriated her. She would push him away when he forced himself on her and yell, "Cut!"—then run to her dressing room. Pinza's garlicky breath would have been hard enough to deal with under normal circumstances, but Lana was very sensitive to odors during her pregnancy. She later lost the baby, which certainly was not because of the garlic she inhaled. Lana's daughter, Cheryl, by her second husband, Joseph Crane, would be her only child.

Marjorie Main was so much fun. She had reached an age where she was having difficulty with her bladder. During a scene, she would hear the call and just walk off the set to the restroom while still reciting her lines. When the director called, "Cut," she seemed not to understand why her lines weren't picked up. Between Marjorie's pee breaks and Lana's fighting with Pinza, it was a pretty tense set. Our director was Don Hartman. Although he would later take over the studio when Dore Schary left, he was too nice to handle this crowd.

Marjorie's husband, Stanley Krebs, had died in 1935. She still carried his urn around with her, so she could speak with Stanley. When she went to the lunch counter, she would hoist up the urn, order an extra meal for Stanley, and chatter away as if he were part of the conversation. She was wonderfully eccentric, and I loved being around her.

Even though I didn't have a lot to do in this film, I so enjoyed being part of this unusual ensemble. My next movie, a musical comedy about the shift from silent films to sound, was a major step forward in my career.

Singin' in the Rain

(MGM, 1952)

"*Smile!* Don't look at your feet!" Gene Kelly shouted at me.

We were rehearsing for *Singin' in the Rain,* which Gene was codirecting with Stanley Donen. It was an important film for MGM, my first leading role since being signed by the studio, and Gene definitely hadn't wanted me as his costar. But Louis B. Mayer himself had chosen me to play Kathy Selden, and there was nothing Gene could do about it, even though he was MGM's biggest star at that time. The word of the studio head was law. Luckily for me, producer Arthur

Freed also wanted me for the role, and he was the most important musical talent at MGM.

I wasn't a dancer, and had three months to learn what Gene Kelly and Donald O'Connor had been doing for years. My lessons started immediately, right after my nineteenth birthday. I had three teachers: Jeanne Coyne, Ernie Flatt, and Carol Haney, all hired by Gene Kelly, who became members of the Freed Unit. Jeanne and Carol were assistant choreographers. Jeanne was also Gene's assistant on the film. She'd divorced Stanley Donen in 1951 and would marry Gene in 1960. She just adored Gene. They had many happy years together. Carol went on to star in *The Pajama Game* on Broadway. Ernie Flatt later became the choreographer for *The Carol Burnett Show*. They would each give me a class every day.

Jeanne and Ernie taught me Donald's and Gene's signature steps. (Gene's favorite tap step was the maxi ford. When he asked if I knew it, I told him I didn't know that car.) They tailored the choreography for "All I Do Is Dream of You," my first number in the film, to my athletic abilities. Gene wanted the taps to be sharp and clear, so he and Jeanne recorded them on a soundstage with a wooden floor. Gene didn't work on that number, as he wasn't in it with me, but he choreographed my other numbers in the film. He came to rehearsals and criticized everything I did and never gave me a word of encouragement. He was a severe taskmaster.

I've never worked so hard. I was dancing for eight hours a day. Making *Singin' in the Rain* and childbirth were the two hardest things I've ever done. The movie was actually harder, because it hurt me everywhere, most of all my brain and my feet. My father had raised me never to start a job unless I planned on finishing it, and I was determined to do my damnedest. The word *quit* was not in my vocabulary. Still, Daddy had never been in a musical film. One day I crumpled in a heap under the rehearsal piano, crying. Fred Astaire came to my rescue. He asked me why I was crying, and I told him the dancing was so hard, I thought I was going to die.

"You're not going to die," he said. "That's what it's like to learn to dance. If you're not sweating, you're not doing it right."

He took me to the studio where he was rehearsing with Hermes Pan, another great MGM choreographer. I watched in awe as Fred worked on his routines to the point of frustration and anger. I realized that if it was hard for Fred Astaire, dancing was hard for everyone. No one ever made it look easier. His kind gesture helped me a great deal.

Shooting the "Good Morning" number took from eight in the morning until eleven at night. When we were finally finished, I collapsed from exhaustion. My feet were bleeding from hours of abuse. I couldn't move. (Ironically, Gene wound up using the first take in the finished film.) My doctor ordered me to rest for two days. Arthur Freed called and told him I should report to work, that the studio doctor would give me "vitamin shots." These were possibly the same "vitamins" that ruined Judy Garland. My doctor insisted that I stay in bed. That decision may have saved me from a life on stimulants.

Aside from falling down with frustration and exhaustion, we had a happy time on the set. Everyone worked well together. Friends dropped by to keep our spirits up.

Like Oscar Levant. Oscar and Gene had become buddies when they made *An American in Paris* the previous year. Oscar was a pianist and composer who acted and was famous for his sarcastic wit. He'd thought that he was going to have Donald O'Connor's part in *Singin' in the Rain,* until Betty Comden called him to talk about something else and let it slip that Gene had cast Donald. Oscar got very angry. But Gene made the right decision: his tap numbers with Donald are some of the best ever captured on film.

Oscar was always stoned when he dropped by the set. We became friends, and in later years he'd show up at my house at three in the morning to sing, play the piano, and smoke cigarettes until he was ready to go home. I had to put a huge ashtray on the piano because he wasn't careful about where his ashes went. His lovely wife understood that Oscar needed to wander about at night until he found an audience. She must have known that the piano was the only thing he was banging.

Oscar wasn't my only pianist visitor. I'd met Van Cliburn at one of the Hollywood parties we attended, and I invited him to stay with me when he was rehearsing for a local concert appearance. All the neighbors would stand outside to listen to him rehearse, because he was one of the most famous classical performers in the world. When he finished a piece, they'd applaud, but he never took a bow. Van didn't require an ashtray when he was playing. He is the dearest man and neat as a pin. I should have tossed Eddie out and married Van, even though he's gay. He wouldn't have left me for Elizabeth Taylor, if only because he probably wasn't her type.

When I look at *Singin' in the Rain* now, I realize something I didn't understand at the time but must have known somehow. Mr. Mayer said I had to do it. Gene Kelly said I had to do it. I didn't know that I *couldn't* do it. So I did it, and I was terrific. But I must admit that I hate my voice in the movie. Right after it premiered, I began intensive lessons with the MGM dialogue coach, Gertrude Fogler. She taught everyone. When Grace Kelly became engaged to Prince Rainier, she'd run to Gertrude for French lessons after she was done filming for the day. After years of training and speaking properly, my voice is placed lower and correctly. In the movie, I *was* that little girl who was thrown into the middle of the great entertainment business.

Part of my transformation from a young girl of the 1950s to a flapper of the 1920s involved my eyebrows. The makeup people plucked out my eyebrows and penciled in thin lines, to suit the fashion of the times. They assured me that my real brows would grow back, but they never did. To this day, I always carry an eyebrow pencil with me, to touch up my drawn-on brows.

The year 2012 marked the sixtieth anniversary of *Singin' in the Rain.* I'm honored to be part of a great work that has stood the test of time. It makes me happy when I hear how young people are being introduced to the film. Schools use it to teach dance. These are things we never thought about in 1952.

There's a scene near the beginning of the film where I throw a cake at Gene, who ducks so that the cake lands on Jean Hagen. (Jean and I had something in common: Mr. Mayer had also chosen her over Gene's objections. She is brilliant as the silent movie star with the squeaky voice and went on to be nominated for an Oscar for this role.) When Gene and Stanley Donen were blocking the scene, I saw four prop cakes laid out on a table. Gene told me I would have four takes to land it.

"I can do it in one take," I said confidently.

Gene and Stanley snickered.

"No, no, I can," I insisted. "I'm Miss Burbank."

They burst out laughing.

I've been in this business a long time now and know how to deliver a punch line, but I was nineteen then and completely serious.

"I'm a Girl Scout," I explained. "I earned forty-seven merit badges. I know I can do this."

Gene gave me a condescending look. I'll show you, Mr. Big Shot, I thought.

I pulled Jean aside. She was dressed in a beautiful evening gown for the scene. "When you deliver your line, stay on your mark and hold your head still," I told her. "If you stay in one place, I know I can hit you in one take." Jean agreed. She didn't want more than one cake in her face.

We reassembled to shoot the scene. When the cameras rolled, Jean delivered her line, Gene gracefully ducked out of place in front of her, and I landed the cake smack on Jean's kisser!

Speaking of kissers . . .

In *Singin' in the Rain*, Gene and I play two people falling in love. In one of the film's many famous scenes, the camera comes down from an overhead crane as we kiss and "You Are My Lucky Star" swells on the soundtrack.

Stanley Donen yelled, "Action!" The camera closed in. Gene took me tightly in his arms . . . and shoved his tongue down my throat.

"*Eeew!* What was that?" I screeched, breaking free of his grasp and spitting.

I ran around frantic, yelling for some Coca-Cola to cleanse my mouth. It was the early 1950s, and I was an innocent kid who had never been French-kissed. It felt like an assault. I was stunned that this thirty-nine-year-old man would do this to me.

Gene had stepped back, not amused. After a few minutes, I calmed down enough to face his now-icy stare and we redid the scene as you see it in the film.

After that, Gene and I became friends. With the help of the MGM teachers, he transformed an untrained high school girl into a dancer. In the early '70s, Gene came to see me when I was starring in *Irene*, my first time ever on Broadway. After the show, he came backstage,

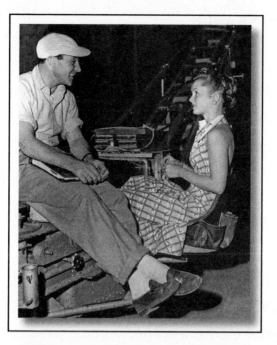

With Gene Kelly during filming for *Singin' in the Rain*.

Grabbing a bite on the lot at MGM between dance
rehearsals for *Singin' in the Rain*—lots of work.
Mother packed my lunch when I went to the studio.

hugged me, told me how proud he was of me, and kissed me—no tongue—in front of the bedazzled cast. I was so moved, I cried. Gene made me a stronger performer who faces every challenge head on—and with a "*Smile!*"

Skirts Ahoy!

(MGM, 1952)

My cameo in this film is an example of the MGM practice of dipping into the talent pool when they needed someone for a scene.

Producer Joe Pasternak made all these light, entertaining movies that everyone loved doing. Pasternak also gave great parties. We used to hang out at his house in Bel Air, a wonderful brick home. He always had a pianist who could transpose songs to any key, so everyone was expected to entertain.

What fun it was when we would all go over to Joe's after working and relax and just be young and silly. Nutty, if you like. Some of the regulars were Mickey Rooney, Ricardo Montalban, Russ Tamblyn, Lena Horne, Kathryn Grayson, Howard Keel, Janie Powell, Vic Damone, Pier Angeli, and Leslie Caron, to name just a few. And Johnny Payne, who would call out at any given time, "Turn off the lights and call the law." Even Billy Daniels came over with his pianist and sang "That Old Black Magic." He was sensational—gorgeous with his gray hair, blue eyes, and beautiful light beige complexion. His performance was the sexiest I've ever witnessed without dropping my pants.

I Love Melvin

(MGM, 1953)

This light musical comedy paired me again with Donald O'Connor. The film was made for commercial reasons, to capitalize on the success of *Singin' in the Rain,* but it was cute. It's basically a thin story about a budding photographer for *Look* magazine pursuing a young actress in spite of her father's objections, that ties together a lot of musical numbers—an MGM specialty.

My opening number is a dream sequence where I sing "A Lady Loves (to Love)" dressed in a sequined outfit with a large net skirt that forms a train. Choreographed by Robert Alton, a famous Broadway director who worked on many MGM musicals (*Annie Get Your Gun, White Christmas, Pal Joey, Show Boat*), this number is reminiscent of the famous "Diamonds Are a Girl's Best Friend" number that Marilyn Monroe later performed in *Gentlemen Prefer Blondes.* I'm surrounded by men dressed in formal evening wear, including top hats and capes lined in scarlet; Marilyn dances with a group of men in tuxedos, who offer her diamond bracelets. (I used to own the beautiful pink gown that Marilyn wears in that number, but as with many things from my collection, a former employee stole it. For legal reasons, I can't give you the details.) It's flattering that someone thought enough of that number to borrow from it. We filmed another version in a farm setting, but the more sophisticated one was chosen to open the film. The second version later appeared in *That's Entertainment! III.*

There were other fun numbers in this film. I play an ingénue who gets a part in a Broadway musical. The football ballet number was filmed with two football teams and me as the ball. Needless to say, when the boys were tossing me around the set, I was happy I had done so well in my gymnastics classes. My stunt double broke her arm during rehearsals for this number.

We went on location to New York City, where Donald and I did a number in Central Park, dancing around a fountain. This isn't an epic film, but it's fun. I loved working with my dear friend Donald again.

The Affairs of Dobie Gillis

(MGM, 1953)

This was one of the many films I did at MGM where I got the job, then went to work. *Dobie Gillis* is about college kids having good times, carefree times. My own life was like that when I made it—no obligations, no worries, just fun. I would go to André Previn's home to listen to music after work. I did whatever I wanted and got a $300 check from the studio every week. Because of the financial freedom this gave me, I was able to help my father retire from the railroad. When I first started at MGM, Daddy would never accept money from me. The railroad paid him $200 a month. Daddy was only in his fifties, but now his health was failing. All his years of hard work had taken their toll. He started fainting under the trains, saved only by his buddies pulling him out. When I heard about that, I told him that I could provide for Mother and him. We all worried about him having a terrible accident. Thankfully, he accepted my offer.

Those were my young and free years. I was the Virgin Mary Frances. I wasn't obligated to any guy. Once Arthur Lowe Jr., the film's producer, took me out to dinner. I had never been to a restaurant where you followed the maitre d' to the table. When asked what I wanted to drink, I answered, "A glass of milk, please." Arthur sweetly told the waiter, "No special vintage on that." Word got out quickly on the lot that I really was a Girl Scout.

Barbara Ruick, Bobby Van, and I became pals while making *Dobie Gillis*. Bobby Fosse worked hard on our numbers together. He was so brilliant even then, but he didn't mix with us during time off the set.

Barbara and I became good friends. She made many records for MGM. We recorded a comic hillbilly tune together, calling ourselves "Iffie and Miffie." Barbara was Miffie. In 1956 she married John Williams, who went on to compose the scores for *Jaws, Star Wars, Raiders of the Lost Ark, Schindler's List,* and so many other big films. They had three children together. Barbara's aunt was the comedienne and radio star Joan Davis, whose television series, *I Married Joan,* was a hit from 1952 to 1955. Barbara and I had wonderful times at Davis's beautiful estate. We stayed friends until Barbara's untimely death in 1974 from a brain hemorrhage while she was on location in Reno, Nevada. She was working on Robert Altman's film *California Split,* which he dedicated to her. What a shock to all of us who loved her. She was so talented.

Give a Girl a Break

(MGM, 1953)

Making this movie was extremely difficult, and I still have a hard time speaking about it. It was like going to war every day. It sounds ridiculous, but there were too many talented people on the film.

Bob Fosse and Gower Champion, both brilliant dancers and choreographers, shared the choreography duties, and it became a competition. On one side were Gower and his wife, Marge. On the other side, the director, Stanley Donen, and Bobby were a team. They challenged Gower on everything. The men were constantly trying to one-up each other. Bobby had been standoffish when we did *Dobie Gillis,* but this was something else. All that jealousy for no reason. The Champions were my good friends, and I was their ally.

Bobby was this amazing talent combined with blind ambition. There was no one like him, and he was right to try to get ahead. Stanley was immediately smitten and seemed determined to help his pal become a star. One day I looked at the rushes of a number I was in with Bobby. The camera was on him; maybe a part of my left ear was visible. Stanley's affection for Bobby had spilled onto the screen and into my two-shot. Even in the love scenes, all you saw was Bobby's face. I'm a team player, but this was ridiculous. Something was going on—and I felt it was wrong, wrong, wrong.

I went to the front office, demanding that someone look at the footage. The footage was reviewed, the scenes were reshot—and my relationship with Stanley deteriorated even further. There's no love lost between us to this day, which is unfortunate. He is a brilliant cinematographer and director who has made many wonderful, important films.

Bobby did the choreography for our numbers together, and he came up with some very strenuous routines. It was the most difficult dancing I'd done since *Singin' in the Rain,* but I was determined to keep up with him. During rehearsals, Bobby, who was so in love with his own well-endowed self, would come up behind me and press his "gift" into my backside to tease me. It was obvious he wasn't wearing a dance belt; I could feel everything he wanted to share. And Bobby didn't respond to subtle discouragement, like being pushed away vigorously.

Fed up, I went to a nearby drugstore one day at lunchtime, to purchase a jockstrap for him, hoping to help him contain his enthusiasm.

"Give me the biggest jockstrap you carry," I told the clerk. "An extra-extra large."

He looked at me, puzzled.

"I have an extra large size," he responded, "but the only color it comes in is black."

Perfect. I bought it.

Back at rehearsal, I placed my present in Bobby's locker. He got the message and never poked me again.

The "Balloon Dance" that Bobby and I do on the roof of a skyscraper is pretty terrific. It looks easy, but it was tricky and dangerous to produce. It took at least two days to film because of the balloons and falling confetti and other special effects. In the finished film, some of the footage is played backward, causing popped balloons to reappear and Bobby and me to slide upward on ramps. Very clever.

And once again, Stanley's fascination with Bobby is on prominent display. The number starts with a large close-up of Bobby, with a miniature Debbie singing "Give a Girl a Break" as he looks around, love-struck. The only other time I personally witnessed a director so smitten with the talent was when George Sidney directed Ann-Margret in *Bye Bye Birdie*. Janet Leigh was very upset that all the close-ups were going to A-M.

Many years later, I attended a charity event at the Beverly Hills Hotel. It was the first time I was in the same room with Bobby since we'd made this movie. He came over, embraced me, pulled me into a huddle in the corner, and told me how sorry he was for his past behavior. He said he realized how young I'd been, that he'd truly just been playing around and didn't mean to upset me. He hoped we could be friends.

From that moment on, I said good-bye to all the bad memories. I was happy to accept his apology. I'd always respected his amazing talent. When I think of Bobby now, I remember all he did to revolutionize dance during his lifetime. He was truly a genius.

Give a Girl a Break showcased Bobby's emerging talent. But the fact remains that, wonderful and cheerful as the finished movie is, it holds no happy memories for me.

The Actress

(MGM, 1953)

The Actress was being made around the time that I was working on *I Love Melvin* and *The Affairs of Dobie Gillis.* I mention it because it represented a deep disappointment in my young life. This was the part I didn't get to keep.

I was delighted when I was cast in the film. Ruth Gordon had written a script, based on her autobiographical play *Years Ago,* about a young New Englander who wants to be in the theater but knows she will never get her father's approval. George Cukor was directing, and Spencer Tracy was cast as the father.

After my screen test, George Cukor wrote to Ruth Gordon:

Sept. 16, 1952

DEAREST RUTH:

I've just come from the stage, where we shot the test with Debbie Reynolds. We did the

opening scene of the play, and the big Telling-
Papa scene, complete with Viola and Juliet. I'm
keeping my fingers crossed. . . . I think we've got
our girl. She has real charm (a mighty rare
commodity among younger actresses),
temperament, individuality, pathos and humour.
What the hell else do you want? Her speech is still
more Glendale than New England, but I'm sure
that the good Miss Fogler could correct that. You
can gather from all this that I have the highest
hopes for Debbie. . . .

Cukor continues, telling Ruth how he pulled
John Gielgud into the rehearsal to help me with the
Shakespearean passages. Gielgud worked with me and
said that I was "damned good—in Shakespeare!"—
and that, within my limits, I'd played those speeches
"most movingly, and with real power."

Rehearsals, costume fittings, and hair and makeup
tests were all done with me. I was excited to be working on a great script about a young girl who wanted to
act. I knew it would be a wonderful experience.

And then Dore Schary called me into his office and
informed me flatly, "You're not going to do the picture.
Don't be upset. Jean Simmons is doing the part. It's all
set. You're out."

Simple as that. He stood up to indicate that it was time for me to leave. Waiting in the outer office was Ida Koverman, who had been Louis B. Mayer's secretary until he was fired. She was crying.

"He's a mean man," she said, trying to console me.

I was stunned. I couldn't understand why they'd done this. Of course Jean Simmons was a fine British actress with a background in theater. She knew more about the Shakespearean parts the actress deals with in the script. But would she be better at playing a girl from New England than a girl from Burbank?

Studios made decisions regardless of what the director or the actors wanted. Mr. Mayer had put me in *Singin' in the Rain* without asking Gene Kelly. Mr. Mayer and Arthur Freed both wanted me for that part, so there was no discussion. MGM did the same thing to Lena Horne. Lena was originally going to play the role of Julie LaVerne in the remake of *Show Boat.* But the studio got nervous about casting an African American as a lead. It was the early 1950s, and Lena was not a big enough star by box office standards to make it worth the risk. So they replaced her with Ava Gardner, who was a very big star.

Lena was deeply hurt and remained bitter about it for many years. She wanted that part so badly, and she would have been spectacular in *Show Boat.* But she

Sept. 16, 1952

Dearest Ruth:

I've just come from the stage, where we
shot the test with Debbie Reynolds. We
did the opening scene of the play, and
the big Telling-Papa scene, complete with
Viola and Juliet. I'm keeping my fingers
crossed....I think we've got our girl.
She has real charm (a mighty rare commodity among younger actresses), temperament, individuality, pathos and humour.
What the hell else do you want? Her
speech is still more Glendale than New
England, but I'm sure the good Miss Fogler
could correct that. You can gather from
all this that I have the highest hopes for
Debbie.

When she began to read the Shakespeare,
she confessed that she'd never seen a
Shakespearean performance, or for that
matter, ever heard Shakespeare spoken
aloud before. You know me....nothing but
the best. John Gielgud appeared at our
rehearsal and took charge. He worked with
her as long as he thought necessary, was
kindness and patience itself. What's more,
he thought she was damned good -- in
Shakespeare. I must say, within her limits,
she played those speeches most movingly, and
with real power.

Mr. Kelly, of the New York Office, has sent
the following information: "Ruth Gordon has
just advised us that she does not have a tape
recording of the play." I know that Ruth
Gordon hasn't got a tape recording of the play,
but she'll make one, will she not?

George Cukor's letter to Ruth Gordon about my audition for
The Actress. I was very excited—until Dore Schary told me
I no longer had the part. *Courtesy of the Margaret Herrick
Library, Academy of Motion Picture Arts and Sciences*

was passed over because of her color. The irony was that Julie LaVerne is a character whose life is destroyed when it is discovered that she is half black.

I knew and loved Ava. She was so down-to-earth. And she was wonderful in the film. But she didn't especially want the part. Lena didn't blame Ava, just as I didn't blame Jean—who, as it happened, fit into the costumes that had been made for me. We were all contract players and had to do as we were told. But that didn't make my disappointment any easier to swallow. I knew I could have done a good job in *The Actress.* To prove it, I did Ruth Gordon's original stage version in summer theaters in 1953 and 1954.

Susan Slept Here

(RKO, 1954)

After I made *Singin' in the Rain,* RKO approached MGM about casting me in a movie entitled *Susan Slept Here.* Howard Hughes wanted me to play the teen-age ward of a Hollywood screenwriter, played by Dick Powell. Dick was almost thirty years older than me, but that didn't matter to Mr. Hughes.

He asked to meet me before he gave me the part. After a short interview, he walked me to my car, a 1932

Chevy that Daddy bought for $50 and gave me when I started at MGM. Mr. Hughes held open the car door, which was hanging from its hinges, and told me that I had the part even though I was jailbait. In fact, I was twenty-one, but Hughes was fond of very young girls with big breasts. I found him to be an interesting, polite, and brilliant man with a quirky side. One of America's richest men, he once left an airplane hangar where he was designing the *Spruce Goose* to travel back to RKO to work on a design for an underwire bra for the busty Jane Russell. The bra stayed up a lot better than the *Spruce Goose* did. Hughes flew the huge plane for one very short trip before it was retired to a hangar in Long Beach, California.

Hughes put Jane under contract and loved looking at her. She told me that she never let him touch her— and still Jane got a check from Mr. Hughes every week until he died in 1976.

Dick Powell and I became friends while making the film. At the time he was married to June Allyson, another MGM star. I hadn't yet met her. Before marrying Dick, June had dated many men, including John F. Kennedy, who happened to be the brother-in-law of Peter Lawford, June's costar in *Good News*.

While we were filming, Dick invited me to their ranch in Mandeville Canyon, just outside Los Angeles.

Dick was a very good businessman who owned a production company with David Niven in addition to his other enterprises. Dick loved that ranch; they even had cattle. During my visit, Dick went out with the horses while June took me on a tour of the house. As we climbed up to the second floor, she stopped by a window in the hallway and instructed me to look at the view—hundreds of acres of beautiful land, a breathtaking vista. When I turned back to her, June had taken about four roses out of a bud vase and was drinking the contents of the vase before replacing the flowers. Apparently the clear liquid was vodka. She had it stashed all over the house, in various containers.

June went to great lengths to hide her drinking, which was strange to me, as Dick was also a big drinker. Every afternoon at five-thirty, no matter what scene we were filming, a tray with two large glasses of milk would appear on the set. Dick and the director, Frank Tashlin, would enjoy their milk, which was half whiskey.

I didn't understand why all these grown-ups went to such lengths to hide their habits. But then, I was a kid who only drank Coca-Cola.

June Allyson and Jimmy Stewart were Daddy's favorite stars. June sweetly signed a picture for Daddy.

He was so touched and delighted. She charmed men, young and old, to the end.

Athena

(MGM, 1954)

Probably the most memorable thing about making this movie was meeting Eddie Fisher. Eddie was then a famous singer with his own TV show, and he was constantly being interviewed. When asked by a reporter what young lady he would most like to meet, Eddie had answered, "Debbie Reynolds." So Joe Pasternak brought Eddie to the set one day and introduced us. We had our pictures taken, then ate lunch in the commissary. The next day Eddie called my house to invite me to his opening at the Cocoanut Grove, a popular nightclub at the Ambassador Hotel in Los Angeles. Johnny Grant, a mutual friend of ours, had given Eddie my phone number. Mother was thrilled—she was a fan of Eddie's TV show.

What can I say about *Athena*? It might have worked in the 1960s or '70s, but it didn't do much for audiences in 1954. The subject was astrology and health foods. Jane Powell plays one of my seven sisters; we frolic with bodybuilders in the health food store owned by our parents. Vic Damone and I do a song called "Imagine" that is definitely not John Lennon's anthem (which, come to think of it, might have fit in this film).

Joe Pasternak threw pages from the script into the air in frustration. So I guess it's no surprise that the audience wasn't crazy about the finished movie.

Hit the Deck

(MGM, 1955)

In *Hit the Deck,* Russ Tamblyn and I do a number called "The Devil's Fun House" that took three days to shoot and left us battered, beaten, and black and blue all over. Rusty plays a sailor trying to save his sister Susan's virtue with the help of two of his sailor friends. Janie Powell plays Susan. The big danger? She wants to be in a show called—what else?—*Hit the Deck.*

Rusty was a doll, the best dancer and tumbler in the movie, and it was great to work with Janie again. Joe Pasternak threw great people into the film, and it turned out fun and wonderful. Ann Miller was a kick in the pants—so funny and silly. We became great friends afterward. She was a great gal.

This was the studio system at its best. We showed up, learned our songs, rehearsed our dances, and had a great time. As the finale says, "Hallelujah!"

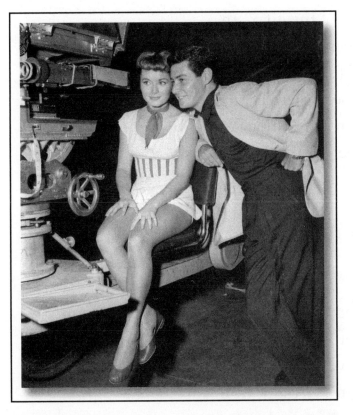

When we were courting, Eddie visited me on the
set of *Hit the Deck*. *Licensed by Warner Bros.
Entertainment Inc. All rights reserved*

The Tender Trap

(MGM, 1955)

My costar in this comedy about a womanizer and
the gal who finally lands him is Frank Sinatra. Frank
was a great kisser. I really enjoyed the scenes where
we made out in his apartment or mine. He was also a
taskmaster on the set.

In the recording studio with Frank Sinatra doing *The Tender Trap* soundtrack. It was so much fun to sing with Frank. We became friends, even though I ignored his advice to break my engagement to Eddie Fisher. *Licensed by Warner Bros. Entertainment Inc. All rights reserved*

Frank was the king in Hollywood, both on and off the screen. He would come to work ready to go, but only wanted to do one take. He was very definite about getting everything right the first time. Our director, Chuck Walters, worked hard to accommodate Frank, making sure that we all knew our lines by the time Frank showed up. Frank kept us on our toes, and the shooting went fast.

There are so many fine actors in this film. Like David Wayne (who was also fun and adorable and so kind to me). I've always thought Celeste Holm was underrated in her career. She was equal to Bette Davis in *All About Eve,* a standout in every movie she did. She lived to be ninety-five and still went out and enjoyed her life.

We didn't shoot much on Mondays because Frank needed to recover from his weekend activities. Frank idolized Humphrey Bogart. Every Friday after work, Frank would join Bogart and his buddies on Bogie's boat. Betty Bacall was the only lady on board for those booze cruises. I would have loved to be invited, but I never was.

One day Frank took me to lunch and asked me a lot of questions about my feelings for Eddie Fisher. I told Frank that I loved Eddie and wanted to marry him.

"You should think twice about this, Schweetie," he warned me. "Schweetie" was his nickname for me, said with a lisp. "It's a hard life, marrying a singer. I know."

Frank's earnest attempt to keep me from heartbreak was very touching. I could tell he was sincere, and I appreciated that he wanted to spare me from a difficult choice. But I really was in love.

Meet Me in Las Vegas

(MGM, 1956)

This movie was released a few months after *The Tender Trap,* and honestly, I don't remember doing it. I was pretty much kept busy going from one film into another, and this was the thirteenth movie I'd done for MGM since arriving at the studio. After a lifetime, I hope I'm entitled to forget a bit performance lasting thirty seconds that I did over half a century ago!

Meet Me in Las Vegas is another Joe Pasternak romp, this one about a cowboy (Dan Dailey), a ballerina (Cyd Charisse), and their magical romance in Vegas. When Dan gambles with Cyd by his side, he can't lose.

Vic Damone and I have uncredited cameos. Dan and Cyd rush past us in the showroom during the rehearsal for Cyd's act, momentarily stopping me from drinking my Coke. I imagine this was a reference to my boyfriend's television show on NBC—*Coke Time with Eddie Fisher.* Dan and Cyd also brush by Frank

Sinatra as he stands next to a slot machine in the casino.

At MGM we were always on call, even when we weren't working on a film. When someone had an idea or needed an extra, we were told to report for work. I was often in the MGM short films that were produced to show in movie theaters with features. Typically, MGM management would inform you: "You're in a movie today. Here's the script. Go to wardrobe, hair, and makeup. Report to the soundstage when you're done." And we did.

Such was the life of a contract player—even for a major star like Frank Sinatra.

The Catered Affair

(MGM, 1956)

This was my first real dramatic role at MGM. After being taken off *The Actress*, I wonder if I was cast in this film because of my increased popularity as one of "America's Sweethearts." No matter. It was a great part with a terrific cast.

I was happy for the opportunity to work with Ernest Borgnine, Bette Davis, and Barry Fitzgerald in this story about a family in conflict over their daughter's wedding. The only trouble was the director. Richard

Brooks didn't want me. He called me "Little Miss Hollywood" and made no attempt to hide his disdain for me.

Every day Richard was rude to me. Bette noticed and took me into her dressing room. "He's a prick," she said. She told me that if I needed someone to talk to, or help in any way, to come to her.

Brooks's abuse didn't sit well with the rest of the cast or crew either, and they found ways to show their support for me. Once he slapped me across the face in front of everyone. I don't know what I'd done to anger him that time. I was always professional. As he lifted his arm to wallop me again, the assistant director, Hank Moonjean, stepped in front of me to stop him. Later that day, a camera "accidentally" ran over Richard's foot, breaking it. He was in obvious pain. Everyone took their time removing the heavy piece of equipment.

There was no reason that I could see for Richard to treat me the way he did. I was just a young girl. Like my character, I was engaged to be married. I'd been told that he was a very good director, yet he was so difficult with me.

Bette Davis and Ernie Borgnine play my parents. They took extra time to coach me for my scenes, rehearsing with me to make sure I was doing well. They taught me to be as natural as possible. I learned so much from them. Sometimes Bette would call me into her dressing room and say, "I think you're overplaying this. Just do it easy and relaxed." Ernie would say the same thing: "Just play it naturally." Richard would say, "Do it any way, your way. You're not doing it my way, so I don't care."

Bette always referred to me as "Daughter," her booming voice caressing those two syllables as only she could. She was happy to share her tricks and technique. We became lifelong friends. I adored her. Ernie also became my friend for life.

When I wasn't being coached by Bette or Ernie, I "sat about" with Barry Fitzgerald, who plays my favorite uncle. What a thrill it was to spend every day with my quirky and fantastic pal Barry. Knowing how keen I was on doing impressions, he taught me how to imitate him—by pushing out my lower lip and wheezing in a lilting Irish brogue, with eyes twinkling. When I did my impression of him on my 2011 United Kingdom tour, it brought the house down every time I mentioned his name.

Finally there was Rod Taylor, who is so wonderful as my fiancé. I've always felt that he was underrated as an actor.

I'm very proud of the work we did in this movie. The National Board of Review voted *The Catered*

Affair one of the year's best films in 1956. They also gave me their Best Supporting Actress Award. Except for my problems with Richard Brooks, I have only happy memories of making it.

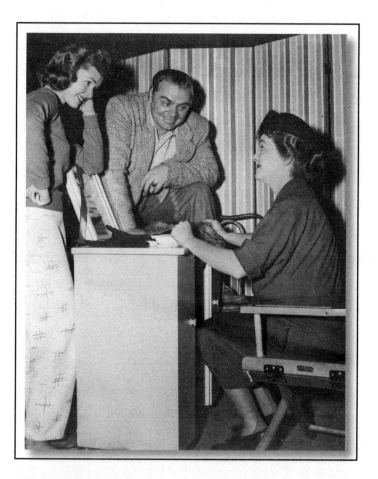

With Ernest Borgnine and Bette Davis during
The Catered Affair. They taught me so much, and
became my lifelong friends. *Licensed by Warner Bros.*
Entertainment Inc. All rights reserved

With "Uncle Barry" Fitzgerald during *The Catered Affair*.

Dressed as Barry Fitzgerald for a CBS comedy special with Frank Gorshin. Barry taught me how to impersonate him.

Bundle of Joy

(RKO, 1956)

Let's just say this sweet movie about a shopgirl mistaken for the mother of an abandoned baby was another difficult shoot, without the benefit of great talents like Bette Davis and Ernie Borgnine to help me. I was pregnant with my daughter, Carrie, which made it necessary for me to be shot behind counters, holding the baby in front of me, or in a big fur coat. I managed to do the dance numbers, although in most of the scenes I'm shot over someone's shoulder or from behind.

My husband was cast as the son of the owner of the department store where my character works. Eddie was very ambitious. He expected to follow in Frank Sinatra's footsteps as a crooner who made a name for himself as an actor. Eddie had everything but Frank's talent and experience.

Eddie needed a strong director, but unfortunately Norman Taurog was in the early stages of Alzheimer's. No one knew anything about the disease in those days, so we just coped with his unexplained memory losses and constant repeated instructions. Eddie wasn't a trained actor and didn't want to admit that he was a beginner. And he hated being wrong. So he blamed me whenever he made mistakes. I coached Eddie, but sometimes his arrogance got in the way of his art. We fought a lot.

One day while driving to the studio we were having a particularly heated argument about the little gold cross I wore on a necklace. We'd had this fight on other occasions. Eddie's manager, Milton Blackstone, once said he thought my wearing this symbol of my Christianity conveyed that I hated Jews. Come again? I explained to Milton—and to Eddie, who was present—that I didn't hate people of the Jewish faith or any other faith. And besides, Jesus was a Jew. Now Eddie had brought it up again on our ride to work. I got so mad, I told him to pull over and let me out of the car. It was early in the morning in Hollywood. I watched Eddie drive away, then walked the remaining two or three blocks to the studio gate.

If you adore this movie, I'm happy that you can't see the chaos that was on the other side of the camera. The best things about making it were the baby and singing "Lullaby in Blue" with Eddie.

Tammy and the Bachelor

(UNIVERSAL, 1957)

Jacques Mapes was a set designer at MGM when I started there. He worked on *Singin' in the Rain*, although I believe we became friends before that. Jacques's partner was Ross Hunter, the producer on *Tammy and the Bachelor.* Jacques and Ross used to come to dinner at my family's place on Evergreen Avenue in Burbank. Mother would make enchiladas and tacos that she served on paper plates. We all shared many happy moments in the little house that Daddy built for us with a loan from the FHA. When Ross began work on *Tammy,* Jacques told him that I would be perfect for the title role. I believe he was right. Tammy was a perfect part for me. As a Texas girl who'd relocated to Burbank, I felt that I was very much like this girl from the bayou transplanted to a different way of life.

Tammy and the Bachelor was released after *Bundle of Joy,* but production was completed before I began work on my film with Mr. Fisher. During the filming, I was already pregnant with Carrie, but I wasn't showing yet, so no special setups were required.

I didn't need any coaching for this part. Tammy and I were kindred spirits. Much as I loved my character, though, I had a lot of trouble with the Bachelor, who is played by Leslie Nielsen. Leslie was very gifted, but fancied himself a method actor. His heroes were James Dean, Marlon Brando, and other members of the Actors Studio, like Paul Newman. Newman had come to Hollywood, become a big star, then returned to the East Coast to do serious theater work. Leslie wanted to do the same.

The fact is, most of the time Leslie was a pill to work with. I always thought he would be great at comedy if he would just relax and play for laughs. How ironic that, decades later, he became one of our most beloved comedic actors with his hit *Airplane!* and the *Naked Gun* movies. Serious Leslie would never have expected to be famous for a silly line like "Don't call me Shirley."

Working with Leslie wasn't the only challenge on *Tammy.* I also had to deal with a goat and Walter Brennan.

The goat and I worked very closely. She was certainly more fun than Leslie. I had to learn to milk her for our scenes together. I cut my nails so I wouldn't hurt her udders. Once I got the hang of it, we got along pretty well. The goat just stood there chewing her cud. Her expression reminded me of Walter Brennan.

Walter plays my grandfather on the bayou. In one scene, I noticed that he wasn't looking at me while we talked. After we finished the take, I asked him where he'd been looking.

"Your ear," he replied.

"Why?" I asked in surprise.

"Because that way more of my face is on camera. Don't look at the other actors. Look in three-quarters, so your face is more prominent. Stick with me. I'll teach you some tricks."

And Walter did teach me. He shared his bag of tricks for how to make the most of a scene.

Walter was one of the greatest scene-stealers I've ever known—in the major leagues along with Thelma Ritter and Walter Matthau. You couldn't turn your back on any one of them. It's hard to rank them; they were all superb at their craft. I'd say it was a three-way tie for who could get the most out of their camera time.

In one of the most touching scenes in the movie, I recite the family history to a group of party guests, a very long speech. I tell the story of how I became the mistress of the house after showing up at the door selling fresh eggs. When the young gentleman who owned the plantation answered, I won his heart. We lived there happily ever after.

My single of Ray Evans and Jay Livingston's song "Tammy" became a big hit and earned me a gold record. The song was in the Top 40 for twenty-three weeks, five of them at number one. It was nominated for an Academy Award as Best Song, but lost to "All the Way" from *The Joker Is Wild*. Everyone was thrilled for me except my husband, who felt threatened by my having a hit record. Since I'm an actress, not a recording artist, I couldn't understand his jealousy.

The success of the single also saved the movie. My recording wasn't released until after the film had failed at the box office. When the song was a hit, Universal rereleased the movie and it made millions.

In early 1958, I was asked to sing "Tammy" at the Academy Awards. I agreed to do this even though my son, Todd, was only a month old. As I mentioned earlier, Mike Todd, Eddie's best friend, was killed in a plane crash just a few days before the ceremony. I was also very close to Mike, and this tragedy almost kept me from performing. But somehow I got through it. I went to the show, sang, and went home, too upset for the festive mood at the Oscars.

People often ask me why I didn't play Tammy in the two sequels. Ross Hunter did ask me to reprise my role, but by then I was pregnant with Todd and the studio couldn't wait for his arrival. So they cast Sandra Dee for *Tammy Tell Me True*. Sandra was fine, but I felt that this decision wasn't the best, that the audience deserved to continue their relationship with Tammy having the same actor in the role. As it turned out, if Universal had waited, I would have been filming during the biggest scandal of the 1950s, when Eddie left me for Elizabeth Taylor, which would have been great for the

Leslie Nielsen, the goat, and me. I got along all right with the goat. Leslie had a problem. *Photofest*

Universal publicity department, if not for me. But it wasn't meant to be.

This film is very dear to me. I've identified with Tammy ever since I first met her. Girls copied the ponytail hairstyle designed for me in the movie, and many parents named their baby daughters Tammy or Debbie. I've met thousands of them over the years, which always makes me happy. For the past four decades, I've closed my nightclub act with "Tammy." So far, the audiences and I still love to hear it.

This Happy Feeling

(UNIVERSAL, 1958)

After the great success of *Tammy and the Bachelor*, Ross Hunter borrowed me again from MGM for this comedy about the romantic confusions surrounding a retired actor who may be returning to the stage. Unfortunately, it isn't one of my more memorable works. The script is funny because Blake Edwards was so funny and creative. I admire everything he's written. He was so talented, one of a kind. It was so much fun doing his scenes.

European Curt Jurgens was cast as the actor and my older love interest. Chemistry is everything, and Curt and I together simply don't have any onscreen. Offscreen he was lovely to me. Once Curt invited me to his home in Holmby Hills for dinner. It was like going to Versailles. Curt was a kind, gifted man, and I was privileged to know him.

The Mating Game

(MGM, 1959)

A lot went on during the making of this movie, and some of it actually had to do with the movie. This was my first film after the Eddie-Debbie-Elizabeth incident. My life was a whirlwind. When I wasn't fighting off the paparazzi in my front yard hoping to capture a picture of me with my two kids, one under three and the other just a few months old, I was enduring daily headlines begging me to "let Eddie and Elizabeth be happy." In the midst of all that, I was doing a movie about a Maryland farm family under siege from the IRS for not paying their taxes. To say I was overloaded would be an understatement. I was a busy lady.

Despite that plot description, *The Mating Game* is a comedy. Paul Douglas plays my father and Una Merkel my mother, a part she played more than once with me. The adorable Tony Randall is the IRS auditor whose calculations almost cost us the farm.

There was a lot of strenuous activity in this shoot, including an opening scene I share with a seven-hundred-pound hog. I roughhoused with the other kids and practiced twirling a rope for a scene where I tie up Tony in our living room. At the end, Tony and I are so happy together that we jump from the second floor of the barn into a haystack. I kept flying out the barn window and waiting in the hay for Tony, who was clinging to the wooden window frame, terrified. I jumped at least three or four times, never to be followed. Finally the stage managers shoved Tony out of the loft window after me. New Yorkers!

Tony was a delight during the making of this film. Like Leslie Nielsen, he was a classically trained actor from the East and very interested in doing serious roles. And here he was, stuck in a barnyard with the world's most famous jilted wife. Unlike Leslie at that time, Tony had a great sense of humor.

Tony loved singing opera. He would break into song as soon as the director yelled, "Cut!" favoring everyone with one of his beloved arias. The two of us had dressing room trailers that shared a common wall. Once, during a break, I was in my trailer going over my lines for our next scene, balancing one or both children on my lap and occasionally glancing at my picture on the front page of the newspaper. Suddenly, the trailer started moving up and down—*thump, thump, thump*—almost like a rhythmical earthquake. From the neighboring trailer I heard Tony's baritone in full throttle. The thumping and the singing seemed to be connected.

Finally I couldn't take any more. I decided to pay Tony a visit. As I approached Tony's trailer, I could see it moving in time with the loud *thumps*. Throwing open his door, I was stunned to find Tony jumping up and down on the couch in his dressing room, singing at the top of his lungs, stark naked. I was momentarily taken aback by the size of Tony's equipment. His voice wasn't the only huge thing in the room.

Tony ignored me completely. He continued to sing, thump, and swing. I'm not surprised that he was able to sire children well into his old age. He must have packed quite a wallop with that thing. Smiling, I went

I had my hands full when my sweet babies visited me on the set of *The Mating Game. Photofest*

back to my trailer, my lines, and my kids. You had to love a guy who got so thrilled by nude opera jumping. Tony and I remained friends until he died. His talent was only outdone by his sweetness.

Please don't assume that all I thought about was the size of everyone's manhood just because I've told you about Tony Randall and Bob Fosse. In Hollywood, it's something of a preoccupation. In my day, Milton Berle was said to be the biggest. When challenged in a contest, Milton would supposedly take out just enough to win. Personally, I didn't care how large it was—"Big Miltie" was still attached to Uncle Miltie.

It Started With a Kiss

(MGM, 1959)

I was glad to leave the country and go on location to shoot this comedy. I wouldn't have to read Hedda Hopper telling her readers that I was still standing in the way of Eddie and Elizabeth's happiness because I wouldn't give him a quickie divorce.

My costar is Glenn Ford, who plays a newlywed air force sergeant whose wife, a fashion model, joins him in Spain and brings along the custom-made car he unknowingly won in a raffle.

Eva Gabor plays a Spanish royal. We became good friends while working together on this picture. Eva wanted me to meet her fiancé at the time, a gentleman named Mr. Brown. I went back to the hotel with Eva, where we found him soaking in the bathtub. I didn't know we were walking into the bathroom. After my episode with Tony Randall, you'd think I would have learned to knock. "Don't get up," I said quickly, in case he was too polite to stay seated when meeting a lady.

One day Glenn Ford and I were rehearsing our lines, and he decided that I was kissable and came at me. I ran—round and round the room several times,

A quiet moment with Glenn Ford in *It Started With a Kiss*, when he wasn't chasing me. The car went on to be used as the Batmobile in the 1960s TV series *Batman*. *Licensed by Warner Bros. Entertainment Inc. All rights reserved*

until I got tired. Finally I stopped. And he crashed into me, knocking me down.

We both started laughing.

"Stop chasing me," I said. "I'm not going to bed with you, so get over it. We'll work on our lines, but nothing else."

Glenn was always on the make for me. At the time, he was going through a rough divorce with Eleanor Powell. We had divorce in common, but I was not interested in him as a lover. We became friends, and I adored him.

I had to learn my way around a bullring for this movie. It was a fun shoot, mostly uneventful aside from dodging the bull—and Glenn Ford.

Say One for Me

(20TH CENTURY FOX, 1959)

My breakup with Eddie turned out to be a boon to MGM. Suddenly all the other studios wanted me, which meant MGM just had to decide who to lend me out to and how much to charge. Somehow my salary didn't increase much. But I didn't mind as long as I was working.

Before I met Eddie, I was deeply in love with Robert Wagner, and making this movie so soon after my marriage dissolved was a real heartache for me. RJ had moved on and so had I, but being around him reminded me of my fantasy life. Well, RJ wasn't interested, so get over it, Debbie. RJ had to dance in the movie and worked hard to get his positions right. Mostly I kept to myself, though I still have a crush on RJ to this day. There is no one more terrific.

Bing Crosby was a very big star when we made this film, as well as one of the most successful recording artists of all time. His version of "White Christmas" was the biggest-selling single of that era. Bing liked to record at six in the morning when his voice was low. He wouldn't even warm up.

Bing was then married to Kathy Crosby, his second wife, an actress and singer who performed under the name Kathryn Grant. They gave parties where I met people like the great baseball manager Leo Durocher, whom I wouldn't otherwise have expected to meet.

Many years later, my charity, the Thalians, planned to honor Bing, Bob Hope, and Dorothy Lamour, who had starred together in the seven popular "Road" comedies (*Road to Singapore, Road to Zanzibar, Road to Morocco, Road to Utopia, Road to Rio, Road to Bali,* and *The Road to Hong Kong*). Everyone told me that I'd have trouble getting Bing to come to accept his award. Bob Hope teased me that I would never get him to agree to it. So I decided to call Bing. In those days you could go directly to anyone, even the biggest stars. You didn't have to go through their agent or manager or hairdresser like you do now—if you can even get them on the line.

I was then appearing on Broadway in *Irene*, and Bing was on vacation in Scotland, playing golf. Just as I was going onstage, I got word that he was on the line. Long-distance phone calls weren't as easy to place then as they are now, so of course I took the call. They held the curtain until I finished. When I asked Bing to be our honoree, he agreed, but only if he could accept the award before dinner. He didn't want to wait around all night to receive it. I agreed to his simple request.

"I've got to go hit my balls," he said and hung up.

I think he was talking about golf, although with a five-hour time difference in Scotland, it would have been the middle of the night.

I once overheard Bing on the phone, when we were making *Say One for Me*, telling the person at the other end to "go ahead and fire him, but don't let him know it came from me." I think he was talking about our director; I'm not sure to this day. Bing was tough, but he could also be generous. That same year I recorded my first album, *Debbie*, and Bing was kind enough to give me the following quote for the record sleeve:

Someone recently said, and with reasonable accuracy
I would think, that good singers make good actors.

Evidence in support of this belief is available in the recent performances of Sinatra and Martin, for instance, but I would like to put forth also the proposition that the reverse is quite true: good actors make good singers. Assuming they can carry a tune. We all know that Debbie is better than a good actress—she's VERY good, and we all know she can sing with a lilt and a listenable quality that's genuinely pleasant and agreeable. Witness "Tammy." It was small surprise to me then that when I listened to this beautiful album she has etched for Dot, I found myself captivated and enchanted. Quite obviously Debbie had spent a great deal of time selecting the songs to be included, because she's made them her own, and invested them with a sincerity that's inescapable—of contrasting moods to be sure, but the moods are there, and to me, mighty effective. And that, *mes amis*, is artistry.

Thank you, Bing.

The Gazebo

(MGM, 1959)

Back to MGM for another fun film with Glenn Ford, this one a black comedy about a TV writer-director (Glenn), his Broadway musical star wife (me), blackmail, and murder. Carl Reiner plays a detective trying to find out what is buried under the gazebo in our backyard. Although Carl is one of the funniest people alive, he told me that he didn't think he had a future in acting and was going to New York to work on a screenplay. I encouraged him to make that choice.

When he returned to Los Angeles, he gave me the script he had written, called *The Thrill of It All.* I gave it to Ross Hunter, with my recommendation that he make the picture, which Ross did. The movie stars Doris Day and James Garner. Of course, Carl would have gotten it made and become the brilliant success that he is without my help, but I was happy to play a small part.

Glenn Ford and I continued our nonromantic friendship, which lasted until his death in 2006. His son, Peter, took care of him when he was in bad health. For years Glenn was too ill to get out of bed. I told Peter that he should paint naked breasts on the ceiling so Glenn would have something pleasant to look at. He didn't take my advice.

The Rat Race

(PARAMOUNT, 1960)

The Rat Race was a departure from my usual musical comedies. I play a dance hall girl/model who becomes involved with a musician, played by Tony

Curtis. The film was shot in New York. To prepare for my role, I spent time in establishments where young ladies danced with men for money. I was staying by myself and felt very lonely, and I was far outside my comfort zone.

Don Rickles plays an abusive club owner. He was so scared about doing well and worked hard to be good. I reassured him whenever I could. One day I bought him a teddy bear as a gift. He was just the opposite of his onstage comic persona. He couldn't have been sweeter or more willing to learn, and he is wonderful in the film.

Tony Curtis was married to my good friend Janet Leigh at this time. Tony was a smart actor, fast with his saxophonist character, and always good to work with. I think we did a good job on this movie.

Pepe

(COLUMBIA, 1960)

I made this movie as a favor to the director George Sidney, who was then married to my friend and MGM coach, Lillian Burns Sidney. The Mexican star Cantinflas plays a young man whose horse is sold to a Hollywood star. He encounters many other stars on his way to retrieve it. I'm one of them. Cantinflas and I do a complicated dance number that he worked very hard to do well.

I'd finally divorced Eddie in 1959 and was now dating the heir to a large fortune from a chain of shoe stores. Harry Karl was very distinguished and made a big play for me, doing everything he could think of to sweep me off my feet. On our first date, we'd gone to the ballet to see *Swan Lake*. Harry gave me diamond earrings and a matching pearl-and-diamond pin made in the shape of swans. He showered Carrie and Todd with gifts and attention. He represented security for my family, and I was planning to marry him.

Lillian thought this was a bad idea, which she let me know at the hotel pool one afternoon. The pool was four feet deep across the length of it, which was good because Lillian wasn't much over four feet tall, and I'm just over five feet myself. Lillian pointed out that Harry's track record wasn't good. He'd married his last wife, actress Marie McDonald, twice. His marriage to another wife lasted less than a month. Lillian warned that Harry might love me, but he loved gambling more.

I told her that I wanted a father for my children, both under five years old, and that I believed Harry would be a good provider. Since I refused her marital advice, Lillian advised me to make sure I got a bigger engagement ring than the one he gave Marie McDonald.

Frank Sinatra had tried to get me to reconsider marrying Eddie when we were making *The Tender Trap*, and now Lillian Sidney put up a red flag about Harry. When I lost everything except my memorabilia collection because of Harry Karl, I sold an apartment I had bought in Century City as an investment to Cantinflas, who had become a good friend. At least I listened to Lillian about the engagement ring, which I lost when we had to sell everything in our divorce settlement.

But those sad events were still to come. By the end of that summer of 1960, it was clear that Harry and I would get married. And shortly after that, I started work on a movie with another older gentleman.

The Pleasure of His Company

(PARAMOUNT, 1961)

I remember calling Fred Astaire on the phone to urge him to take top billing in this movie about a young girl who is about to be married, even though that was originally my credit. I respected him so much, that was the only way it could be done. After a few minutes of listening to me insist, he said, "All right, Debbie, if that's what you want." I think he was happy to get off the phone.

Tab Hunter plays my fiancé. Tab and I had been friends since we were teenagers. The studios used to put us together for premieres and publicity occasions. One night in my parents' kitchen in Burbank, Tab tried to kiss me good-bye. I told him not to. I thought it would be like kissing my brother. And I was right—Tab is like my brother. It was the early 1950s; there was no discussion about being gay back then. But I knew that Tab was, and that I felt friendship for him, not romance. I got the sense that he felt the same about me. We always laughed and had fun when we were together. Tab's a wonderful man who's married to another wonderful man now. I'm glad we've been friends for so long.

Fred Astaire plays my father, and we do a little waltz at the wedding reception. I was so nervous, dancing with the great Fred Astaire. What was I going to do?

"You don't have to dance," he told me. "Just stay with me. Move with me. Follow me and trust me."

So I did—I put my trust in the best. And it was like dancing on air, a complete joy. I felt as light as a feather. Fred had his hand on my back. He had very long fingers. His figure was lean, athletic, and beautiful, even at the age of sixty.

Dancing with Fred Astaire in *The Pleasure of His Company*. Fred was the sweetest, most gentle of men. I adored every moment with him. *Photofest*

He really was the sweetest man I've ever known. If I'd thought he would go for a younger girl, I might have made a move. Instead, I danced with him, thinking what a great pleasure it was to be in his company.

The Second Time Around

(20TH CENTURY FOX, 1961)

Although this movie was actually made before *The Pleasure of His Company*, when Harry was still courting me, it was released afterward. I play a widow who moves her young family from New York to the wild Arizona territory in the early 1900s and ends up becoming sheriff. Thelma Ritter plays the owner of the ranch where my character lives.

Like Walter Brennan, Thelma was a terrific scene-stealer. In one scene, she had no dialogue at all; she was just positioned behind me, hammering nails into a shoe. As I delivered my lines downstage of Thelma, I could hear her literally spitting nails. Her mouth was full of them. She was pounding and spitting, totally upstaging my action.

I asked her to stop.

"What's the matter?" she responded. "Can't ya compete?"

"Not with that, Thelma," I admitted.

She agreed to stop, but it didn't matter. Even quiet, Thelma is still the most prominent thing in that scene. She was a master.

Andy Griffith plays my leading man. At one point, he had to ride to Thelma's ranch, where she and I were waiting for him on her porch. Andy rode in, this big man bouncing along, howling with every step his horse made—"Son of a bitch! Ouch! Owwww!"—until he finally came to a stop in front of the porch, slipped, and fell off the horse.

Thelma and I had to bite our tongues to keep from laughing.

Someone from the crew took Andy to get protection for his male parts, which were taking a beating.

The second take didn't fare much better: Andy kept bouncing and screaming and slipping off the horse, while Thelma and I stood on the porch laughing, no longer able to control ourselves. By the end of the fourth take, Andy was in so much pain, but we finally had the shot—which lasts only a few seconds on the screen.

Juliet Prowse, a celebrated dancer who was a contract player at Fox at that time, plays one of the townspeople. She was then having an affair with Frank Sinatra, who had asked her to marry him, but also to give up her career. Juliet was unwilling to do this. I felt compelled to say something to her.

"Marry Frank," I advised Juliet. "He's a wonderful man. At the end of a year he'll want you to go back to work because you'll drive him so crazy dancing around the house."

Juliet didn't see it that way and broke the engagement.

I gave the wrap party for the cast and got everyone gifts. I raided the Fox prop shop for Andy and found a real, stuffed palomino. I gave it to him with a card that read, "A little something you can practice on." Andy loved it.

He loved it so much that he loaded it onto the top of his station wagon when he decided to leave the party. By then he'd had a few drinks. On the drive home, he was pulled over by the highway patrol, who inquired as to where he thought he was going with this horse—unusual even by California standards. Andy told the cops that the horse was his friend. If Roy Rogers could stuff Trigger, Andy should be able to travel around with his pet horse. Miraculously, the police let him move on. After that, Andy would take his new friend with him to parties.

How the West Was Won

(MGM, 1963)

While I was making *The Second Time Around*, Henry Hathaway called to invite me to lunch. So my first encounter with Henry was in the Fox commissary. Before I went, I asked several of my friends, including

Glenn Ford, about him. They warned me that Henry was the toughest director, especially in the way he treated women.

Henry was a tall, silver-haired man, with a weathered look; his gruffness was hidden at first by his polite manners. He began by explaining the part in his film that he wanted me to do: a seventeen-year-old crossing America with her pioneer parents to find a better life in the West. Flattered that he thought I could play seventeen when I was in my late twenties, I still turned him down. I was working on *The Second Time Around* and knew that there would be other projects after I finished shooting that. Henry couldn't believe it when I told him no and insisted on knowing why. So I told him that I'd heard about his reputation, and he blew up—proving my point while denying it—and informed me that I *would* do the part. It seemed that I had no choice. But I made him agree to treat me well and not scream at me. He insisted (at the top of his voice) that he never yelled. Time would tell.

I didn't see him again until I reported to our first location, in Paducah, Kentucky, in May 1961. Henry welcomed me by yelling that I needed to get ready immediately to shoot a scene. When I returned in hair, makeup, and costume, he ordered me to walk "from that hill over there and look out there." I asked him what the scene was about. He told me to just do what he'd said. So I did, and he seemed happy.

A few days later, Henry came at me, screaming and swearing, in the middle of filming.

"Please don't yell at me, Mr. Hathaway," I said. "I'll faint."

He kept yelling.

I closed my eyes and hit the dirt.

Everybody rushed to help me. I just lay there, limp.

Henry was livid, screaming that I was faking. As three crew members carried me off, Henry realized he was about to miss his shot, which required the sunset.

Finally he apologized, still insisting that I was faking. This had remarkable healing powers. I "awoke" from my fainting spell and finished the scene.

The next day he repeated his performance, yelling at me as though nothing had changed, and I repeated mine. "Stop this!" he demanded as I dropped to the ground. But this time he laughed when the two words "I apologize" once again had their magic effect.

After that, we got along well together. I'd say, "I'm going to faint, Mr. Hathaway," and he'd calm down. Henry wasn't used to ladies who stood up to him.

Originally, I was only supposed to be in the first part of the movie, my story ending when my family perishes crossing the rapids. But Henry wound up liking me so much that he kept writing extra scenes into the film for me. By the time we were done, I had aged from seventeen to ninety, taking my character all the way to California and the end of the movie. By then I was crazy about Henry too.

Henry really knew his shots and how he wanted them to look. He wouldn't let the actors use stunt doubles, although we were assisted by unseen stuntmen when it was necessary. As a result, we were often in real physical danger. Two stuntmen drowned shooting a rapids scene in Oregon meant to match the scene that Thelma Ritter and I almost drowned in. Another lost his leg in a train chase near the end of the movie.

In one scene, Thelma and I are in a covered wagon during a stampede caused by an Indian raid. Six horses pull our wagon, galloping faster and faster. Thelma has the reins and is clutching them as hard as she can, cursing a blue streak while I cling to the wagon frame beside her, terrified. Any viewer who can read lips will be treated to her choice profanity as we race onscreen across the ground toward the ravine. We don't have any actual dialogue, but Thelma is swearing throughout the whole furious chase. Although you can't see it in the finished film, we're headed toward the Dallas Divide in the Black Canyon near Telluride, Colorado.

The wranglers wanted to stop the horses before we went over the cliff, but Henry refused to let them—until the very last second. And then the wranglers had to use every ounce of force they could command. It was a harrowing experience, way too close for comfort. But Henry got what he wanted.

This was a big job for everyone who worked on the film. Being on location together for so many months really helped us to bond. My friendships with Agnes Moorehead, Thelma Ritter, and Carroll Baker became even closer than they had been, and those with Jimmy Stewart, Robert Preston, and Gregory Peck were strengthened.

The work was hard, but it was worthwhile. The shoot lasted almost a year. *How the West Was Won* went on to receive Academy Award nominations for Best Picture, Best Art Direction, Best Color Cinematography, Best Color Costume Design, and Best Original Score, and to win Oscars for Best Writing (James R. Webb), Best Film Editing (Harold F. Kress), and Best Sound (Franklin Milton). It was shot in Cinerama using three cameras next to each other, which was hard for the actors because we always had to look at the camera instead of engaging with each other. The saga moves from western New York to the Pacific Ocean; it's nearly three hours long, and looks wonderful on the big screen—an epic film made by one of Hollywood's truly epic directors.

My Six Loves

(PARAMOUNT, 1963)

I finished *How the West Was Won* in March 1962. The next day I began working on *My Six Loves*. In this charming comedy, I play a Broadway star who goes on vacation only to find herself taking care of six abandoned children. At that time in my career, I had approval of the director. So I chose Gower Champion, and he didn't disappoint me on this project. He worked like a demon, knew the camera like crazy, and was a delight to be around. Many years later, Gower would save me by stepping in to direct my Broadway show *Irene.* I love his work.

We all had a good time on this shoot. My costar, Cliff Robertson, was a total gentleman who was respected by everyone. It tickled me that he spent more time in the makeup chair than I did. The cast included Alice Pearce, who'd been brought to Hollywood from Broadway by Gene Kelly to reprise her role in the film of *On the Town* and who went on to win an Emmy for her role as the nosy neighbor in the hit series *Bewitched.* Everyone got along well and had a lot of laughs.

David Janssen, who had been in the service with my brother, Bill, was another dear friend who worked on this film. David was a tortured soul. His mother had been a chorus girl in Los Angeles who had an affair with Clark Gable, and David was convinced that Gable was his real father. There certainly was a resemblance. It was a big issue for David. I believe it contributed to his alcohol abuse, which may have led to his early death.

During the shoot, I was pregnant with my third child, my first with Harry Karl. When we finished filming, Harry and I went to Europe for a combined business trip and vacation. In Rome, I felt the baby stop moving. It dropped down about three inches. I knew immediately that I had lost this child. When I got home, my fears were confirmed. Abortion was illegal, and a cesarean section would have impaired my health, so I had to carry the dead fetus until it either aborted itself or was stillborn.

I was in my seventh month and wound up carrying the baby to term. People would say, "You look wonderful. What are you going to name the baby?" And I'd answer with a broken heart, "I haven't decided yet," knowing that the baby was already gone. Devastated, I asked Harry to handle the baby's burial. I couldn't bear to know any more about our lost child. Even though this was heartbreaking, we still hoped to have more children.

Mary, Mary

(WARNER BROTHERS, 1963)

In the fall of 1962, I was signed to do the movie version of Jean Kerr's hit Broadway comedy *Mary, Mary*, about a recently divorced couple forced to spend time together by an IRS tax audit in a blizzard. But it wasn't until months later that I read the script. When I did, I was overcome by insecurity. I went to Jack Warner and told him I couldn't do it. He wasn't having any of it.

"I'm not good enough," I insisted. "I'm not right for the part."

He reminded me that he was paying me $350,000—a far cry from the $60 a week I'd been getting when my career started.

"You think I'd waste all that dough on you if I didn't think you could do it? I *know* what you can do!"

Maybe if I hadn't been married to the then very rich Harry Karl, hoping to have more children and not really needing to work, I wouldn't have thought twice about it. Or maybe it had something to do with the fact that stars from the Broadway cast were also doing the movie—except for Barbara Bel Geddes, who'd been nominated for a Tony Award for playing Mary. I kept telling myself that I didn't have the proper training, that I just did cute and adorable, that I wasn't serious. You'd think that George Cukor, Bette Davis, Ernest Borgnine, and John Gielgud having told me I was good would have sunk in, but apparently it hadn't.

I went to my friend Lillian Sidney and asked her to coach me. She'd been indispensable to Louis B. Mayer and worked with so many MGM greats, and I knew that she wouldn't go easy on me. When she agreed, I finally felt that I'd be able to do it. After that, Lillian worked with me on most of my film roles.

Our producer-director was Mervyn LeRoy, who was a very famous and powerful man in Hollywood. He was on the Hollywood Museum board as well as many other show business committees and associations. He was similar to Mike Todd—rough around the edges of his strong personality. Mervyn was at the end of his directing career and spent a lot of time on the phone in his little office on the soundstage. We couldn't get him to come out of that room to do a take. When he did, he'd interrupt shooting to go off to his little toilet—just like Marjorie Main on *Mr. Imperium*. I didn't understand this behavior when I was young. Now that I'm eighty, I have more sympathy.

My part required me to smoke. Michael Rennie, the elegant British actor, plays a jaded movie star who shows up the day after the storm. He was kind enough to teach me, lighting my cigarettes with his gold lighter and coughing with me between setups. It took me many years after that to quit smoking. I didn't start again until I was going through my second divorce.

Barbara Bel Geddes had been so good in the stage version. Her voice went up at the end of every sentence. You may notice that I do that trick in the movie. It was my tribute to her, although I doubt that she would have recognized it.

The Unsinkable Molly Brown

(MGM, 1964)

I first saw The Unsinkable Molly Brown on Broadway with the original cast: Tammy Grimes as Molly and Harve Presnell as her husband, Johnny Brown. I knew immediately that I could play Molly and lobbied for the film role as soon as I could. When I contacted the producer, Larry Weingarten, he told me that the director, Chuck Walters, wanted Shirley MacLaine for Molly. That would have required Shirley to be released from her contract with producer Hal Wallis at Fox, whereas I was already under contract at MGM. I offered to test for the part. They refused. In desperation, I offered to work for free. They still refused.

Resigned, I created a nightclub act, to reinvent myself until good movie roles came along. In 1962 my friend and accompanist Rudy Render had been to a run-through of Mitzi Gaynor's club act and was so impressed that he urged me to do my own. The Sands in Las Vegas had offered me an engagement, but I was always busy with the children or making movies. Harry knew the lawyer at the Riviera Hotel, Sidney Korshak. He got in touch with Sidney, and I was booked for my first Vegas gig.

In the beginning of 1963, I was pregnant again. After the painful episode the year before, I was excited to be having another child. The baby was due at the end of the summer. We set the Vegas opening for March, so I could take time off before the baby arrived.

My nightclub act was a huge success. When I returned to Los Angeles, I was surprised to receive a phone call from my agent, Al Melnick, telling me that Hal Wallis would not release Shirley from her Fox contract to do *Molly Brown* and MGM had offered me the part—although for a lot less than my usual fee, probably because I'd said I would do it for nothing.

Even so, I was thrilled. Shirley would have been great, but I knew that she would continue to get wonderful roles. She was much more respected as an actress than I was. I was still thought of by many people as "cute," or "the kid," which is hard to maintain after you hit thirty. Cute can be the kiss of death for a movie career.

My next hurdle came from Chuck Walters. We'd worked well together when he directed me in *The Tender Trap,* but he said he wanted to meet with me before we signed the *Molly Brown* contract. He came to see me at home, which made me wary. After some small talk, he asked me to turn down Molly Brown, saying that I was "too short" for the part. This absurd statement reminded me of a story I'd heard about Helen Hayes being flattered by producers, then told she was too short to play Queen Victoria in *Victoria Regina.* Hayes countered with the question, "How short is the part?" and was hired. Hayes was known as the First Lady of the Theater, and her Queen Victoria was one of her most famous roles. There was no way I wasn't going to play Molly after all I had been through to get the part. I recounted the story to Chuck, who laughed and dropped the subject. I had waited years to use that line.

Filming was set to begin in October 1963, after the new baby's due date. In late May, Harry and I decided to go on vacation. While we were in Europe, the same thing happened that had happened with my earlier pregnancy. We rushed home, and I was admitted to St. Joseph's Hospital in Burbank. Once again my baby was pronounced dead, but this time I refused to carry it to term. Labor was induced by flooding my system with drugs to make my body reject the fetus. The pain was excruciating. The experience left me depleted and emotionally devastated.

I began to prepare for *Molly Brown* in earnest, rebuilding my health with hormone and vitamin shots, until I was finally able to join the production. Meanwhile, Lillian Sidney worked with me on every line and its underlying emotion.

We shot the first scenes in Colorado, of Molly as a young girl. Since I was still carrying some of my pregnancy weight, it gave my character the look of a sturdy youth. By the time Molly matured into a Denver society woman, I had lost the weight and looked more like the sophisticated lady Molly wanted to be.

Harve Presnell reprised his role as Johnny from the Broadway production. I wanted my friend Agnes Moorehead to play the part of the Grand Duchess, but Chuck insisted on casting the British actress Martita Hunt. Angela Lansbury's mother, Moyna Macgill, was cast as one of the European aristocrats.

Martita Hunt was a stitch. Her high, mannered voice perfectly suits her part. Martita enjoyed her liquor straight, without any ice. As her drink was being poured, she would say, "Follow the finger," and slide it up the side of the glass until she had a full tumbler of scotch or whatever hard liquor she was drinking.

One afternoon we were filming the staircase scene where Molly Brown introduces her noble European friends to Denver society. Each person is announced and comes down the stairs to join the receiving line at the bottom. Martita came back from lunch a bit over-served that day. On the first take, she wavered and fell down the stairs. She gamely got up, rearranged her tiara, and tried again—with similar results. The decision was made to put her in a harness that could be attached to wires and guided from above.

The stagehands put a leather belt around Martita's waist, under her white satin gown, and cut a slit for the hook to which they would fasten the guide wire. Martita was then suspended at the top of the staircase like a fish on the end of a line, and lowered down the stairs to get the shot. This worked beautifully. As she neared the bottom, Harve Presnell ran over to take her hand and guided Martita the rest of the way.

In the dance number "He's My Friend," Martita puts her foot out to trip one of the guests. When the guest hits her foot, Martita almost spins off her chair. She was a great lady and lots of fun.

Another English actor, Hermione Baddeley, plays Buttercup. All the British actors would come to the parties at her house on Mulholland Drive and have a grand old time. They really knew how to coochie-coo.

But it wasn't all fun and games on this shoot. By the time we returned from Colorado, Chuck Walters could see in the dailies that I wasn't "too short for the part" and actually began to help me with my performance, which I greatly appreciated. MGM was putting all its resources into *Doctor Zhivago* at the same time we were filming *Molly Brown*. They'd cut at least $1 million from our budget, and we were running out of money to complete the picture.

Chuck suggested that we cut "He's My Friend," a bear of a dance number that would take days to film. The cast had been rehearsing it while I was doing other scenes. To save the number, we decided that we would use more than one camera, to reduce the shooting time. I went into an intense few days of rehearsal to catch up with the cast, who were weeks ahead of me.

Somehow we managed to pull off the entire scene in one day. At the end of the number, we all do somersaults, ending in standing position in front of the Grand Duchess's chair. If you watch closely, you can see me wobble. I don't know where I got the strength to even pull myself up, but I knew we didn't have the time or money to reshoot the scene. When we were done, two of the dancers collapsed in exhaustion. It was worth it, though. It's a great number. Peter Gennaro's choreography really captures the essence of the film.

On November 22, my musical director, Rudy Render, called the set while we were filming, to tell me that President Kennedy had been shot in Dallas. We stopped everything and listened to the radio, to find out that the worst had happened. The president had been killed. Everyone was devastated. It didn't seem

Dancing in the "He's My Friend" number. MGM wanted us to cut it to save money. So we shot it in one day, which almost killed all of us. But we did it! *Licensed by Warner Bros. Entertainment Inc. All rights reserved*

real. I was fortunate to have met John F. Kennedy. He was very supportive of my Hollywood museum project. His death was a great loss to the country.

The Unsinkable Molly Brown was released in June 1964 and did very good business. The film was nominated for many awards. In addition to a Golden Globe nomination, I was nominated for the Oscar as Best Actress. I'm very proud of this, even though I lost the award to Julie Andrews for her performance in *Mary Poppins. My Fair Lady* deservedly won most of the Oscars that year.

Molly Brown is my favorite of all the roles I've played. I love something about almost every part I've done, but I identified with Molly as soon as I met her. In the sometimes blurry line between art and real life, Molly is the woman I've become as the years have passed. I'm right there with her when she declares, "I ain't down yet!" Molly Brown and I have spent a lot of time together. I'm very proud of this film and all the hard work that everyone did to make it a success.

Goodbye Charlie

(20TH CENTURY FOX, 1964)

Lillian Sidney didn't want me to do this film about a playboy who is murdered by a jealous husband and comes back to life in the body of a woman—me—then gets murdered again and comes back as a Great Dane. She felt it was a one-joke story. Lillian was still my coach, and I respected her opinion. But after my hard work on location in *Molly Brown,* I was happy to do a lighter film at home. Also, my brother, Bill, needed another film to complete his seven-year apprenticeship as a makeup artist. *Goodbye Charlie* gave him the extra time on set he needed to get into the union.

Once again, I was able to choose my director, and I wanted to work with Vincente Minnelli. Vincente had done some of MGM's most important films (including *Meet Me in St. Louis, An American in Paris, Lust for Life,* and *Gigi,* to name just a few). I was excited about the prospect of working with him. But Vincente was past his prime. In his early sixties, he was forgetful and repeated himself. He may have had the beginnings of Alzheimer's. One day he spent several hours arranging black bobby pins on a black couch. He had great difficulty helping us understand what he wanted in a scene.

Tony Curtis plays Charlie's best friend. One scene takes place in the kitchen of Tony's house, with me fixing breakfast for us, after I've convinced him that I'm Charlie. I'm more at home on a soundstage than in a kitchen, so Daddy built me a replica of the kitchen where I could rehearse with my props. This might not sound important, but when you're doing a scene, handling the props needs to look natural and come across as the character's second nature. I had a lot of practice with pots, pans, coffeemakers, and utensils, so I could look real with things most people use every day. The scene was very funny when it was finished. I'm always glad when I have time to prepare.

As the jealous husband who murders Charlie, Walter Matthau was a challenge to work with. He took the part where he wanted to go with it. I wouldn't say that he was a method actor, but rather an actor with his own method. He stole every scene that he was in. You either ran to keep up or the camera was going to be on him, because he was terribly funny and very clever. He loved to do accents, probably because he excelled at them. Walter was such a powerful presence, and shameless about rewriting lines to suit his character. He went off script often, which made him hard to follow. I always try to stay on script, even though I love to improvise, because the writers deserve respect for the work they've done. Sometimes changes are necessary, but for the most part I always follow the screenwriter's plan.

In one scene, Walter and I were doing comedic dialogue when he went totally off the script into a story that only he knew. All of a sudden he picked me up, threw me over his shoulder, and twirled me around. The entire crew applauded, but not because of Walter's routine. They saw my exposed buttocks covered only by panty hose—I wasn't wearing panties because I didn't want a panty line. Today I would laugh, but then I was so embarrassed that I turned red and ran for my dressing room, cursing Walter with every step. We didn't reshoot the scene, and Walter's improv isn't in the finished film. But somewhere somebody has a copy of that footage.

Tony Curtis was good to work with again. He was always prepared, always knew his lines, and was especially good at comedy. At that time I didn't realize that Tony had been telling people around town that my marriage to Eddie Fisher broke up because I was a lesbian and a lousy lay. I'm not a lesbian. I may have been a lousy lay, but Eddie was my first love. It would have been nice if he had taken the time to show me what to do to make him happy. Obviously, Eddie felt the need to blame our failed marriage on me. But of all the things he could have said about me, I was surprised to hear this rumor. When I finally learned about it, I confronted Tony.

"That's what Eddie told me," he said.

"You're going to believe Eddie," I said, "who divorced me and left me for Elizabeth?"

Tony said something like "Well, I'm sorry if it upsets you, but that's what Eddie said to me. And Eddie's my friend."

In other words, I wasn't.

I guess everyone chooses sides in a divorce, and Tony had chosen Eddie's.

There was such a backlash from most people against Eddie when he left me and our children for Elizabeth that he spent the rest of his life being the bad guy. But Eddie had earned that title, and I was sorry that Tony spread his lies.

The Singing Nun

(MGM, 1966)

After the huge success of *Molly Brown,* I was offered a lot of films. I accepted *The Singing Nun* because it gave me the opportunity to stay in Los Angeles with the children. I also got to work with Greer Garson, my dear friend Agnes Moorehead, and Ricardo Montalban. A lot of big stars dressed in habits for this movie.

I play the title character, Sister Ann. The story is loosely based on the life of a French nun named Soeur Sourire, or Sister Smile, who had a worldwide hit record with her song "Dominique."

Greer Garson plays the mother superior of the convent. It wasn't a big role, but she wanted to do it. Greer had won the Academy Award for Best Actress for the 1942 movie *Mrs. Miniver.* (She was famous for giving the longest acceptance speech in Oscar history.) But television was taking over the entertainment business, and movie parts were becoming scarce for aging actors, even for Academy Award winners.

Greer was British, with a fabulous voice. Everyone catered to her on the set. We served tea every day. We didn't have big trailers, so we redecorated a small trailer in her favorite color, blue. The furniture was reupholstered, and there were always fresh flowers in her room.

I'd been in awe of Greer when I was a new contract player at MGM and she was one of the biggest stars. Her English background was obvious when you went to her Bel Air home for afternoon tea. She had a very grand manner but didn't act like she was above everyone. She taught me how to be gracious. To the end of her life, she was charming and always adorable to me. I loved working with her.

Hayes Goetz, a coproducer, was kind enough to schedule my scenes so I had Wednesday afternoons off to go to Girl Scout meetings with Carrie. I felt that I was giving my daughter some stability and good values by involving her in the Scouts. I thought I was doing the right thing. Now Carrie says she hated it. Our Scout troop was a group of girls who came from very privileged homes. We sometimes went camping with troops from poorer neighborhoods in Los Angeles. We'd go on Harold Lloyd's estate, where he let us use acres of green grass for our activities. One Christmas Mrs. Lloyd invited all of us into the house for cookies and lemonade. There were Christmas decorations everywhere and a tree that had to be thirty feet high. The girls from both troops thought they were in a museum.

The Singing Nun was moderately successful at the box office. Soeur Sourire insisted that the movie was fiction. Unfortunately, her real life was much more difficult than what we portrayed in our version.

Divorce American Style

(COLUMBIA, 1967)

When Norman Lear called me early in 1966 to tell me about a movie he'd written about a divorce, my own marriage to Harry Karl was having problems. We were less intimate. It took me several interviews to get this role. Every time I went in to talk with Norman, who was also directing the film, he lowered his offer. Finally we agreed on a price that was much lower than my usual rate. Norman was very serious, which isn't uncommon for some comics. He put his wife, Frances, in charge of the wardrobe. I don't know where she spent the money because we all look like we're in off-the-rack clothes from J. C. Penney. Bob Mackie was her assistant. As I recall, she wasn't very nice to him, and no one is nicer or more talented than Bob.

The best part of this movie for me was the weekends. During the week Dick Van Dyke, Jason Robards, and I worked like mad, but when we were done on Friday, my security guard, Zinc, would drive us to my beach house in Malibu. We'd drink and sing and laugh all night. Jason would sing along to the soundtrack from *Mame*. He was a happy drunk. I don't know if his wife, Betty Bacall, appreciated his drinking songs, but I found him the most entertaining company. Lucky Betty, to be married to Bogie and then Jason. What wonderful men. When the party was over, Zinc was available to drive anyone home.

In the movie, the couple who divorce go through some mishaps and then get back together. Harry and I got as far as the mishaps. It seemed we weren't aging well together. Neither has this movie, but at least it got some good reviews.

How Sweet It Is!

(NATIONAL GENERAL, 1968)

In a way, this comedy about an American couple in Paris trying to resist temptations was as true off the screen as on it. Lots of film people have on-set affairs and romances, but I must say that this was the only time I was attracted to someone in the cast. One of the men my character encounters in Paris is played by the gorgeous French actor Maurice Ronet, who really did it for me. Even if I had ideas about Monsieur Ronet, though, I wouldn't have acted on them, because I was still married to Harry Karl. Although we were having problems, I was still committed to my husband. Besides, Maurice was gay, and I wasn't Elizabeth Taylor! Leave it to me to have two strikes before anything even could get started.

This was a fun film to make. I spent a lot of time in a turquoise bikini. In one scene, producer Garry Marshall wanted me to be nude in bed with James Garner, who plays my husband. I refused to be completely naked. I argued with Garry, who finally let me do the scene wearing panties and pasties. James was supposed to be nude also, but he kept his shorts on the whole time. As the scene started, James was to turn toward me and give me a kiss. Sounds simple enough. Then I heard "Action," followed by an oddly familiar buzzing noise. Jim had decided to play a joke on me during our love scene. He'd brought a huge vibrator to bed with him. I rolled over and grabbed it out of his hand. I swear it felt like a baseball bat. And I used it like one, chasing and clobbering Jim with it—while still dressed in pasties and panties.

Jim would come to our house for parties. He'd make small talk with everyone and then go into my son's room and play slot cars with Todd while Harry and I and the other grown-ups were partying in the living room. He's a sweet friend.

Our director, Jerry Paris, was funnier than anyone I ever worked with. He was always kidding. He went on to be a very successful television director of hit series, including *Happy Days, The Mary Tyler Moore Show, The Odd Couple,* and two of Dick Van Dyke's series. He's probably best known for his portrayal of Jerry Halpern, the dentist on *The Dick Van Dyke Show.* Jerry was sweet to everyone and so well liked. He had a short life and will be forever missed.

Jerry's closest friend was Garry Marshall, who wrote and produced the film along with Jerry Belson. There's nobody like Garry—one of the great comedy minds and the greatest friend you could ever want. He is luckily married to a true doll, Barbara. He's a loving husband and friend.

What's the Matter with Helen?

(UNITED ARTISTS, 1971)

In the summer of 1970, Curtis Harrington came to me with a book called *Best of Friends,* about two ladies in the 1930s who move to Hollywood from a rural town, hoping for a fresh start after their sons are convicted of murder and imprisoned. The complex story examines the lives of these women, one an overweight psychopath and the other a dancing teacher. Curtis was known for his edgy horror movies; in 1963 *Time* magazine called him "Poe with a megaphone" for his film *Night Tide.* I loved the book he showed me, and when a deal with NBC requiring them to bankroll two movies for me made it possible, I decided to do it. The script included musical numbers, which also appealed to me.

Otto Preminger had just made a movie called *Such Good Friends,* based on a best-selling novel of the same name, so we couldn't use our book's title. Since Henry Farrell, our scriptwriter, had done the screenplay for the huge hit *Whatever Happened to Baby Jane?* it was decided that we would try to capitalize on the connection by calling our movie *What's the Matter with Helen?* I hated this.

I play the dance teacher, Adele, and Shelley Winters was cast as her troubled friend, Helen, who turns out to be a murdering crazy woman. And that's what Shelley became—every minute of the shoot. Shelley was a method actress. I had no problem with that, having worked with many actors who follow the teachings of Lee Strasberg's Actors Studio. But whatever your school of acting, you don't have to be nuts to play nuts. Shirley terrorized the entire cast and crew. She thrived on all her craziness and made everyone's life miserable.

Even before filming began, Shelley got into terrible fights with Morton Haack, our very talented costume designer, who'd done such beautiful work on *Molly Brown.* One day during a fitting, Shelley screamed at Morton that he was trying to make her look fat while making me look thin—I was down to 104 pounds, which worked for my character. Morton reminded Shelley that she *was* fat, which Shelley in her saner moments admitted, usually when stating that she was going on a diet (which she never managed to do). Furious, Shelley ripped off all her clothes, stomped out of the fitting room stark naked, and left the set. She refused to wear anything that Morton designed for her after that. Shelley so soured Morton on working with actors that he quit the movie, returned to London, and never made another picture.

Shelley was irrational about every detail in the film. She wouldn't show up on time, so I offered to pick her

up on my way to work. It was a tense few months of
production, which almost caused me to have a break-
down. I hyperventilated at one point, but fortunately
was fine the next day.

Because of my deal with NBC, I was an uncredited
producer on *What's the Matter with Helen?* I was also
taking no salary, thinking that if the movie turned
out to be successful, the money would come in later.
Shelley's behavior did nothing to endear her to me, and
after three weeks I decided to fire her. But the cost of
reshooting her scenes with another actress would have
put us way over budget. So we had to keep her, even
though Geraldine Page was ready to step in.

But Shelley didn't make it easy. In one of the last
scenes of the movie, her character goes into a jealous rage because my character is getting married. To
prevent me from leaving, Shelley stabs me to death. I
told the prop masters to get rid of all the real knives so
Shelley couldn't actually do me in. I couldn't risk her
slicing me up just to stay in character.

Dennis Weaver plays my love interest and was a
total delight. He was also a great kisser, even better
than Frank Sinatra. Since my marriage to Harry Karl
was breaking up and I wasn't getting any sex at home,
I thoroughly enjoyed my love scenes with Dennis.
He couldn't have realized how much I liked making

out with him, as he was happily married and wasn't a player. I remember him fondly to this day.

When filming was finally completed, I vowed never to speak to Shelley again, but I couldn't keep my promise. I'd known her for so many years. At the wrap party, everyone reminisced about memorable moments from the shoot. I enjoyed reminding Shelley about her insane antics. She protested that she'd never ripped doors off their hinges, made hysterical scenes, or acted like a maniac; that I was making it all up. Only when the crew gleefully chimed in, "Yeah, Shelley, you really did that," did she acknowledge that just maybe she might have been a wee bit out of line.

Shelley was never easy to take as a friend, even when we weren't working together. Hugh O'Brian once escorted me to a party in Malibu that Shelley also attended. When we went into the living room, there was Shelley, with her full skirt spread out, covering two young men who were servicing her. Hugh and I left immediately, not wishing to spend time around Shelley's doubleheader.

What's the Matter with Helen? didn't do well at the box office, but I think it's one of my better performances. I just hated making it. I hated working on a project that I believed in with a temperamental actress who made life miserable. Cuckoo and crazy—that's what was the matter with Shelley! Still, in spite of all the difficulties, I love the finished film.

Little did I realize it would be my last appearance in a starring role for quite some time. My next part was also a lead—but you never see my face in the movie.

Charlotte's Web

(PARAMOUNT, 1973)

I got this movie thanks to Lillian Sidney. She was having dinner with Richard Sherman, the younger half of the Sherman Brothers songwriting team. He told Lillian that he hadn't yet settled on an actress to do the voice of Charlotte in the animated film of E. B. White's classic children's book about a barnyard spider who befriends a piglet doomed for slaughter.

"Stop looking," Lillian said. "Debbie would be perfect."

Even though I'm not crazy about spiders in real life, I love Charlotte, so I was happy to read for Richard and his older brother, Robert. As we worked in the studio, I kept reading more scenes. Finally I just said, "Why don't you just use this? I can finish it today."

They agreed, and together we did it that day. They were such a talented team. In 1965, I'd had the honor of presenting Robert and Richard with an Academy

Award for their song "Chim Chim Cher-ee" from *Mary Poppins.* I was late getting to that awards show because Sydney Guilaroff spent three hours doing my hair. We arrived at the Santa Monica Civic Auditorium just as the doors were closing. A few minutes after I presented the Sherman Brothers with their Oscar, Julie Andrews won her Best Actress Award for the same film. My children were happy when Mary Poppins won instead of their mother, because they enjoyed Julie's movie so much.

Charlotte is a very special part for me, and I'm happy that children continue to enjoy this version of her story to this day.

That's Entertainment!

(MGM, 1974)

MGM's decision in 1970 to get rid of all their expendable things—including musical charts, tapes, and unused film scenes—caused a lot of us to worry about saving our history for future generations and was the reason I began my collection. My friend Jack Haley Jr. was an avid collector and film historian who also bought costumes and other items at the MGM auction. *That's Entertainment!* was filmed on the lot that I had tried to buy from MGM to establish a theme park like Walt Disney's.

What a spectacular love letter to film history this movie is! With care, knowledge, and passion, Jack manages to tell the story of MGM's musical films from the 1920s to the 1950s, with tributes from their stars still living at the time, in one great film celebrating the studio's fiftieth anniversary. Few people who grew up in the 1950s and '60s had ever seen a Busby Berkeley number or the old classics. In 1974 there were no home videotape machines or cable TV. If you didn't catch one of these jewels on the late night movie, you missed decades of brilliant films that were made by some of our best artists. In a stroke of genius, Jack introduced Eleanor Powell, Fred Astaire, Gene Kelly, and so many other MGM giants to a whole new audience. I believe the resurgence of interest in *Singin' in the Rain* came from Jack's use of the great musical numbers from the film in *That's Entertainment!* My favorite number features Fred Astaire and Eleanor Powell in *Broadway Melody of 1940,* tap-dancing to "Begin the Beguine." It doesn't get any better than perfection.

At the time *That's Entertainment!* was made, I was performing on Broadway in *Irene,* so my part was shot in my dressing room at the Minskoff Theatre. When the movie opened, I was on hiatus from *Irene* and was able to attend the premiere in Westwood, near the UCLA campus. MGM stars of every era filled the theater. Fred Astaire attended with his sister, Adele, his original dancing partner. At the party afterward, everyone was thrilled when they went onstage to dance.

With my dear friend Jack Haley Jr. He appreciated the value of film history, and *That's Entertainment!* renewed interest in musicals like *Singin' in the Rain*. Jack was also a memorabilia collector who worked with me on several attempts to create a Hollywood museum. I adored him. *Licensed by Warner Bros. Entertainment Inc. All rights reserved*

Suddenly a very drunk Donald O'Connor scrambled after them and inserted himself into their routine.

Edie Wasserman, the wife of Universal Studios' president, Lew Wasserman, grabbed me, insisting, "Debbie, you've got to stop this."

"Stop what?" I said. "I can't stop Donald O'Connor from dancing."

"We want to see Fred dance with Adele. You've got to go up there and stop Donald."

Taking a deep breath, I stood up, climbed onstage, and moved behind Donald. Grabbing his shoulder, I spun him around and tried to dance with him. He hauled back to punch me, missing me by inches.

Jack Haley was the first to reach us, followed by two big men who picked Donald up and carried him down the stairs, out the back door, and onto Wilshire Boulevard, where they put him in his limo.

I returned to my seat, upset and embarrassed to be part of this scene, and left shortly after Fred and Adele finished their dance, still shaking. I had never been that close to a fistfight—and with one of my best pals!

It took a long time for Donald to forgive me. He said that I was wrong to interfere, that he'd wanted to dance with Fred and Adele. Eventually he admitted that he had been in a great mood because he had downed an entire bottle of Scotch.

That's Entertainment, Part 2

(MGM, 1976)

That's Entertainment, Part 2 is narrated by Gene Kelly and Fred Astaire. They do special numbers together as they introduce the many musical selections. The film built on Jack Haley Jr.'s devotion to film.

Dan Melnick replaced Jackie as the producer. The numbers in this sequel are wonderful, but it's hard to top the first one. Even though the movie was well received, it wasn't as successful as the original. Still, it's a continuation of the great history of the MGM years we all love. And who can resist Kelly and Astaire, especially when they're dancing together?

A year had passed between *Charlotte's Web* and *That's Entertainment!* It was another two years before *That's Entertainment, Part 2* was released. My last contract with MGM ended in 1973. By then, the old Hollywood studio system was a thing of the past. Harry Karl and I had also divorced around the same time. I devoted the next years to raising my family and touring to earn enough money to support us and pay off Harry's gambling debts. By 1981, I was finally able to start saving again. In February 1983, I was back on Broadway, replacing Raquel Welch as the star of *Woman of the Year*. Carrie was a few blocks away, starring in *Agnes of God*. Later that year I taped a television special pairing stars with cars in Reno, Nevada, and met Richard Hamlett at a party. We married in 1984. You already know how that turned out. I'll just say that it was a while before you saw much of me onscreen again. Here's what I remember about those films.

Kiki's Delivery Service

(STUDIO GHIBLI, 1989)

I was a voice actor for a very minor role in this animated Japanese film that was later dubbed into English. It's about a young witch who runs an air courier service, my first film work of any kind in fifteen years. Movie musicals had long since gone away, and parts for middle-aged musical stars were nonexistent. Thankfully, I had my stage work to fall back on. Many actors my age just stopped working.

Richard and I were still together, I thought happily. My next appearance was a cameo in a hit film released the same year that we bought the hotel and my beautiful granddaughter was born.

The Bodyguard

(WARNER BROTHERS, 1992)

This was Whitney Houston's film debut, about the life of a hugely successful pop singer, and was very much tailored to her talents. In addition to playing her bodyguard, Kevin Costner was a producer. He asked me to appear as myself in a scene on the red carpet outside the Academy Awards.

The shoot took a day and was very easy and pleasant. I met Kevin's parents, who were visiting the set that day. They were so sweet and reminded me of my parents. I also briefly met Whitney Houston, who was so nice to me. Who knew that we would lose her all too soon? She had the voice of an angel sent from God.

Kevin sent me a beautiful bouquet of flowers afterward. You can't teach people class. You either have it or you don't. Kevin has it—as did Whitney, who also had beauty and grace.

Heaven & Earth

(WARNER BROTHERS, 1993)

I made *Heaven & Earth* while I was still involved in the excitement of redoing my hotel to get it ready to open to the public. I was very surprised when Oliver Stone considered me for the part of Tommy Lee Jones's mother in this final film of his Vietnam trilogy. I went to meet him in his Venice Beach office. Oliver is not a traditional member of show business society. He produces and directs his own movies, in his own way, and is so gifted and creative that his movies are terribly successful. He creates waves. I thought it was a privilege to be considered for this film.

When I met Oliver, I asked him to come over and stand by me so I could give him a hug, as if he were my son. I was surprised that he did it, sort of with a smile on his face.

"Well, you are sweet," I said, patting his face. "I thought I would be afraid of you, but I'm not. Now you can sit down, dear, you're perfect for the director."

Oliver looked at me as if I weren't real, then said, "Well, I guess you're to be the mother."

We talked about the character, how she had gray hair and a Southern accent. I told him that I was from Texas, so that would work.

"I agree with you," he said. "You've got the part."

I spent a lot of time in the background during the three-week shoot. I wanted this to be a different kind of role for me, which it was. The gray wig completely changed my look.

It's a serious story about the struggles of a Vietnamese village girl during and after the war. Everyone on the set was so serious. In one scene, Tommy Lee and I had to put something in a car trunk. I climbed into the trunk and closed the lid, knocking on the inside as if I couldn't get out. When Tommy Lee opened the lid, I smiled and said, "Hi, there!"

"You're really something, Debbie," he said. "You're really funny."

I was so happy to finally get a laugh out of him.

I really enjoyed working with Tommy Lee. He's a brilliant actor who can do anything. He has a very winning personality.

When the film was edited, Oliver called me and said he hoped I wouldn't be upset, but most of my part was cut because the film was too long. I wasn't upset at all. I had a great time working with these wonderful talents. Tommy Lee and Oliver were very kind to me, and it was an honor for me to perform in an Oliver Stone film.

A few years later, Carrie and I were staying at a hotel in Santa Monica called Shutters. We were walking on the beach and passed Oliver, who was carrying his little child on his shoulders. I said hello, but Oliver didn't acknowledge me. He just walked right on, in his own world, happy and not wanting to be disturbed. He heard me but he didn't hear me. I understand that, and I totally respect it. Sometimes, as an artist, you don't open that door that keeps you safe from the outside world.

That's Entertainment! III

(MGM, 1994)

In the middle of my increasing troubles at the hotel, I was asked to do this third installment of *That's*

Entertainment! Jack Haley Jr. was no longer involved. The movie was made to capitalize on his success with the first *That's Entertainment!* and I find this a very commercial picture. The producers went to the MGM vaults and found every dance number or fun scene that hadn't been used in the first two installments in the series.

This included my solo performance of "You Are My Lucky Star" that had been cut from *Singin' in the Rain*—and rightly so, because it wasn't up to the quality of the rest of the movie. The song was in a key too high for me. It's fun to watch, but certainly has more of a place in *That's Entertainment! III* than in *Singin' in the Rain.*

Mother

(PARAMOUNT, 1996)

This was the first starring role offered to me in a long time. Still, the decision to do *Mother* was a difficult one. My hotel was in trouble, and I felt that leaving to go on location in Los Angeles could cause more problems. But at Carrie's insistence, I met with Albert Brooks, and he gave me the job on the spot.

Albert knew exactly how he wanted me to play the character he'd written. Right before filming began, though, my stomach ruptured. My X-rays looked like I'd been drinking Drano instead of champagne. Albert was patient with me when I reported to work only a few days after getting out of the hospital. He's a brilliant writer and producer and a great guy, and I worked hard to keep up with him. I'll always appreciate his patience during the shoot. (For a complete account, see chapter 11.)

This movie continues to be one of my favorites. I'm very proud of the work we all did together.

Wedding Bell Blues

(CINEPLEX ODEON FILMS, 1997)

My main involvement in *Wedding Bell Blues* was providing the location for this romantic comedy about three girls who visit Las Vegas to find husbands and land at my hotel just off the Strip. The details were handled by my son, Todd. They filmed me performing in my Star Theater, but that's my only scene with the girls. I hope they had no idea that everything was falling apart around me.

This was during a very low point in my life. I was under great stress and barely alive. As the three girls in the movie were looking for husbands in Vegas, I was fighting for my life by getting rid of mine.

In & Out

(PARAMOUNT, 1997)

By the time I made *In & Out*, Richard was gone from the hotel but not my life. He continued to cause problems for me from the other side of the country.

Scott Rudin, a coproducer of *In & Out*, and Herb Nanas (his partner on *Mother*) recommended me for this role as Kevin Kline's mother. After I met with the director, Frank Oz, in New York City, they gave me the part.

In spite of some artistic differences I had with Mr. Oz, which we worked out, the film was a delight because the cast was so superb. For the complete story, see chapter 12.

Fear and Loathing in Las Vegas

(RHINO FILMS/SUMMIT ENTERTAINMENT, 1998)

I guess you can say that I snuck into this movie based on Hunter S. Thompson's book *Fear and Loathing in Las Vegas: A Savage Journey to the Heart of the American Dream*. When hipsters Johnny Depp and Benicio Del Toro drive up to a hotel in Las Vegas in a drug-induced haze, my picture is on the marquee as the entertainment. They decide to check out my show.

"That's a hot chick," Johnny says as he gets out of the convertible and looks at my poster. Inside, he leans against my picture by the showroom and you hear someone singing.

It *could* be me.

I've never met Johnny, but I'm tickled that he says I'm hot in Terry Gilliam's fantasy movie. Thank you, Johnny. He is one of my favorite actors. When he was learning sword fighting for one of the *Pirates of the Caribbean* movies, he and his coaches rented space in my North Hollywood dance studio for rehearsals. I was on the road, but was told that Johnny was delightful and polite to everyone who worked there. I was so disappointed that I didn't get to see him. He's just wonderful. I'm glad we're in a film together, even if I wasn't there— which sounds like my romantic life in a nutshell.

Zack and Reba

(ITASCA PICTURES, 1998)

In this dark story about teenagers and young people who have issues with departed loved ones, I play the grandmother of a young man whose wife has died. In an attempt to stay close to her, he carries her skeleton around with him. He becomes romantically involved with a young lady whose fiancé has just committed suicide.

My character reminded me of an older Molly Brown, but with bad wardrobe and hair. In the film, I shoot at birds from my bedroom window in the wonderful Victorian house that was our set in the Salt Lake City location.

There aren't a lot of good things to say about this movie other than that I loved working with Michael Jeter, who was so funny and delightful. Brittany Murphy was dear, but I didn't have many scenes with her. The most challenging part was working with my fictional grandson, played by Sean Patrick Flanery, who was difficult for me to reach. He seemed to want to be James Dean, but he wouldn't rehearse our scenes with me. James Dean always worked hard and studied with many teachers.

All in all, my difficulties working with Sean were completely overshadowed by my joy in being around Michael Jeter and the lovely director, Nicole Bettauer. They at least provided a little relief from the disaster with the hotel.

Rudolph the Red-Nosed Reindeer: The Movie
(LEGACY RELEASING, 1998)

Another animated film, this one about Santa's popu-lar reindeer with a shiny red nose. I do the voices of

Blitzen's wife and Rudolph's mother, Mitzi, as well as Mrs. Claus and Mrs. Prancer.

Rugrats in Paris: The Movie
(PARAMOUNT, 2000)

Again, as a voice actor, I have little to report, other than I was delighted to be part of this lovely film about the popular Rugrats characters. My hotel was gone, I'd divorced Richard, and I had hopes for building a permanent museum for my Hollywood memorabilia collection.

And who wouldn't want to play someone named Lulu Pickles?

My next three films were made during the period when most of my acting work was in television in *Will & Grace, These Old Broads,* and the Disney Channel series *Halloweentown.* If you're wondering why I haven't mentioned that series before, it's because it was all work and no good stories.

Connie and Carla
(SPYGLASS ENTERTAINMENT, 2004)

Two ladies who share a love for musical theater witness a mob hit, which causes them to hide out in Los Angeles as drag queens. I was cast as one of the Hollywood idols the girls use as inspiration, performing some numbers with a bevy of drag artists called the "Belles of the Ball."

Basically playing my stage persona, I enjoyed making this picture. My only trouble was with one line. I had to tell Nia Vardalos and Toni Collette that I was ready to do my act: "I've got sheet music, gorgeous gowns, and a great underwire bra." For some reason, I couldn't get this line out. It took many takes until I could say it correctly. "Sheet" was sometimes "shit." This embarrassed me horribly, even though everyone was good to me during our work together. Other takes were ruined when the girls started to giggle because they could tell I was going up on my line.

Our director, Michael Lambert, was so nice to me, saying I was a great broad in spite of my "off" afternoon with that damn line.

During breaks in filming the nightclub scenes, I entertained everyone with sing-alongs while we waited for the next setup. My favorite was "Thing Be."

First I got everyone to practice singing "Thing be"—over and over.

The audience in the nightclub scene sang, "Thing be. Thing be."

As they continued their chorus, I sang: "The color of her hair is a fiery, fiery red."

("Thing be. Thing be.")

"Oh, the color of her hair is red."

("Thing be. Thing be.")

"The color of her hair is a fiery, fiery red."

("Thing be. Thing be.")

"So what color would her . . ."

("Thing be. Thing be.")

You can see this in the DVD extras. It was a fun shoot.

Light of Olympia

(SANTOON PRODUCTION, 2008)

Yet another film where I'm a voice actor.

I adore doing voice-overs. You can be creative and yet feel free as an actor. You're on your own, so to speak. I especially love accents. At the very least, I look for an unusual-sounding voice for the character I'm portraying. It's really fun. Just like in *Singin' in the Rain*, voice acting gives me a "glorious feeling."

One for the Money

(LIONSGATE, 2012)

In this movie based on Janet Evanovich's first Stephanie Plum mystery from the popular series, I play Jersey girl Stephanie's grandmother. I had to do an accent that wasn't too broad (like a New Yorker's) but still made you think you were near the Turnpike.

During the weeklong shoot in Pittsburgh, I got to work on a small but fun part, which is the kind I like at this stage of my life. My memory isn't what it was in the 1950s, when I could memorize whole pages of dialogue in one sitting. Now I have to keep a little card in my hand for reassurance. Also, the director needs to know my limitations. Julie Anne Robinson was wonderful, letting me read over my material just before the scene, then calling "Action" when she saw I was ready.

It's been difficult adjusting to the way movies are made now. They are so much faster at lighting, sound, and staging than they were when I was at MGM. I'm working to keep up. I was happy to play this feisty lady who supports her granddaughter's antics, and Katherine Heigl was a delight, as was the fantastic actress Debra Monk, who plays my daughter.

Behind the Candelabra
(WARNER BROTHERS, 2013)

I made *Behind the Candelabra* a year after the auction that broke my heart and saved my life. I was thrilled to be offered this part in a movie with a major director and big stars.

Liberace and his family were friends of mine for many years. Lee (as he was known) was a superbly talented man whose private life remained relatively secret until the AIDS crisis in the 1980s. When I was asked to play the part of Lee's mother in Steven Soderbergh's film based on Scott Thorson's book *Behind the Candelabra: My Life with Liberace,* I was happy for the chance to play someone I knew so well.

Lee and his mother lived next door to each other. He had a slot machine installed in the living room of her Vegas house, and Frances was always at it. To practice for my scenes with the machine, I put together a big box and my mother's old-fashioned meat grinder and worked on my lines while pulling the handle.

My first scene is with Matt Damon, who plays Lee's lover, Scott. Matt has the most beautiful blue eyes and was very patient as we went over our lines together.

Before filming began, Steven Soderbergh and I met at the Four Seasons Hotel in Beverly Hills. To prepare, I put on one of my mother's dresses, a gray wig, and a pair of glasses that would make any grandma happy, then waited for my new director in the bar of the hotel. When Steven came in, I waved to him. He probably thought I was an old hooker. He seemed a little surprised that I'd come in drag.

Once we sat down together, Steven let me do most of the talking, which I adored.

"Is this look all right for your film?" I asked him.

I wanted his approval for the character's appearance, which was a shocking transformation for me.

"It's fine," he said.

Steven is a man of few words.

We agreed that I should wear a prosthetic nose for the part, as Frances Liberace's features were much more prominent than mine. We talked at length about my friend and his mother.

Steven is a wonderful director. He is soft-spoken but observes everything. He's very knowledgeable about his shots, how he wants his scenes to play, and knows how to work with actors. I was thrilled to be directed by him. He's so calm and easy on the set, using positive energy and feedback. He makes everyone comfortable in their work because he knows what he wants.

My last scene is at the Hilton Hotel in Las Vegas. Sitting in the showroom where Lee performed for so many years, I had time to reminisce about my friend and the happy times we'd spent there. When all the news was full of reports that Lee was gay, I told people that I wasn't surprised. After all, I had taught him how to fly. When he was doing his act at the Hilton, Lee would enter from the back of the showroom and fly over the audience to the stage. But first he had to solve a problem: his feet remained behind him and he kept landing on his face. Lee's manager, Seymour

Heller, asked for my help. By then, I had mounted so many shows myself that I was considered an expert at handling technical glitches. Fixing Lee's entrance was simple. The rigging pitched him forward. Once that was corrected, Lee landed perfectly.

Watching Michael Douglas play Lee was a treat. He worked so hard perfecting Lee's smile and voice

I knew Frances Liberace. She and my mother-in-law, Mrs. Karl, had the same heritage. I felt close to being able to perform her personality quite well. I'm told that I did. I wanted an authentic look to play Lee's mother. She had heavy features and a thick accent. This is what I might look like wihout the face cream I've used for decades.

and mannerisms and did a superb job of re-creating Lee's difficult piano performance. Doing that scene many times had to be exhausting, but Michael never complained.

During a break in filming, Michael's lovely wife, Catherine Zeta-Jones, brought their children to my booth to introduce them to me. Dylan was twelve years old, and Carys was nine. I was so surprised and pleased when they started singing "Good Morning" from *Singin' in the Rain*. Naturally I joined in. These beautiful children who knew my work touched me deeply.

When we'd finished shooting, Steven announced that it was my last day so that people could say good-bye to me. I stood up and thanked everyone and offered to teach them an old vaudeville song. Then I led them in a chorus of "Thing Be"—just like I'd done on *Connie and Carla*. That always works well with a crowd and is a fun way to say good-bye.

Thank you for listening to my tales of the real—and the unreal—things that have happened to me. Now that we've reached the end of this story, I realize that I've seen a few endings before.

I caught the end of vaudeville when MGM sent seventeen-year-old Debbie on the road with Carleton Carpenter.

I witnessed the end of the studio system, and with it the end of the spectacular movie musicals produced by the great Louis B. Mayer, Arthur Freed, and Roger Edens, with directors like Gene Kelly, Vincente Minnelli, and George Cukor. Working with talents like Gower and Marge Champion, Donald O'Connor, Bob Fosse, Fred Astaire, and all my costars and friends at the studios. I cherish the memory of them all.

There were many who shared my love of Hollywood history. Jack Haley Jr., Mary Pickford, and other dear friends tried to save our memorabilia for future generations. Now strangers will have to carry on that mission.

For anyone who wants to become an actor today, the world is a very different place. The studios used to keep our secrets, protect us from the press, and choose our movie roles. They sent us on trips to every corner of the world. We met presidents and royalty. They educated us, dressed us, and gave us experiences few people have ever had. And in return for all this, we worked every day in a job that we loved—and got paid for doing it!

In many ways, my life has been like a fairy tale. I kissed a lot of frogs, but I got a prince and Princess Leia. After thrilling triumphs and some terrible setbacks, I'm still here.

I hope we all live happily ever after!

Acknowledgments

I wish to dedicate this book to my children, Carrie and Todd Fisher. Without their encouragement and loving support, along with my faith in God, I never would have managed to survive many of these heartbreaking moments in my life.

When I was offered the opportunity to do this book, I thought, Who could I ask to help me write this? Who would be funny, sincere, and honest? Who is a clever writer who also knows me? So I asked my good friend Dori Hannaway. I believe she's written a wonderful and funny book. I'm so thrilled she said yes. I send her my deepest thanks and appreciation for her work and friendship.

Donald Light, Jen Powers, and Margie Duncan— you have my gratitude. No one could have better friends. Thank you for all you do every day, not just when I'm writing a book.

Dan Strone, my literary agent at Trident Media—you have no equal. Thank you for all your hard work and insight at every stage of this journey.

Thank you, Rick Hersh, for introducing me to the amazing Mr. Strone.

Debbie and Dorian thank:

Kseniya Zaslavskaya of Trident Media, who helped make this project go as smoothly as possible.

To our fantastic editor at William Morrow, Jennifer Brehl, thanks for all your guidance and support.

Thanks also to the rest of the team at William Morrow: Susan Amster, Cindy Buck, Elissa Cohen, Lauren Cook, Michele Corallo, Karen Dziekonski, Cathy Felgar, Lynn Grady, Brian Grogan, Doug Jones, Tavia Kowalchuk, Emily Krump, Shelby Meizlik, Rachel Meyers, Michael Morrison, Mary Ann Petyak, Sharyn Rosenblum, Mary Schuck, Beth Silfin, Liate Stehlik, Mary Beth Thomas, and Nyamekye Waliyaya.

Thanks to Lorie Pagnozzi for her beautiful book design.

Special thanks to everyone who helped us by sharing their recollections: Theresa Dowling, Esq.; David

Rudich, Esq.; Rip Taylor; Fred Pierson; the late Hank Moonjean; John Bowab; Margie Duncan; Ruta Lee; Donald Light; Sandy Avchen; Phyllis Berkett; Nancy and Joe Kanter; Bootie Bell Chewning; Anne Russell; Bonnie Basso; and David Crabtree.

At the Academy of Motion Picture Arts and Sciences, thanks to Randy Habercamp, May Haduong, and Lawreen Loeser.

And thanks to the Academy's staff at the Margaret Herrick Library, especially Faye Thompson, Matt Severson, Stacey Behlmer, and Jenny Romero.

For their help with reading the manuscript and giving us their most welcome corrections and changes, thanks to Michael Miller, Donald Light, Jen Powers, Cary Fetman, Nikki Smith, Tom Wilson, Carol Hannaway, Ken Sweigart, John Snell, Dr. Joanne Steuer, John Hazelton, and Leonard Maltin.

Many people helped with the wonderful photographs: Julie Heath, Kim Paine, Leif Adams, Jeff Briggs, and Stan Taffel at the Warner Brothers Photo Archive; Ron Mandelbaum and Howard Mandelbaum at Photofest; Peter Kersten at Getty Images; Elisa Marquez at AP Photos; and Cindy Braun at the Paley Center for Media.

Thanks to Peter L. Skolnik, Esq.; Andy Howick; and Michael Orland for their help.

Special thanks to Tom Wilson. You are picture perfect! Your insight and knowledge were invaluable.

Thanks to John Sala, who is one degree of separation from everyone in Hollywood.

We thank Carol Hannaway for her beautiful cover design, her tireless work restoring Debbie's photographs, and her invaluable help with the photo insert.

Last but never least, we thank Patrick Merla for his keen editing and unrelenting support from the first page to the final pass. Patrick's skills and tenacity with every detail have helped make this book what it is. We couldn't have done it without him.

The Films of Debbie Reynolds

June Bride (Warner Brothers)
   Released October 29, 1948
   Starring Bette Davis and Robert Montgomery
   Directed by Bretaigne Windust
   Produced by Henry Blanke
   Written by Ranald MacDougall

The Daughter of Rosie O'Grady (Warner Brothers)
   Released April 29, 1950
   Starring June Haver and Gordon MacRae
   Directed by David Butler
   Written by Jack Rose and Melville Shavelson

Three Little Words (MGM)
   Released July 12, 1950
   Starring Fred Astaire and Red Skelton

Produced by Jack Cummings
Directed by Richard Thorpe
Written by George Wells

Two Weeks With Love (MGM)
Released November 10, 1950
Starring Jane Powell, Ricardo Montalban,
Louis Calhern, Ann Harding, and Debbie
Reynolds
Produced by Jack Cummings
Directed by Roy Rowland
Written by John Larkin and Dorothy Kingsley

Mr. Imperium (MGM)
Released March 2, 1951
Starring Lana Turner, Ezio Pinza, and Marjorie
Main
Produced by Edwin H. Knopf
Directed by Don Hartman
Written by Edwin H. Knopf and Don Hartman

Singin' in the Rain (MGM)
Released March 27, 1952
Starring Gene Kelly, Donald O'Connor, Jean
Hagen, and Debbie Reynolds
Produced by Arthur Freed

Directed by Gene Kelly and Stanley Donen
Written by Betty Comden and Adolph Green

Skirts Ahoy! (MGM)
Released May 28, 1952
Starring Esther Williams, Joan Evans, Vivian
Blaine, and Barry Sullivan
Produced by Joe Pasternak
Directed by Sidney Lanfield
Written by Isobel Lennart

I Love Melvin (MGM)
Released March 20, 1953
Starring Donald O'Connor and Debbie Reynolds
Produced by Don Weis
Directed by George Wells
Written by George Wells, Ruth Brooks Flippen,
and László Vadnay

The Affairs of Dobie Gillis (MGM)
Released August 14, 1953
Starring Debbie Reynolds, Bobby Van, Barbara
Ruick, and Bob Fosse
Produced by Arthur M. Loew Jr.
Directed by Don Weis
Written by Max Shulman

Give a Girl a Break (MGM)

    Released December 3, 1953

    Starring Marge Champion, Gower Champion,
        Debbie Reynolds, Helen Wood, and Bob Fosse

    Produced by Jack Cummings

    Directed by Stanley Donen

    Written by Vera Caspary, Frances Goodrich,
        and Albert Hackett

Susan Slept Here (RKO)

    Released July 14, 1954

    Starring Dick Powell, Debbie Reynolds, and Anne
        Francis

    Produced by Harriet Parsons

    Directed by Frank Tashlin

    Written by Steve Fisher (play) and Alex Gottlieb
        (play and screenplay)

Athena (MGM)

    Released November 4, 1954

    Starring Jane Powell, Edmund Purdom, Debbie
        Reynolds, Vic Damone, and Louis Calhern

    Produced by Joe Pasternak

    Directed by Richard Thorpe

    Written by William Ludwig and Leonard
        Spigelgass

Hit the Deck (MGM)
    Released March 4, 1955
    Starring Jane Powell, Tony Martin,
        Debbie Reynolds, Walter Pidgeon, Vic Damone,
        Gene Raymond, and Ann Miller
    Produced by Joe Pasternak
    Directed by Roy Rowland
    Written by Sonya Levien and William
        Ludwig

The Tender Trap (MGM)
    Released November 4, 1955
    Starring Frank Sinatra, Debbie Reynolds,
        David Wayne, and Celeste Holm
    Produced by Lawrence Weingarten
    Directed by Charles Walters
    Written by Julius J. Epstein (screenplay) and Max
        Shulman and Robert Paul Smith (play)

Meet Me in Las Vegas (MGM)
    Released March 9, 1956
    Starring Dan Dailey, Cyd Charisse,
        Agnes Moorehead, and Lili Darvas
    Produced by Joe Pasternak
    Directed by Roy Rowland
    Written by Isobel Lennart

The Catered Affair (MGM)
  Released June 14, 1956
  Starring Bette Davis, Ernest Borgnine, Debbie
    Reynolds, Barry Fitzgerald, and Rod Taylor
  Produced by Sam Zimbalist
  Directed by Richard Brooks
  Written by Gore Vidal (screenplay) and Paddy
    Chayefsky (teleplay)

Bundle of Joy (RKO)
  Released December 12, 1956
  Starring Eddie Fisher, Debbie Reynolds,
    and Adolphe Menjou
  Produced by Edmund Grainger
  Directed by Norman Taurog
  Written by Robert Carson, Norman Krasna,
    Arthur Sheekman, and Felix Jackson

Tammy and the Bachelor (Universal)
  Released June 14, 1957
  Starring Debbie Reynolds, Leslie Nielsen,
    and Walter Brennan
  Produced by Ross Hunter
  Directed by Joseph Pevney
  Written by Oscar Brodney

This Happy Feeling (Universal)
    Released June 18, 1958
    Starring Debbie Reynolds, Curt Jurgens,
       and John Saxon
    Produced by Ross Hunter
    Directed by Blake Edwards
    Written by Blake Edwards

The Mating Game (MGM)
    Released April 29, 1959
    Starring Debbie Reynolds, Tony Randall,
       and Paul Douglas
    Produced by Phillip Barry Jr.
    Directed by George Marshall
    Written by H. E. Bates (novel) and
       William Roberts

It Started With a Kiss (MGM)
    Released August 19, 1959
    Starring Glenn Ford, Debbie Reynolds,
       and Eva Gabor
    Produced by Aaron Rosenberg
    Directed by George Marshall
    Written by Charles Lederer (screenplay)
       and Valentine Davies (story)

Say One for Me (20th Century Fox)
   Released June 19, 1959
   Starring Bing Crosby, Debbie Reynolds,
      and Robert Wagner
   Produced by Frank Tashlin
   Directed by Frank Tashlin
   Written by Robert O'Brien

The Gazebo (MGM)
   Released December 18, 1959
   Starring Glenn Ford and Debbie Reynolds
   Produced by Lawrence Weingarten
   Directed by George Marshall
   Written by George Wells (screenplay), Alec Coppel
      (play and story), and Myra Coppel (story)

The Rat Race (Paramount)
   Released July 10, 1960
   Starring Tony Curtis, Debbie Reynolds,
      Jack Oakie, and Don Rickles
   Produced by William Perlberg and George Seaton
   Directed by Robert Mulligan
   Written by Garson Kanin

Pepe (Columbia)
   Released December 21, 1960

Starring Cantinflas, Dan Dailey, and Shirley Jones
Produced by George Sidney
Directed by George Sidney
Written by Leslie Bush-Fekete, Claude Binyon,
  and Dorothy Kingsley

The Pleasure of His Company (Paramount)
  Released June 1, 1961
  Starring Fred Astaire, Debbie Reynolds,
    Lilli Palmer, and Tab Hunter
  Produced by William Perlberg
  Directed by George Seaton
  Written by Samuel A. Taylor (screenplay and play)
    and Cornelia Otis Skinner (play)

The Second Time Around (20th Century Fox)
  Released December 22, 1961
  Starring Debbie Reynolds, Steve Forrest,
    Thelma Ritter, and Andy Griffith
  Produced by Jack Cummings
  Directed by Vincent Sherman
  Written by Oscar Saul and Clair Huffaker
    (screenplay), and Richard Emery Roberts (novel)

How the West Was Won (MGM)
  Released February 20, 1963

Starring Carroll Baker, Gregory Peck, Lee J.
Cobb, George Peppard, Debbie Reynolds, James
Stewart, John Wayne, Henry Fonda, Richard
Widmark, Walter Brennan, and Harry Morgan
Produced by Bernard Smith
Directed by John Ford, Henry Hathaway,
and George Marshall
Written by James R. Webb

My Six Loves (Paramount)
Released April 3, 1963
Starring Debbie Reynolds, Cliff Robertson,
and David Janssen
Produced by Gant Gaither
Directed by Gower Champion
Written by Peter V. K. Funk (novel), Joseph
Calvelli, John Fante, and William Wood

Mary, Mary (Warner Brothers)
Released October 24, 1963
Starring Debbie Reynolds, Barry Nelson, and
Diane McBain
Produced by Mervyn LeRoy
Directed by Mervyn LeRoy
Written by Richard L. Breen (screenplay) and
Jean Kerr (play)

The Unsinkable Molly Brown (MGM)
    Released June 11, 1964
    Starring Debbie Reynolds, Harve Presnell,
        and Ed Begley
    Produced by Lawrence Weingarten
    Directed by Charles Walters
    Written by Helen Deutsch, based on the libretto
        by Richard Morris

Goodbye Charlie (20th Century Fox)
    Released November 18, 1964
    Starring Debbie Reynolds, Tony Curtis, Pat Boone,
        and Walter Matthau
    Produced by David Weisbart
    Directed by Vincente Minnelli
    Written by Harry Kurnitz (screenplay) and George
        Axelrod (play)

The Singing Nun (MGM)
    Released March 17, 1966
    Starring Debbie Reynolds, Ricardo Montalban,
        and Greer Garson
    Produced by John Beck
    Directed by Henry Koster
    Written by John Furia (story and screenplay)
        and Sally Benson (screenplay)

Divorce American Style (Columbia)
  Released June 21, 1967
  Starring Dick Van Dyke, Debbie Reynolds,
    and Jason Robards
  Produced by Norman Lear
  Directed by Bud Yorkin
  Written by Norman Lear (screenplay) and
    Robert Kaufman (story)

How Sweet It Is! (National General)
  Released August 21, 1968
  Starring James Garner, Debbie Reynolds,
    and Maurice Ronet
  Produced by Jerry Belson and Garry Marshall
  Directed by Jerry Paris
  Written by Jerry Belson and Garry Marshall
    (screenplay) and Muriel Resnik (novel)

What's the Matter with Helen? (United Artists)
  Released June 30, 1971
  Starring Debbie Reynolds, Shelley Winters,
    and Dennis Weaver
  Produced by George Edwards and
    Edward S. Feldman
  Directed by Curtis Harrington
  Written by Henry Farrell

Charlotte's Web (Paramount)
    Released March 1, 1973
    Starring Debbie Reynolds, Paul Lynde, and
        Henry Gibson
    Produced by Joseph Barbera and William
        Hanna
    Directed by Charles A. Nichols and Iwao
        Takamoto
    Written by Earl Hamner Jr. (story), based on
        E. B. White's book

That's Entertainment! (MGM)
    Released May 23, 1974
    Starring Frank Sinatra, Fred Astaire, Bing Crosby,
        Gene Kelly, and all the MGM stars
    Produced by Jack Haley Jr.
    Directed by Jack Haley Jr.
    Written by Jack Haley Jr.

That's Entertainment, Part 2 (MGM)
    Released May 16, 1976
    Starring Fred Astaire, Gene Kelly, and all the
        MGM stars
    Produced by Saul Chaplin and Daniel Melnick
    Directed by Gene Kelly
    Written by Leonard Gershe

Kiki's Delivery Service (Studio Ghibli)
    Released July 29, 1989
    Starring Kirsten Dunst, Phil Hartman,
        and Debbie Reynolds
    Produced by Hayao Miyazaki and
        Toru Hara
    Directed by Hayao Miyazaki
    Written by Hayao Miyazaki (screenplay) and
        Eiko Kadono (novel)

The Bodyguard (Warner Brothers)
    Released November 25, 1992
    Starring Kevin Costner, Whitney Houston,
        and Gary Kemp
    Produced by Kevin Costner, Lawrence Kasdan,
        and Jim Wilson
    Directed by Mick Jackson
    Written by Lawrence Kasdan

Heaven & Earth (Warner Brothers)
    Released December 25, 1993
    Starring Tommy Lee Jones, Joan Chen, and
        Haing S. Ngor
    Produced by Oliver Stone, Arnon Milchan,
        A. Kitman Ho, and Mario Kassar
    Directed by Oliver Stone

Written by Oliver Stone (screenplay), Le Ly
Hayslip with James Hayslip (book), and
Jay Wurts (book)

That's Entertainment! III (MGM)
Released May 6, 1994
Starring Gene Kelly, June Allyson, Lena Horne,
and Debbie Reynolds
Produced by Bud Friedgen, Michael J. Sheridan,
and Peter Fitzgerald
Directed by Bud Friedgen and Michael
J. Sheridan
Written by Bud Friedgen and Michael J. Sheridan

Mother (Paramount)
Released December 25, 1996
Starring Albert Brooks and Debbie Reynolds
Produced by Herb Nanas and Scott Rudin
Directed by Albert Brooks
Written by Albert Brooks and Monica Mcgowan
Johnson

Wedding Bell Blues (Cineplex Odeon Films)
Released June 13, 1997
Starring Illeana Douglas, Paulina Porizkova,
and Julie Warner

Produced by Ram Bergman, Mike Curb, Dana
   Lustig, and Carole Curb Nemoy
Directed by Dana Lustig
Written by Dana Lustig and Annette Goliti
   Gutierrez

In & Out (Paramount)
   Released September 19, 1997
   Starring Kevin Kline, Joan Cusack,
      Tom Selleck, Matt Dillon, and Debbie
      Reynolds
   Produced by G. Mac Brown, Scott Rudin, Suzanne
      Santry, and Adam Schroeder
   Directed by Frank Oz
   Written by Paul Rudnick

Fear and Loathing in Las Vegas (Rhino Films/Summit
Entertainment)
   Released May 22, 1998
   Starring Johnny Depp and Benicio Del Toro
   Produced by Patrick Cassavetti, Laila Nabulsi,
      and Stephen Nemeth
   Directed by Terry Gilliam
   Written by Terry Gilliam, Tony Grisoni, Alex Cox,
      and Tod Davies, based on the book by Hunter
      S. Thompson

Zack and Reba (Itasca Pictures)
Released October 1, 1998
Starring Brittany Murphy, Sean Patrick Flanery, Thomas Jane, Michael Jeter, and Debbie Reynolds
Produced by Ken Jacobsen, Randy James, and Miles Levy
Directed by Nicole Bettauer
Written by Jay Stapleton

Rudolph the Red-Nosed Reindeer: The Movie (Legacy Releasing)
Released October 16, 1998
Starring John Goodman, Alan Arkin, Eric Idle, Whoopi Goldberg, Bob Newhart, and Debbie Reynolds
Produced by William R. Kowalchuk Jr.
Directed by William R. Kowalchuk Jr.
Written by Michael Aschner, based on the story by Robert May

Rugrats in Paris: The Movie (Paramount)
Released November 17, 2000
Starring Christine Cavanaugh, Elizabeth Daily, Cheryl Chase, and Debbie Reynolds
Produced by Arlene Klasky and Gabor Csupo

Directed by Stig Bergqvist and Paul Demeyer
Written by Jill Gorey, Barbara Herndon, Kate
Boutilier, J. David Stern, and David N. Weiss

Connie and Carla (Spyglass Entertainment)
Released April 16, 2004
Starring Nia Vardalos, Toni Collette, and
David Duchovny
Produced by Nia Vardalos, Tom Hanks, Rita
Wilson, Gary Barber, Roger Birnbaum,
and Jonathan Glickman
Directed by Michael Lembeck
Written by Nia Vardalos

Light of Olympia (Santoon Production)
Released June 2008
Starring Joey D'Auria, Phyllis Diller, Tom Gibis,
and Debbie Reynolds
Directed by San Wei Chan
Written by Tommy Cannon and Sarah Kinney

One for the Money (Lionsgate)
Released January 27, 2012
Starring Katherine Heigl, Jason O'Mara, Daniel
Sunjata, John Leguizamo, Sherri Shepherd,
and Debbie Reynolds

Produced by Sidney Kimmel, Wendy Fineman,
   Tom Rosenberg, and Gary Lucchesi
Directed by Julie Anne Robinson
Written by Stacy Sherman, Karen Ray, and Liz
   Brixius (screenplay) and Janet Evanovich (novel)

Behind the Candelabra (Warner Brothers)
   Released May 2013
   Starring Matt Damon, Michael Douglas, Rob
      Lowe, Dan Aykroyd, Debbie Reynolds, and
      Scott Bakula
   Produced by Jerry Weintraub
   Directed by Steven Soderbergh
   Written by Richard LaGravenese

HARPER **LUXE**

THE NEW LUXURY IN READING

We hope you enjoyed reading
our new, comfortable print size and found it
an experience you would like to repeat.

Well – you're in luck!

HarperLuxe offers the finest in fiction and
nonfiction books in this same larger print size and
paperback format. Light and easy to read, HarperLuxe
paperbacks are for book lovers who want to see
what they are reading without the strain.

For a full listing of titles and
new releases to come, please visit our website:

www.HarperLuxe.com

HARPER **LUXE**

SEEING IS BELIEVING!